Elizabeth
&
Margaret

Elizabeth & Margaret

The Intimate World of the Windsor Sisters

Andrew Morton

GRAND CENTRAL
PUBLISHING

New York   Boston

Grand Central Publishing
Hachette Book Group
1290 Avenue of the Americas, New York, NY 10104
grandcentralpublishing.com
twitter.com/grandcentralpub

First Edition: March 2021

Grand Central Publishing is a division of Hachette Book Group, Inc. The Grand
Central Publishing name and logo is a trademark of Hachette Book Group, Inc.

The publisher is not responsible for websites (or their content) that are not
owned by the publisher.

The Hachette Speakers Bureau provides a wide range of authors for speaking events.
To find out more, go to www.hachettespeakersbureau.com or call (866) 376-6591.

Library of Congress Control Number: 2020950981

ISBNs: 978-1-5387-0046-4 (hardcover), 978-1-5387-0047-1 (ebook)

Printed in the United States of America

LSC-C

Printing 1, 2021

To Ali and Lydia:
Sisters and Friends Forever!

Contents

Introduction

Sister, Friend, Judge

Things were different now. No more "Lilibet" this and "Lilibet" that, the easy informality of two sisters united against the world. Now there was a distance between them, calibrated and barely acknowledged, but a distance nonetheless. The gap shrank when they were together, alone. But with servants and others around, there was a formality. When others referred casually to "your sister," Princess Margaret would snap haughtily, "You mean *the queen*." They had once shared a bedroom; now they were separated by a platoon of pen-pushing gatekeepers who, since Princess Elizabeth's recent elevation to sovereign, measured out every minute of her busy schedule. There was no longer any question of barging in unannounced—a habit their uncle, Louis Mountbatten—war hero, adviser, schemer, and general meddler—found difficult to break.

Margaret had chosen her moment well. On that wintry December day in 1952, the new queen was reviewing coronation details before heading to Sandringham for the family's annual Christmas gathering. Margaret was ushered in past the Canalettos and the Gainsborough portrait *Diana and Actaeon* by a red-jacketed flunky and suitably announced before entering the opulent Belgian Suite at Buckingham Palace. She called her sister "ma'am" before she dropped a diffident curtsy and kissed Lilibet on both cheeks. Then, at her sister's urging, she took a seat on the gold silk chaise in the sitting room. They were unmistakably sisters, both in modest day dresses decorated with a string of pearls and a well-chosen brooch. During their childhood they had been dressed identically by their charges. From time to time the pattern continued.

Margaret had a confession to make. She told her sister that she had fallen in love with Group Captain Peter Townsend, their father's former equerry who now enjoyed the ancient title of comptroller of the queen mother's household, which meant he was second in command of day-to-day administrative issues regarding the recently widowed monarch. Tall, slim, with piercing flinty gray-blue eyes and an unwavering gaze, he was every inch the matinee idol—and a bona fide war hero to boot. He was one of "the Few," a Battle of Britain pilot who saved the nation from Nazi conquest, his blue RAF uniform decorated with the medals that attested to his gallantry.

Since the premature death of their father, King George VI, in February that year, Margaret had increasingly relied on Townsend as she tried to cope with the darkness that overwhelmed her. Whisky, pills, tranquilizers, and cigarettes did little to help with the pain. It seemed that only Peter—soothing, calm, gentle—could lighten her moods.

They had shared a mutual attraction long before the king died. His death merely drew them closer together. In those early carefree days, Margaret had made Peter laugh, and he made her feel safe and secure. They confided and consoled, and eventually their friendship became more—much more.

It wasn't the fact that Peter was sixteen years her senior and had two boys of school age that had prompted Margaret to see her sister. No, the reason why she was sitting there, hands clasped, demure, with none of her normal theatricality, was to explain the implications of his impending divorce from his wife, Rosemary.

Since he had sued for divorce the previous November, they had quietly, privately and very tentatively discussed their own union at some distant date in the future. Even though he was, at least for public digestion, the innocent party, there was no escaping the fact that Peter Townsend was now about to be a divorcé. The D word hung like a primed grenade between them as both realized its dread import. Ironic that the matter was first raised between the sisters in the Belgian Suite where their uncle David, Edward VIII, lived during his brief reign before he abdicated the throne for the love of a twice-divorced American, Wallis Warfield Simpson.

Under the Royal Marriages Act of 1772, Princess Margaret, who was third in line to the throne behind Prince Charles and Princess Anne, had to obtain the queen's permission before she married any man, let alone a divorcé. Both knew that the teachings of their church were hostile to divorce. As defender of the faith, the queen had standards that she could not deviate from. Indeed, if Queen Mary, who was now ailing, had been let in on the secret, they both knew what her verdict would be. They could hear her now.

But times were a-changing. Would Lilibet grant her younger sister, who was currently third in line to the throne, permission to marry a divorcé? She held Margaret's happiness—her life— in the palm of her soft pink hand. Her big sister had spent her life judging her. Now that she was the queen, she ruled her life. It was a momentous decision that would define and shape the lives and reputations of both women forever.

~

Margaret watched her sister intently, surprised that she was not more surprised following her brief recitation of events. Clearly while she thought she and Peter had been discreet, they had not been discreet enough, and tongues had wagged. If her sister had a picture of what had been going on, others would also be sketching in added details.

~

While the queen did not betray her emotions, this was unwelcome news coming so close to the coronation in June. Nothing could be allowed to deflect from that moment, seen by many as both the high point and defining moment of a sovereign's reign. She knew and liked Peter Townsend and had appreciated his calm manner with her often querulous father, King George VI, who, at moments of sentiment, had described the war hero as the son he had never had.

She was torn. During her own long night of the soul, when her father had asked her to accompany him to South Africa and leave her sweetheart, Prince Philip, behind, it was "Margo" who had been the most loyal of loyal little sisters, always taking her side and praising Philip in front of their parents. And Townsend was no Wallis Simpson, loathed by the royal family; he was a popular figure inside the palace, admired and respected for his wartime record, unruffled demeanor, and organizational abilities.

There was much to ponder. She was no longer just Margo's big sister. She was the queen, with constitutional obligations and duties. Margaret was not formally requesting permission to marry. Yet. She hoped that Peter might be included in more family get-togethers to pave the way for others to view them as a suitable match. They were prepared to take things gradually. Margaret hinted to her sister that she would settle for these small allowances, rather than a full-fledged backing for marriage.

Elizabeth looked out of the window into the palace garden beyond. Margaret smiled inwardly, knowing that it was her sister's tendency to look out of the window before she made a decision. As the Sevres clock ticked sonorously on the mantelpiece, the queen told her sister that she had an idea.

Elizabeth
&
Margaret

1

Rising of the Sun and the Moon

Perhaps the only thing David and Bertie shared completely was a keen interest in fashion. One was a flashy dresser who gravitated toward Fair Isle sweaters, two-tone shoes, and turned-up trousers. The other dressed more conservatively and focused on the tailoring of a dress or a suit, spending hours with ateliers and cutters, sketching out designs, trying out new ideas for court dress, state occasions, and even pantomime costumes.[1]

Aside from that commonality, they were worlds apart in demeanor and temperament; one bred for the sunlight, the other for the shadows. One was more youthful and jaunty, with smooth, rarely shaved skin and a slight build but an energetic gait and spirit. The other was frail, nervy, and prone to irrational bursts of temper and suffered from a slew of debilitating ailments, ranging from stomach problems, to a serious stammer, nonstop blinking, and twitches that caused his mouth to droop. One partied till dawn, seduced single—and married—women,

and loathed his father. The other bowed down to his father's bidding, settling into a sensible marriage and "a more rooted royal
style." Their father always lamented that one child "was heading
down the wrong tracks" while the other perpetuated the proper
image of the monarchy, "a model of dreamlike domesticity."[2]
Even Wallis Warfield Simpson, the American paramour of the
Prince of Wales, noticed the polar temperaments of the two
brothers: her lover "all enthusiasm and volubility...the Duke
of York quiet, shy."[3]

The choices made by these two brothers, David, the eldest
son and heir to the Windsor dynasty, and Bertie, his younger
sibling by only eighteen months, would intimately shape the
future of the House of Windsor and in the process profoundly
alter the destiny of Bertie's daughters, Elizabeth—Lilibet, as
she was known in the family—and Margaret. Their grandfather, King George V, experienced an eerie foreboding about
the future of his family even as he celebrated his Silver Jubilee
in 1935. With his eldest son and heir, the Prince of Wales, now
forty and no nearer marrying and securing the dynasty, the king
stated sorrowfully, "After I am dead, the boy [the future Edward
VIII] will ruin himself within 12 months. I pray to God my
eldest son will never marry and have children, and that nothing
will come between Bertie and Lilibet and the throne."[4]

The king's prayer would be answered. It was Edward VIII's
abdication to marry a twice-divorced American, Wallis Warfield Simpson, that would transform the lives of his brother
and his brother's daughters, changing the family dynamic forever. Their uncle's decision placed them firmly in the lifelong
embrace of the monarchy, further shaping who they were and
what they became.

As with David and Bertie, in the popular imagination, every generation of the House of Windsor is stalked by a shadow. The good versus the naughty royal. The rebellious extrovert versus the sensible introvert. William the straight shooter, and Harry the wild child. Diana the demure, and Fergie the roustabout. The sun and the moon. These stereotypes often mask as much as they reveal. And yet, each set of royal siblings—like all siblings—feeds off this asymmetry, occupying the psychic space left by the other.

As Princess Margaret told her writer friend Gore Vidal, "When there are two sisters and one is the queen who must be the source of honor and all that is good, the other must be the focus of the most creative malice, the evil sister."[5] Certainly her behavior on occasion made her sister shine, Margaret easily slipping into the black sheep stereotype. That reputation barely disturbed the ash on her ever-present cigarette holder. As she once remarked, "Disobedience is my joy."[6]

Margaret was sufficiently self-aware to be able to draw the subtle distinction between the media's portrayal of her as someone jealous of the queen's position versus the more layered conflict of a young woman overshadowed by her older sister: "I have never suffered from 'second daughter-itis.' But I did mind forever being cast as the 'younger sister.'"[7] As a friend perceptively noted, "She sees herself as the king's daughter rather than the queen's sister."[8] That is to say, part of the main royal family, not a subsidiary branch, which was the case after Elizabeth became queen. Margaret never indicated that she wanted to switch places with her sister, telling anyone who would listen that her role in life was to support her sister with the immense burden of her position. As she once remarked, "Isn't it lucky that Lilibet is the eldest?"[9] While Margaret chafed at the restraints of royal life, Elizabeth dutifully embraced them.

The two sisters were contradictory and conflicted, butting heads over matters both small and monumental, but they also loved one another. This push-and-pull between affection and distance, deep love and primal jealousy, went to the heart of the private world that Elizabeth and Margaret shared.

༄

Both sisters entered the world on the twenty-first day of the month, but that was the only similarity about their births.

Elizabeth was born on April 21, 1926, in Mayfair, London, to then Prince Albert, duke of York and Elizabeth Bowes-Lyon. That year was proving a challenging one for Britain, teetering on the edge of industrial chaos and a historic general strike. By the time of her birth, strong public interest had already built up because her imminent arrival offered a diversion from the national crisis. A crowd milled outside 17 Bruton Street when Elizabeth finally arrived via cesarean section at 2:40 in the morning. In accordance with ancient tradition, home secretary Sir William Joynson-Hicks was present to witness the birth in order to prevent child swapping.[10] Soon enough, the bonny blue-eyed baby became a potent symbol of family, continuity, and patriotism.

Just about a month later, on May 19, she was christened Elizabeth Alexandra Mary in a ceremony at the private chapel at Buckingham Palace, officiated by Dr. Cosmo Gordon Lang, the archbishop of York. Such was the interest in the baby princess that excited onlookers broke through the police cordon outside the palace in an attempt to catch a glimpse of the famous infant. Her distinguished name implied her future destiny as queen—even though, under the 1701 Act of Settlement, she appeared unlikely to ascend the throne once Uncle David produced an heir. Still, everyone spoke as if she represented the country's great promise, with one newspaper observing, "The possibility that in the little stranger to Bruton Street there may be a future Queen of Great Britain (perhaps even a second Queen Elizabeth) is sufficiently intriguing."[11]

The new baby catapulted her parents from a relatively quiet royal life to the front pages of newspapers and magazines. Weeks after her birth, the pavement outside the Yorks' London residence was still thronged with so many fans that she occasionally had to be smuggled out of the back door in her pram for her daily airing. In time her mother became concerned about this surge of attention. She later wrote to her mother-in-law, Queen Mary: "It almost frightens me that the people should love her so much. I suppose that it is a good thing, and I hope that she will be worthy of it, poor little darling."[12]

This extraordinary amount of attention was not limited to the man and woman in the street. From the start, her irascible grandfather King George V doted on her. Stories soon circulated about how the angelic little girl had won the affections of the unbending sovereign. Though he was notorious for intimidating his own children and senior staff, Elizabeth was the exception. The archbishop of Canterbury recounted that on one occasion, the monarch, who was playing a horse, allowed his granddaughter to pull him around by his gray beard as he shuffled on his knees along the floor. "He was fond of his two grandsons, Princess Mary's sons," recalled the countess of Airlie, "but Lilibet always came first in his affections. He used to play with her—a thing I never saw him do with his own children—and loved to have her with him."[13] He monitored her every small advance, sending a wireless message to his son and daughter-in-law, who were on board the *Renown* sailing to Australia, to inform them that his granddaughter had cut her first tooth. The king was enraptured by her. One Christmas at Sandringham, three-year-old Elizabeth was listening to the carol "While Shepherds Watched Their Flocks by Night" when she noticed the lyric "to you and all mankind." She innocently announced: "I know that old man kind. That's you grandpapa. You're old and you are very, very kind."[14]

∽

Baby Elizabeth always listened attentively when Grandpa England stressed the virtues of decency, duty, and hard work, values that were further reinforced by an inflexible household regime and a dedicated team of staff in the nursery, including her nurse, Clara Knight, known as Alah; Margaret "Bobo" MacDonald, a copper-haired Scotswoman; and later Bobo's sister, Ruby. At the firm request of her grandmother, Queen Mary, Elizabeth was trained to be a model royal from the beginning. "Teach that child not to fidget!" became her grandmother's recurring demand. Alah painstakingly coached the three-year-old Elizabeth on the necessity of standing absolutely still, like a marble statue. The pockets in all her dresses were sewn shut to make sure she wouldn't shove her hands in them and slouch or be tempted to fiddle with them. She learned to answer a salute, wave her white-gloved hand from a balcony or open car, pose graciously for photographers, and control her bladder for hours. Later she was taught the proper form of address for the archbishop of Canterbury and the prime minister. If she performed to Alah's exacting standards, she was rewarded with a biscuit.[15] Misbehavior would earn a slap across the back of her legs. Even by the standards of the day, her childhood was stifled and emotionally threadbare, the adults in her life encouraging a docile conformity.

As a toddler, Elizabeth learned that she needed to act with grace, bow and curtsy to adults, and never lose her composure or act too familiarly toward anyone. Everything in her rigidly controlled life was run like clockwork, from breakfast at 7:30 a.m. to bedtime at 7:15 p.m. sharp.[16] In short, she began life as a sheltered, privileged child, drilled in the need for self-discipline and respect for the demands of her position.

While there were obvious limitations in her regimented and rather repressed childhood, there were perks too, though some were more obvious to adult sensibilities. Elizabeth would travel in limousines between the various royal castles, palaces, and houses while carefully attended by a small army of butlers, footmen, maids, and chauffeurs. At Christmas and on her birthday she was inundated with gifts, many sent by adoring members of the public who themselves were of modest means. At age four, she acquired her first Shetland pony, Peggy, from her grandfather and began riding lessons soon after. Whenever she appeared in public, throngs of people would stop, smile, cheer, and even wave flags. It was thus a childhood that alternated quickly between great attention and great isolation, and Elizabeth was raised as a small adult rather than as a child. Then, when she was just four years old, her position of ascendancy in the nursery came under challenge.

❦

While Elizabeth was born in the center of fashionable Mayfair in a comfortable town house at 17 Bruton Street, her sister arrived on August 21, 1930, during a violent thunderstorm in the family's "haunted" ancestral home, Glamis Castle, a storied Scottish pile that came complete with dark, winding corridors, steep stone steps, drafty bedrooms, and its own "monster," said to be a disfigured creature hidden away in a secret room. Elizabeth had been a "wanted" first child, but the duke and duchess had hoped for a boy as their second.[17] They hadn't even considered female names. Though the parents liked the sound of Ann Margaret, at the behest of Queen Mary, they settled on naming the child Margaret Rose, as Margaret was the name of a Scottish queen.

On the morning after Margaret's birth, Alah told Elizabeth a big surprise awaited her in her mother's room. After touching her newborn sister's hand, Elizabeth grew so excited that she grabbed the doctor, David Myles, and led him to the room, proclaiming: "Come and see my baby, my very own baby!"[18] She was so excited that she was found later in front of her toy cupboard. Beside her were a blue velvet frog, a woolly rabbit, a pair of prized dancing dolls, and several picture books, the excited child announcing that she was getting things ready for the baby to play with.

Such devotion was not merely a reaction to the immediate excitement of Margaret's birth. At her christening on October 30, she wore the same lace dress that her sister had four years earlier. Gazing at her sister with adoration, Elizabeth whispered, "I shall call her Bud. You see she isn't really a rose yet."[19] Those words carried more significance than intended: Margaret Rose would always remain the bud, representing unfulfilled potential, someone restrained by convention and longing to burst forth. Even though Margaret, Elizabeth, and their mother would come to be called "The Three White Roses of York,"[20] the truth was that only Elizabeth had been born a royal "rose" in that she was ultimately destined to be the queen.

The arrival of this second daughter focused the world's attention even more closely on Elizabeth as the likely heir to the throne. A waxwork figure of her on her pony was installed at Madame Tussaud's. Chocolates, dinnerware, tea towels, and hospitals were named after her. Her face was emblazoned on a six-cent stamp in Newfoundland. A popular tune, titled

"Nursery Suite" and composed by Edward Elgar, honored her as well as her sister and mother. The Australian government named a piece of Antarctica "Princess Elizabeth Land." Her doting father began comparing the young girl to the illustrious Queen Victoria. "From the first moment of talking," he told the writer Osbert Sitwell, "she showed so much character that it was impossible not to wonder that history would not repeat itself."[21] For the baby Margaret, still too young to pronounce Elizabeth's name correctly, her older sister was simply "Lilibet."

Within just a few years, in 1933, Lilibet confidently informed her younger sister: "I'm three and you're four." Confused, Margaret responded: "No, you're not. I'm three, you're seven." The toddler had no idea that Elizabeth was referring to their positions in the line of succession. At seven, Elizabeth already had the throne on her mind, unlike her uncle and even her own father. She solemnly told her Scottish governess, Marion "Crawfie" Crawford, "If I am ever Queen, I shall make a law that there must be no riding on Sundays. Horses should have a rest, too."[22]

⁓

While Elizabeth was busy contemplating future edicts, rumors circulated that Margaret was deaf and dumb because the public was not allowed to see her. This annoyed King George so much that, when the royal family were standing on the balcony of Buckingham Palace after a royal wedding, he bent down and whisked her off her feet and stood her on the balustrade. Years later Margaret told her confidant Christopher Warwick that she had no head for heights and found the whole experience "terrifying." His action, however, had the effect of dramatically dispelling the rumors.

Inside the family, it was apparent that Margaret was a beauty with an intriguing and willful personality. Her mother proudly gushed to Cosmo Lang: "She has got large blue eyes and a will of iron, which is all the equipment that a lady needs! And as long as she can disguise her will, and use her eyes, then all will be well."[23]

From the beginning it was clear that Margaret was daddy's little girl, despite not being as well behaved as her older sister. She would often sneak downstairs after lunch in the nursery, push "her small fat face" round the dining room door, and climb onto her father's knee to steal a sip of soda or spoonful of sugar.[24] Crawfie, their governess, recalled: "She was a plaything. Warm and demonstrative, made to be cuddled and played with."[25] She also displayed an early ability to play off one parent against the other. When she was four, she went up to her mother, looked at her affectionately, gave her a kiss and told her, "Mummy darling, I really do believe that I love Papa much more than I do you."[26]

Elizabeth wasted no time in keeping a watchful eye on her exuberant baby sister, viewing it as her solemn duty to protect Margaret from the outside world. On one occasion, when a buck-toothed chaplain came to visit and asked Elizabeth if he could see Margaret, her older sister replied, "No, I think your teeth would frighten her."[27]

∽

During their early childhood, the two sisters led an insulated and carefree life at 145 Piccadilly, a stone-fronted, five-storied house that came to be known as "the palace with a number and without a name."[28] Their father wanted the children raised in a peaceful, loving environment—unlike the regime that had been imposed by his own martinet of a father. As a child, Bertie had been forced to wear painful leg braces to correct his knock knees and had been beaten into writing with his right rather than left hand, even though he was a natural leftie. By age eight, perhaps because of such unthinking abuse, he had acquired a debilitating stammer. Now that he had finally found warmth and comfort with Elizabeth Bowes-Lyon, the daughter of the earl of Strathmore and Kinghorne, Bertie was determined to create an intimate home life for his daughters and raise them without pretention. The public noted how the Yorks projected the image of a perfect family: "a neat, hard-working, quiet husband, an adoring mother with a lovely smile, and the well-behaved little girls, just two of them in ankle socks . . . like the characters in an Ovaltine advertisement."[29]

Bertie's wife, Elizabeth, proved the perfect partner in this enterprise, widely admired for her charm and femininity. After seeing her in the royal box at the theater, the novelist Virginia Woolf described her as, "a simple, chattering, sweet-hearted, round-faced young woman in pink. Her wrists twinkling with diamonds and her dress held on the shoulder with diamonds."[30] But this pristine surface masked the duchess's strong-minded, indomitable nature. She was fiercely protective of her family and lived by an uncompromising code of Christian morality. The household staff knew that her decisions were final and that her loyalties were firm. Still, she managed to exercise admirable patience, never losing her cool when handling her husband's frequent mood swings and unpredictable flashes of anger, known as "gnashes." Some considered his behavior a form of epilepsy.

Surprisingly, despite the presence inside of a famous royal family, there was no special security at 145 Piccadilly. The curious could simply walk up the stone-flagged path and ring one of the two bells, marked "Visitors" and "House." Once inside, the butler would lead them across the soft brown carpet to a spacious and airy morning room with windows overlooking the family's verdant garden, where Princess Elizabeth rode her tricycle. A short walk away was Hyde Park, where the family's golden Labradors were exercised.[31]

The sisters' lessons were held in the duchess's sitting room off the main drawing room, filled not only with chintz-covered sofas and a Persian carpet, but also gigantic maps and books. Their imperious grandmother had a ruling hand in the girls' education, requesting a curriculum schedule from Crawfie and demanding alterations without letting her daughter-in-law know. She insisted that history be given greater emphasis than arithmetic, because the princesses "would probably never have to do even their own household books," and because history would be especially important for the future queen.[32] Every Monday morning, they would receive half an hour of religious instruction, which left a particularly deep impression on the younger sister. They said their prayers first thing in the morning and last thing at night.

Queen Mary's iron control over the girls' education stemmed from her general disapproval of their upbringing. To her, maintaining appearances mattered more than anything, and the sight of royal children playing unnerved her: "Shouldn't they get a more intellectual indoor game than Racing Demon? I am distressed by their late and fluctuating bedtime."[33] She took special issue with Margaret, whom she called "espiègle," or "playful rascal": "Princess Margaret's character is more complicated and difficult [than Elizabeth's]." The dislike was mutual: Margaret grew up intimidated by their stiff and imposing grandmother, who would often tactlessly ask, "When are you going to grow?"[34] Whenever they had to visit Queen Mary, Margaret recalled getting a "hollow, empty feeling in the pit of my stomach."[35]

Elizabeth, on the other hand, was deeply enamored of their grandmother, regarding her as the keeper of the royal flame. It was Queen Mary who impressed upon Elizabeth that duty trumped personal considerations, that public performances were more important than individual needs. Her training in the nuances of rank, precedent, title, and position started at an early age. On one occasion a footman addressed Princess Elizabeth as "My lady." She replied: "I'm not a lady I'm a princess." Her grandmother interceded and said to her: "Quite right, you were born a princess and it will be many years before you learn to be a lady."[36]

While educational decisions were made with Elizabeth in mind, it was actually Margaret who proved the more precocious, naturally gifted student. She would constantly try to narrow the age gap between herself and her sister, to prove that she was just as smart and deserved just as much attention. When Elizabeth started French lessons with Madame Marie-Antoinette de Bellaigue, Margaret would eavesdrop at the door, and her expertise at mimicry gave her a far better accent than Elizabeth. She also displayed an early talent for acting, doing a near-perfect impression of Shirley Temple. When they started piano lessons with Miss Mabel Lander, Margaret again demonstrated greater curiosity and artistic inclination than her restrained sister. Elizabeth could carry a tune, but it was Margaret who clearly boasted the better voice, her sharp musical ear translating to perfect pitch. According to one account, when she was only nine months old, she had already learned to hum the waltz from *The Merry Widow.*

While Crawfie tried her best to tailor their educations to suit their ages, such customization was nearly impossible since all classes were held in the same room. Furthermore,

Margaret was so talented and competitive that no one could tell her to study a subject or do a task differently from her sister. She would constantly compare her assignment to her sister's, convinced that she had been stuck with the duller alternative. Crawfie responded by allowing Margaret to study years ahead of her age. Lilibet thus received a decent education that also helped sate Margaret's burning curiosity and natural intellect. A friend stated that partly because of these shared studies, Elizabeth turned out "relatively young [for her age]," while Margaret developed a sharp and sensitive mind.[37] Temperamentally, too, Margaret was far more inquisitive than her sister. "Very matter of fact and uncurious," was how their friend and future classmate Alathea Fitzalan Howard described Elizabeth.[38] The comparison between the two sisters was a theme she returned to. In a later diary entry, she observed: "I wish [Lilibet] could get away from the little-girl atmosphere that Margaret inevitably gives her. I adore Margaret but it is such a pity she keeps her sister back, and it does make [Lilibet] younger in many ways than a lot of nearly 16 girls."

Though most sisters with a four-year age difference would not be raised so closely, Elizabeth and Margaret were treated more like twins who dressed exactly the same, shared the same room, enjoyed the same activities, and, by and large, were taught the same lessons. Their father was the final arbiter over what they wore, fussing over his daughters in a way that was quite possessive. When they were bridesmaids for the wedding of the duke and duchess of Gloucester, the duke of York requested that their skirts be shortened because "I want to see their pretty little knees."[39] This extreme closeness made it harder for Margaret to handle the few moments when Elizabeth enjoyed certain privileges, such as horse riding alone with their father or an instructor, and being allowed to stay up thirty minutes later at night—though this curfew meant little in practice.[40]

Even as Queen Mary tried to control their lessons, the Yorks themselves placed limited emphasis on studies, not wanting their daughters to be regarded as "too intellectual." As Crawfie recalled, the duke and duchess "wanted most for [their daughters] a really happy childhood, with lots of pleasant memories stored up against the days that might come."[41] In this secure and loving home, the girls enjoyed plenty of playtime, though they tended not to have much company aside from occasional visits from their cousins.

Most of the girls' days were spent with each other and with their governesses, who would often whisk them through the back door to Hamilton Gardens. In one rare instance, Elizabeth did befriend Sonia Graham-Hodgson, the daughter of her grandfather's doctor, Harold Graham-Hodgson. "Sonia was the one friend whom the Queen chose for herself," Crawfie remembered. They would play French cricket, skip, and hopscotch and even took dancing lessons together. Sometimes, the duke of York would join them for a hide-and-seek game called Sardines. Sonia remembered Elizabeth as "a thoughtful and sensitive child, and naturally well-behaved. She never seemed aware of her position and paid no attention to those who stood by the railings to watch her play."[42] Their friendship was so special that the eight-year-old Elizabeth dedicated an unfinished novel, The Happy Farm: "To Sonia, My dear little friend and lover of horses."[43] For a long time she was Elizabeth's best friend.

Though Sonia was her closest friend outside the immediate family, Elizabeth spent most of her time with her younger sister, playing in the sunlight that streamed through the glass dome at the top of the staircase. Behind a black lacquer screen, the sisters kept two scarlet brushes and dustpans, which they used to sweep the carpet every morning. They could choose from an array of toys, curios, and miniature animals arranged neatly in a glass cabinet, "each of them tiny enough to be pushed by a ladybird."[44] The cabinet also contained china cottages and palaces, model soldiers and ships, finely blown glass creatures, and a minuscule silver cradle containing a petite doll. This last treasure was only one in a collection of dolls, some of which had belonged to Queen Victoria's children. Several came with a complete range of accessories: gloves, fans, sunglasses, tortoiseshell brushes, beaded bags, and shoes.[45] Though they seemed to be any little girl's dream, Margaret shuddered in horror. She said later how much she hated dolls because "they're like dead babies."[46]

The sisters also lovingly managed what they called a "horse market," another vast collection of wheeled toy horses that they would polish and maintain. Every night before bed, Lilibet would unsaddle, groom, and water them. Soon enough, these toy horses yielded to the real thing, as the princesses were taught to ride by their parents and later by their groom Horace Smith. Even at this tender age, it was Lilibet who was horse-mad. Margaret was never as fond of horses and dogs as her older sibling.

As a family, the Yorks loved music and dancing, playing their gramophone at top volume or singing songs around the piano after tea. The children would begin their day with high jinks in their parents' bedroom, and every evening would end with more fun at bath time in a bright room filled with sponge animals. The duke would frequently bathe his daughters himself. Aside from the Bible, they would read books together like *Alice's Adventures in Wonderland*, *Black Beauty*, and *Peter Pan*, or "anything about horses and dogs."[47] Sometimes, their father would join the girls for midmorning games in Hamilton Gardens behind their home. Using the statue of Lord Byron as "home base," they would play tag and hide-and-seek for hours among the shrubs and bushes.[48]

Yet although the sisters shared a close, sometimes claustrophobic, environment, clear differences quickly emerged. Early on, Elizabeth focused her attentions on horse riding—a hobby that aligned well with her inborn obedience. Even at a young age, she wanted everything in perfect order, keeping a large box of wrapping paper and ribbons saved from Christmases or birthdays—a sign of what would become her well-known frugality as queen. Always neat and methodical, Lilibet would sometimes wake up in the middle of the night just to check that her shoes were properly stowed away. Meanwhile, Margaret filled the role of entertainer, caring little about behaving well after she realized that she could gain attention through performances. As their cousin recalled, "She quite often got away with a lot just by being able to make a joke out of something. She had a mischievous sense of humor," whereas Elizabeth "was always the more serious of the two."[49]

Any time the family returned home from a theater performance, Margaret would immediately begin casting everyone in various roles and order them to reenact their own character. Elizabeth preferred a quiet and solitary day of riding, but Margaret loved playing charades, mimicking people, singing, playing the piano, and attending the theater. She even invented imaginary friends, including one named Inderbombanks. Crawfie recalled that Margaret often suffered from terrible dreams, involving everything from talking cats to green horses, and she would recount them in great detail to avoid doing chores. Essentially, Margaret was a highly theatrical child, loath to share the spotlight with anyone.[50]

This carefree childhood was marred by the death of their grandfather, George V, on January 20, 1936. Their mother took the girls for a walk in the light snow to explain that Grandpa England had fallen gravely ill and passed away. Elizabeth already knew the import of the moment, tearfully asking later, "Oh, Crawfie...Ought we to play?"[51] Only Elizabeth accompanied her parents to the lying in state at Westminster Hall and later the State funeral. Meanwhile, according to Crawfie, the five-year-old Margaret "was much too young to pay attention to what was going on."[52]

It soon became apparent that the sisters' temperaments were fundamentally different, not simply because Margaret was "too young." Elizabeth could be depended upon to do what was asked, keeping her toys and clothes in perfect order—a reflection of her disciplined deportment. Margaret remained impish and high-spirited, even biting and tormenting her gentler sister whenever she did not get her way. Elizabeth once chided, "Oh Margaret, with you it's always what I want."[53] This would have consequences. Occasionally, the two got into scraps, usually when forced to wear the same unflattering hats. Snapping each other's straps, they would cry out, "You brute! You beast!"[54]

As expected, it was Margaret who would initiate these harmless scuffles, but she knew how to weasel her way out of the consequences. Crawfie wrote, "Lilibet was the one with the temper, but it was under control. Margaret was often naughty but she had a gay bouncing way with her which was hard to deal with. She would often defy me with a sidelong look, make a scene, kiss and be friends and all forgiven and forgotten. Lilibet took longer to recover, but she always had the more dignity of the two."[55] Indeed, Margaret was a "born comic" with a distinctive way of endearing herself to others. One of their mother's friends remembered, "Princess Elizabeth was always charming and unselfish. Princess Margaret, naughty but amusing."[56]

As Elizabeth entered her pre-teens, she evolved more firmly into the role she had already begun to assume since Margaret's birth: someone "to whom one could always explain things." She would always listen to sensible argument. Meanwhile, Margaret moved in the opposite direction. According to one observer, she "would not listen to reason. She was lively, high spirited . . . and wayward. But because she also had an entrancing charm, she always got away with it."[57] As their father would famously conclude, "Lilibet is my pride; Margaret is my joy."

Yet, both had their own burdens to carry. Elizabeth knew from a young age that she would have to live up to her family's and society's expectations of her. Meanwhile, Margaret constantly anticipated the humiliation of being second best. Elizabeth had been trained in the cool detachment of a monarch, while Margaret was left to express herself more freely. But partly because of this very fact, she always felt defensive about being demeaned and belittled. She was particularly sensitive to the comment that she was "too young," which she was told whenever she couldn't attend the same grand events as her sister. Still, for all their differences, Elizabeth would always remain maternally protective toward Margaret, defending her from all criticism. In return, Margaret gave her total loyalty to Elizabeth, even amid near-constant sibling rivalry. This complicated dynamic, first established in their nursery and study room, would persist throughout their adult lives.

෨

The Yorks spent many of their weekends at Royal Lodge, their country retreat—a large pink building painted to resemble the duchess of York's childhood home, St. Paul's Walden Bury.

It was a place of freedom and informality, nothing like the stifling atmosphere in which Bertie and his brothers had been raised. It boasted a long staircase with oak banisters and bright crimson carpet, huge Chinese porcelain jardinières bursting with flowers and branches reaching to the ceiling, and horse paintings covering the walls. A pack of Labradors, corgis, and a Tibetan ran about the house, barking and scurrying up the stairs. At the top of the landing was a pair of wooden rocking horses, side by side, belonging to Elizabeth and Margaret.[58]

It was at Royal Lodge that the two girls first met Wallis Warfield Simpson—the woman whose American unorthodoxy would soon upend British tradition. Wallis arrived with their uncle David amid whispered rumors about the nature of their relationship, at least among high society. The overwhelming majority of the British people had no idea about this latest love affair. David came ready to flaunt his two new infatuations: a custom-made American Buick station wagon and his new love. Hailing from Baltimore, Maryland, Wallis looked striking in person, with a thin, attractive figure, perfect posture, a long neck, striking violet eyes, and dark mahogany hair made up into a fashionable and immaculate chignon. Even though she was animated and gay, the visit did not go over particularly well, the only moment of levity occurring when Dookie, the princesses' corgi, wandered in, stole a biscuit from a plate, and left. Wallis later admitted, "While the Duke of York was sold on the American station wagon, the Duchess was not sold on [the king's] other American interest."[59]

The two sisters—now aged ten and six—were escorted into the sitting room by Crawfie, jostling each other aside in an attempt to enter first. The duke introduced them as "Lilibet" and "Margaret Rose"—according to Wallis, the former "a long, slender, very beautifully-made child"; the latter, "an enchanting doll-like child with a small, fat face." As usual, they wore matching outfits: twin royal tartan kilts and yellow pullovers. Wallis recalled, "Both [were] so blond, so beautifully mannered, so brightly scrubbed that they might have stepped straight from the pages of a picture book."[60] They stared at this shocking American specimen with undisguised curiosity. They'd heard various bits of gossip from the household staff about "that woman" and their uncle, but they made sure to remain on their best behavior.

Though the girls remembered to mind their manners, they were keenly attentive to the smallest disruption in their measured lives. As they observed their uncle and Simpson drive away from the property in his fancy American car, Elizabeth asked, "Crawfie, who is she?" The governess avoided answering, only adding to their confusion, as they had previously heard her mention that Uncle David was "besotted by Mrs. Simpson." They had no inkling what "besotted" might mean, or that within just a few months, it was Mrs. Simpson who would alter the course of their lives forever.

On December 10, 1936, after only a 325-day reign, King Edward VIII abdicated the throne to marry Wallis. This decision upended the previously closeted lives of the York family. Margaret, theatrical as ever, was keenly affected by the unfolding crisis, asking Alah fearfully: "Are they going to cut off his head?"[61] Outside the house at 145 Piccadilly, crowds began milling in anticipation of the announcement that Prince Albert, duke of York, would succeed his older brother. After Lilibet awoke and noticed the commotion, a footman told her the reason why—she was now second in line to the throne after her father.

She dashed upstairs to tell her sister. Margaret asked breathlessly, "Does that mean that you will have to be the next

Queen?" Elizabeth replied solemnly: "Yes, someday," to which Margaret retorted, "Poor you."[62] The girls spent the remainder of the day peering down the stairwell at the important guests marching through their home, including Prime Minister Stanley Baldwin. They would then rush to the windows to ogle the thousands of people gathered outside.

Even at age ten, Elizabeth was well aware of the "glass wall" separating royalty from the rest of society. Knowing that this marked a major turning point in her life, she didn't date her diary entry for December 10, 1936, writing simply "Abdication Day" at the top.[63] From that moment forth, she prayed each night that a brother would be born to supersede her in the line of succession. Her sister lamented, again with theatrical overstatement: "Now that Papa is king, I am nothing."[64] When told they would now have to move to Buckingham Palace, Margaret ruefully asked, "You mean forever?" Crawfie answered, "Yes. And you are no longer Margaret of York." "Then who am I?" "You are just Margaret." The little girl repeated, "But I have only just learned to write 'York.' Now I'm nobody."[65]

Their father was left even more appalled by the situation, unable to accept his fate and viewing his brother's decision as an unforgivable betrayal. "This can't be happening to me!" he moaned when a servant addressed him as "Your Majesty." He confided to his cousin Lord Louis "Dickie" Mountbatten: "I never wanted this to happen. I've never even seen a State Paper. I'm only a Naval Officer, it's the only thing I know about."[66] Given the duke's well-known stammer and other disabilities, brief consideration was given to having his younger brother Prince George assume the throne, but that notion was soon discarded. This was not a beauty contest—the duke of York was next in line as the second eldest brother, and his eldest daughter was now heir presumptive.

The Sunday papers indicated which way the popular wind was blowing. They delivered the momentous news with accompanying portraits of "Our Princess Elizabeth." By contrast, Margaret was sidelined to group family photos. The emotional dynamic that had been confined to their home was exposed for the whole world to discuss and ponder. As for Uncle David, their avuncular playmate who had taught them the Nazi salute on the lawns of Balmoral, he was no longer a presence in their lives. When his name was mentioned it was in low, conspiratorial voices and eventually silence. As for Wallis, she was simply referred to as "that woman"—not that the sisters ever heard an adult use that damning phrase in their earshot.

Though the girls initially curtsied to their father when he first became king, that was the only time they did so. Instead their father instructed them to behave toward him as they had before his elevation. As the coronation approached, he again took a detailed interest in their outfits, concerned that they were perfect. The king oversaw the entire process of preparing the girls' clothes for the ceremony, even to the point of securing a specially designed lightweight gilt coronet. It would be their first time wearing long dresses—white lace embellished with silver bows, silver slippers with white ankle socks, and purple velvet cloaks lined with ermine. To complete their delicate outfits, they both wore pearl necklaces and elbow-length, fingerless white gloves.[67]

During the fitting, Margaret threw a tantrum when she saw that Elizabeth's train was an entire foot longer than hers. For once, their mother immediately silenced her younger daughter, coldly explaining that because of Elizabeth's seniority of birth, she enjoyed this privilege. Margaret surrendered—a rare response—but it was a moment that burned. Her tantrum put Elizabeth and the staff on edge about how she would behave during the tedious, three-hour coronation service. Confiding to Crawfie, Elizabeth worried that Margaret was "very young" and might "disgrace us by falling asleep in the middle."[68] She was concerned that any deviation from mature behavior would attract attention and cause unwelcome comment.

On the gray, misty morning of the coronation, the two girls watched with eager anticipation as crowds gathered in front of the palace and along the Mall, "squealing and laughing and peeping out the windows."[69] Soon enough, they found themselves riding in the blue and black Irish State Coach to Westminster Abbey. They were not allowed to giggle or face each other, and at least one of their small gloved hands needed always to be raised. Margaret's seat in the coach was elevated so the crowds could glimpse her through the windows, though of course it was really Elizabeth they wanted to see.

At the abbey, the two princesses were seated next to one another under the watchful eye of their grandmother, whose domineering presence reminded them to behave impeccably during the ceremony. Elizabeth watched the pageantry in fascination, but what she seemed even more impressed by was that "[Margaret] was wonderful....I only had to nudge her once or twice when she played with the prayer books too loudly."[70] Margaret carried her cloak stylishly and deliberately, only occasionally catching attention when she turned the pages of her book with purposeful force.[71] Her mother took no notice. The new queen's mind was elsewhere, reflecting for a moment on the sacred ceremony where a man, her husband, became half-deity, half-priest. Later that day, at a magnificent reception at Buckingham Palace, the new queen consort, perhaps reflecting on the ceremony, was quoted as saying: "We [the royal family] are not supposed to be human."[72]

∽

Symbolizing this transition to their new lives was the move from their palatial but nonetheless cozy home in Piccadilly to cold, impersonal Buckingham Palace. It was only a short walk across Green Park, but it was as if the family were entering a different world. Their new home was so vast that it took a full five minutes to walk from the princesses' bedroom to the garden. The endless corridors were a maze to navigate, so much so that by the time food arrived it would often be cold. There were 775 rooms and a staff of over seven hundred, including a man to wind the clocks and full-time florists to arrange the bouquets.[73] The girls now had their own bedrooms. Bobo shared with Elizabeth and Alah with Margaret. The thrill of enjoying their own rooms did not help them forget their former home. In the early days the sisters often asked if they could simply dig a tunnel back to Piccadilly.

Naturally, their new lives brought change to their daily routine—change that was not entirely welcome. They had to come to terms with the fact that they would now be spending less time with their parents, whose days were filled with matters of state and society. Though the king and queen still spent breakfast with them, their nightly romps soon became a distant memory.

As Crawfie recalled, life at Buckingham Palace created "a glass curtain...between you and the outer world."[74] The girls led an even more cloistered life than before, with no friends outside their small circle. Often times, they would simply stare out their windows at the people passing below. Aside from the nursery staff, the sisters relied on each other and grew even closer. They also continued to dress alike, which had become a source of both security and tension.

Their identical clothes could not mask how much their father's elevated position forced Elizabeth, now eleven, to mature even more quickly. She began developing new interests, especially in politics and political personalities, as she watched numerous officials, both domestic and foreign, visiting her father. Margaret was more captivated by the summer garden parties held on the palace lawns and attended by as many as three thousand guests. She loved to pick out the curious and the distinctly odd, much to her amusement. Elizabeth, as ever concerned about the social niceties, would order her "not to point and laugh" or to "be in too much of a hurry."

Her frequent reprimands spoke to the greater expectations that rested on her shoulders. If she had to grow up in unexpected ways, then the least her sister could do was to buckle down. During this transition the newly crowned King George VI spoke to Elizabeth more seriously, conscious that every moment was a teachable one. When his father was king, he never shared any aspects of statecraft with either him or his brother, the Prince of Wales. It was a source of regret and concern.

She was now granted privileges denied to Margaret. To prepare Elizabeth for her eventual duties, her studies expanded to include lessons in history and the constitution with the vice provost of Eton College, Henry Marten. Naturally, Margaret wanted to join in too but was told it was unnecessary for her to learn history. Instead her lessons included music and dance. Her exclusion from the afternoon tutorials burned deep—Margaret was bitter and frustrated that she was being kept from the world of ideas and critical thinking. As an adult she became something of an autodidact, but she was scattered in her intellectual pursuits. She always felt that she would have enjoyed a richer and more orderly intellectual life if she had been allowed to study more academic subjects during her youth.

Elizabeth was aware of her sister's jealousy and did what she could to mollify her. When their parents agreed to the inauguration of the 1st Buckingham Palace Company of the Girl Guides in 1937, it was clear that Margaret was way too young to join the pack. Elizabeth pleaded with guide leader Violet Synge to let her in. "She is very strong you know," she explained, pointing to a "fine pair of hiking legs" adding that she loved getting dirty. To keep the peace, a Brownie pack of fourteen youngsters, the daughters of palace employees and court officials, was created especially for Margaret. The girls went bird watching, erected tents, cooked sausages on an open fire, and slept under canvas. Margaret loved sharing a tent with other girls, whispering and giggling long after lights out, while her elder sister was shy and felt uncomfortable undressing in a group setting.[75]

Elizabeth continued to cultivate her passion for horses and was given riding lessons at Royal Lodge with Henry Owen, her father's groom. Horse riding—a solitary activity—appealed to Elizabeth's reserved nature, and the process of jumping obstacles helped train her mind for the hurdles of adult life. Elizabeth's other teacher, Horace Smith, noted how well suited she was for horsemanship because of her inherent thorough-ness and a conscientious nature, two qualities that her younger sister seemingly lacked.

As Elizabeth approached puberty, there was a natural incli-nation by the king and queen to keep Margaret as the baby of the family for as long as possible. She grew unused to hearing the word *no* and was rarely admonished when she did wrong. In fact, her naughtiness often made her parents laugh.

Margaret delighted in her role as the enfant terrible even if it exasperated her family. Once, at the age of six, she was sent to her room for some insolence. When she was recalled to her mother's boudoir some two hours later, her mother asked, "I'm sure you are good now, aren't you?" Margaret haughtily replied, "No, I'm naughty still. And I'm going to go on being naughty."[76]

Elizabeth, with her ingrained sense of right and wrong, was deeply perturbed by how Margaret's rude behavior would look to others outside the immediate family circle. She often pleaded with her mother: "Stop her, Mummie. Oh, please stop her." Though Elizabeth would often laugh at Margaret's absurdities, she mostly viewed her sister's conduct with a sense of foreboding. In later life, when they had been to church at Windsor and retired for a pre-lunch drink at Royal Lodge, the queen mother's home, the queen would ask her mother, "How is Margaret this morning?" and calibrate her own behavior to her sister's scudding moods.

During their childhood Elizabeth indulged Margaret's mischievousness, in part because she—like her mother—had the rare ability to defuse her father's frequent "gnashes."[77] These outbursts could be sparked by even the smallest of irritations, such as food being served at the wrong temperature or a man walking by without removing his hat. According to biographer Kenneth Rose, these bouts of anger verged on epileptic fits. As a central part of the cloying claustrophobia of their lives, these episodes could be terrifying for the princesses, who worried when their father's introspective moods would morph into fury, even violence. Then he would kick wastepaper baskets across the room or twist a bathroom sponge to shreds in his frustration.

❧

For now, though, private worries were overshadowed by the threat of another world war. In March 1938, German troops marched unopposed into Austria. Rather than guaranteeing peace, the British and French strategy of appeasement had increasingly emboldened the Hitler regime. With war hovering on the horizon, the king and queen sailed to Canada and the United States for a six-week visit in May and June of 1939. The unstated aim was to woo the Americans with an eye to ensuring their economic support should another conflict flare. Before they sailed from Portsmouth, they kissed the girls goodbye, and the girls stood on the quayside, waving them off. When Margaret said tearfully, "I have my handkerchief," Queen Mary instantly retorted, "To wave, not to cry in."[78]

Upon their return from a wildly successful visit, where the royal couple made headlines after eating "hot dogs," the family traveled to Dartmouth in southwest England aboard the royal yacht, *Victoria and Albert*. Accompanying them was the king's cousin, Dickie Mountbatten, whose intentions for the trip soon became quite transparent.

On the yacht, Mountbatten informed the royal family that two of the cadets had contracted mumps and that the princesses should remain in the captain's quarters on shore to avoid exposure. The only cadet available to keep the princesses entertained was Prince Philip of Greece, Dickie's tall, bronzed, eighteen-year-old nephew—the son of former Princess Alice of Battenberg and Prince Andrew of Greece, which made him sixth in line of succession to the Greek throne.[79]

Elizabeth was only a sheltered thirteen-year-old at the time, face-to-face with this "fair-haired boy, rather like a Viking, with a sharp face and piercing blue eyes."[80] She displayed none of the confidence of an heiress presumptive. And who could blame her? She was dressed in the same clothes—ankle socks and puffed-sleeve dress—as her little sister. Elizabeth sat "pink-faced" beside Philip throughout lunch, as he showed off his impressive skill at downing several heaping platefuls of shrimp and a banana split.[81] While Margaret found "anyone who could eat so many shrimps...a hero," Elizabeth seemed infatuated for other reasons.[82] This awkwardly innocent moment would evolve into the first challenge to their sisterly bond, just as violence was about to engulf the world.

2

Sisters at War

A s Germany eyed a Polish invasion and with the world
on the brink of war, an indignant Margaret demanded,
"Who is this Hitler, spoiling everything?"[1] The princesses knew
little about the political and military calculations embroiling
Europe, though they were now the innocent pawns at the heart
of a German plot. It seemed Hitler planned to capture the
royal families of every European country he invaded and use
them as hostages to guarantee the good behavior of the cowed
citizenry, and Britain was no exception.

In August 1940, a whey-faced man named Dr. Otto Begus
received written instructions to report for a special mission.[2]
Begus had fought and been wounded in World War One,
and became a fanatical recruit to Hitler's National Socialist Party. He served in many capacities—spy, saboteur, agent
provocateur—all with the aim of expanding Nazi control over
Austria, Italy, and Ethiopia. Perhaps his most daring escapade
came during the end of the "phoney war" in May 1940, when
he led the failed mission to capture Queen Wilhelmina of the

Netherlands during the German invasion of the Low Countries. Now he had been assigned to detain the king and queen
of England and their two young daughters.

The mission proved more difficult to execute than expected,
however, dependent for its success on perfect timing and total
surprise. Everything was organized around an initial Kom-
mando unit of twenty-four SS parachutists, including Begus,
some of whom had carried out the unsuccessful Dutch operation. Their numbers were augmented with other men selected
for their fitness, courage, and training. According to the draft
plan, the area around Buckingham Palace would first be inten-
sively dive-bombed, paving the way for four hundred parachutists to land in Green Park, Hyde Park, and St. James's Park.[3]
They would then encircle Buckingham Palace and other royal
residences to prevent counterattacks.

Meanwhile, Begus's unit of around one hundred parachutists would drop from low-flying aircraft directly into the gardens
of Buckingham Palace, then rush through the rooms, searching
for members of the royal family and seizing them alive. According to optimistic estimates, this operation would take only ten
minutes. Strangely enough, parachutists were instructed to
salute and politely address their captives: "The German High
Command presents its respectful compliments. My duty, on
the instructions of the Fuhrer, is to inform you that you are
under the protection of the German Armed Forces."[4] It was
Hitler's fervent belief that if the airborne kidnapping attempt
succeeded, Britain would finally be forced to surrender.

While little written evidence exists to confirm Begus's
operation, the prospect of German paratroopers landing at
Buckingham Palace, the Tower of London, and other royal
residences haunted the royal family and military planners. As
historian Andrew Stewart argues, "There was a real concern

amongst Britain's senior military and political leaders about the potential danger posed by enemy airborne forces and this definitely extended to the security of the royal family."[5] The queen, terrified of being captured, learned how to shoot a pistol in the gardens of Buckingham Palace, taking aim at rats flushed out from bombed-out buildings within the palace grounds. Her cousin Margaret Rhodes later recalled, "I suppose quite rightly, she thought if parachutists came down and whisked them away somewhere, she could at least take a parachutist or two with her."[6] Similarly, whenever he traveled, King George VI started carrying a rifle and a pistol in his car. He also supervised the removal of the priceless crown jewels from the Tower of London to Windsor Castle. There, he and his trusted librarian Owen Morshead used borrowed workmen's tools to dismantle the crowns, crosses, and diadems, hastily wrapping them in waterproof bags and sinking them in the castle ponds. It seems that they were later removed, wrapped in cotton wool, placed in leather hatboxes, and concealed in the castle dungeons.

Behind their brave smiles, both the king and queen felt a nagging sense of impending doom. Yet in public they put on a united front, calm, unruffled, and defiant. Hitler was said to have described the queen as "the most dangerous woman in Europe," as her presence among the people of London and elsewhere harnessed the atmosphere of surging patriotism into support for total war against the Nazi regime. Politician and diarist Harold Nicolson caught the mood when he met the king and queen at a private lunch. He wrote to his wife, Vita: "He was so gay and she so calm. They did me all the good in the world...And those two resolute and sensible. *We shall win*. I know that. I have no doubts at all."[7] Anticipating the grim and uncertain days ahead, the queen wrote to her eldest sister, Rose, asking if she would care for the princesses if the worst happened to her or her husband. Rose solemnly agreed: "I do promise you that I will try my very best & will go straight to them should anything happen to you both—which God forbid."[8] Despite these words of reassurance, both the king and queen continued to fret over how to keep their precious daughters safe.

The issue gained added urgency in the wake of Hitler's invasion of the Low Countries and Queen Wilhelmina's narrow escape from capture after boarding a British destroyer. Following that frantic development, the former lord chancellor, Lord Hailsham, wrote to Prime Minister Winston Churchill, urging the king, queen, and princesses to evacuate to Canada, the route of escape used by many of their aristocratic friends: "I observe that the Nazis both in Norway and in Holland made a desperate effort to capture the royal family. No doubt they will do the same in this country if they can." But the king and queen firmly rejected the suggestion that they and their daughters be sent to Canada to escape danger, with the queen resolutely insisting: "The children could not leave without me, I could not leave without the king, and the king will never leave."[9] Privately and quietly, the Canadian government purchased Hatley Castle on Vancouver Island as the residence of the British government in exile, led by the heiress presumptive, who, together with her sister, would have been spirited away from Britain on board a destroyer sailing from Liverpool or by plane via Iceland.

As the Luftwaffe relentlessly bombed London, the royal family tried to present an image of stoicism and good cheer for a battered nation. Though Buckingham Palace suffered nine direct hits during the Blitz, which began in earnest in September 1940, the king and queen remained firm. In a sound bite that could have been crafted by the Ministry of Information, the queen stated, "I am glad we have been bombed. Now we can look the East End in the eye"[10] referring to the continual pounding of that part of London. Amid the death and destruction, the king was celebrated as "a Sovereign standing at the head of his people, sharing their dangers, deeply concerned for their suffering, encouraging them in their continued determination to resist the enemy."[11]

Though their parents refused to ship Elizabeth and Margaret off to Canada, they remained in Scotland during the months leading up to the air war over England. They spent the time riding their horses and playing innocent games, such as catching falling leaves to make a wish. Even the fitting of gas masks seemed just another game, with nine-year-old Princess Margaret regarding the rubber object as a newfangled toy.

Nevertheless, the princesses were aware that outside their insulated surroundings something momentous was afoot. They showed their disgust by pelting the radio with cushions and books whenever they heard the anti-British tirades of Irish-born, pro-Nazi broadcaster William Joyce, known pejoratively as Lord Haw-Haw. With their lives increasingly in limbo, they worried constantly about their distant parents. Once Margaret asked Crawfie, "Do you think the Germans will come and get them?"[12]

On May 12, 1940, the girls were evacuated to Windsor Castle just west of central London. With its deep basements and thick walls, the medieval fortress was virtually impregnable to aerial attack. The rest of the world, however, only knew that the Windsor sisters had been evacuated to "somewhere in the country."[13] Initially, the girls and their governess were told they would stay just for a few days, but they ended up living there for the rest of the war.

When they arrived, a blackout was in force, and the imposing castle seemed cloaked in eerie shadows and ghosts. Elizabeth and Margaret clung to Crawfie as they made their way down the echoing passageways and up the ancient stone steps to their quarters in Lancaster Tower. The gothic gloom was heightened by the absence of decorations; paintings, objets d'art, chandeliers, and other royal treasures had been removed for safekeeping, some stored in disused Welsh mine shafts. Dust sheets covered the remaining furniture, while glazed cupboards had been turned to face the walls so that any shattered glass from bomb blasts could not harm those sheltering from bombing. To add to the Stygian scene, every night heavy blackout curtains were drawn across the windows. Outside, three hundred Grenadier Guards, also known as the Castle Company, served as the first and last line of defense, the men stationed inside trenches protected by barbed wire. Margaret didn't think much of the military preparations, years later describing the defenses as "pathetic," adding they "would never have kept the Germans out but they certainly kept us in."[14]

The castle was governed by a bell warning system. If the bell sounded, castle inhabitants had to make their way quickly to the air raid shelters in the dungeons. Two nights after their arrival, the warning bell rang and the girls headed down to the basement. They arrived late, much to the consternation of members of the household, as Margaret could not find her knickers. Once underground, she refused to sleep on the camp beds, though she eventually dozed off. By contrast, Elizabeth never once closed her eyes, alert to every sound and nervous about what the war might mean for her family and for Britain.

The next morning Clive Wigram, who had been appointed governor of the castle, informed the princesses and their

governess that they would be staying at Windsor for the foreseeable future. As the king and queen instructed, this was
to be their new home, and the girls would lead as normal a
life as possible. They had to carry on their classes, and they
could play within the confines of the castle walls. Crawfie was
instructed to monitor radio broadcasts and newspaper coverage
to spare the sisters from additional stress. "Stick to the usual
programme as far as you can Crawfie," ordered the king.

೧∾

Their new lives, though, were a long way from "the usual."
They lived in cold, drafty rooms; at bath time, hot water was
strictly rationed; lights were low-voltage or nonexistent; and
they ate meals prepared under the tyranny of the ration book.
This was a system where everyone registered with a store, and
when something was purchased it was marked off in their
ration book to ensure that everyone received the same amount,
be it food or other commodities such as gasoline.

When Cabinet minister Sir Stafford Cripps came to dine,
he asked for an omelet, which made a big dent in their ration of
one egg a week. Knowing that they would have to go without,
the princesses scowled and made faces behind his back as he
tucked into what would have been their meal.

Drills were a regular occurrence, all the more urgent as
the sisters could feel the vibrations of the bombs hitting London some fifteen miles away. As Margaret recalled, the enemy
aircraft "always seemed to come over when we had just got to
sleep." The girls would then have to rouse themselves, throw
on some clothes, grab their tiny suitcases containing their most
prized possessions, and rush down the subterranean passages
"smelling disgustingly damp"[15] to their allotted sleeping quarters. It was perhaps appropriate that the first pet they acquired

was a chameleon, which fed off the flies and spiders they caught for it in this netherworld.

For two consecutive nights in October, the princesses suffered the unnerving sound of "whistle and scream" bombs, along with the repeated thud of antiaircraft guns mounted around the castle. These disturbing noises and the constant anticipation of another air raid was starting to show in the two young princesses. Their mother expressed her concern to Queen Mary, writing that her daughters appeared careworn and "different." "Though they are so good & composed there is always listening & occasionally a leap behind the door and it does become a strain."[16]

Yet, the girls counted their blessings, aware that thousands of children had been parted from their parents and sent to the countryside or to one of the dominions. It was this large-scale evacuation of some three million children that was the subject of Elizabeth's first radio broadcast in October. It was a heartfelt four-minute chat about the challenges endured by the evacuees, many sailing to a strange land for temporary adoption by families they had never met. After many hours of practice, she pleasantly reminded her worldwide audience that children were full of cheerfulness and courage in spite of the "danger and sadness of war." The broadcast ended with Elizabeth urging her sister to join her in wishing everyone good night. Princess Margaret interjected a short "Goodnight, children"—enough to cement the image of a united front. Their playmate Anne Coke, listening to the broadcast from her temporary home in Scotland, reacted like many children: "They were our heroines. There were the two Princesses still in England, in as much danger as us all."[17]

The very next day, October 14, 1939, Elizabeth learned that a German submarine had penetrated the defenses of the northern naval base at Scapa Flow and sunk the *Royal Oak* battleship, with the loss of over eight hundred lives. She jumped up, horrified, and exclaimed: "Crawfie, it can't be! All those nice sailors!" Even at Christmas, the *Royal Oak* tragedy still weighed on Elizabeth's mind. She felt guilty, telling Crawfie, "Perhaps we were too happy. I kept thinking of those sailors and what Christmas must have been like in their homes."[18]

The princesses started a vegetable garden in the grounds, covering their produce with netting to stop rabbits; learned to knit socks and gloves for the war effort—a pastime Elizabeth struggled to master—and continued French lessons with Madame Marie-Antoinette de Bellaigue. Their teacher, who taught the princesses until 1948, later recalled that Elizabeth already displayed "a strong sense of duty mixed with *joie de vivre* in the pattern of her character."[19] Her merry little sister saw the language lessons as an opportunity to sing French country and nursery songs and play the piano.

Aside from such shared moments, Elizabeth's education was changing significantly. Twice a week, like some character in a Jane Austen novel, Henry Marten would arrive at Windsor Castle in a pony and trap, a Gladstone bag full of books and papers by his side. Though he was rather hesitant to teach the princess details about the constitutional decline of the monarchy, they were studying in a place that breathed history and where, in the skies above, Britain was fighting for survival. In March 1945 Marten was knighted by the king on the steps of Eton College, where he was the vice provost and later provost or headmaster. The accolade was granted for his work as Princess Elizabeth's tutor but also his lifetime service to the college, during which he wrote several standard history textbooks.

While Elizabeth studied with Henry Marten, Margaret was once again left to her own devices, a situation that was, as she later told her official biographer Christopher Warwick, "I don't mind telling you a bone of contention."[20] Fellow biographer Kenneth Rose noted: "The undemanding course of study at the hands of the governess Crawfie left an unsatisfied appetite in the younger of her two pupils." To add insult to injury, she was not allowed to take singing lessons, hobbling her natural ability. As her cousin Margaret Rhodes observed, "She missed her vocation; she should have been in cabaret."[21] Margaret was left to focus on an undemanding, ladylike curriculum of reading, writing, dancing, and drawing—typical finishing school fodder for girls of her class.[22] "Margaret did resent her lack of education very much," argues royal historian Hugo Vickers. "She blamed her mother for it very much. I don't think she ever forgave her to be quite honest."[23] Years later, Margaret agreed that this seemed to be a shortsighted policy, given the plain fact that twice in recent royal memory the second son, namely George V and George VI, had assumed the throne, and both were shockingly unprepared. In these desperate and dangerous times, Margaret was just a heartbeat away from becoming the next queen.

The growing educational divide between the sisters was amplified when the king and queen decided to travel from Buckingham Palace to Windsor Castle every night in a bulletproof car. The presence of her parents meant that Elizabeth spent more time with her father discussing, superficially at first, current affairs and matters of state.

When important visitors—whether ambassadors or politicians—came calling, the queen would urge Elizabeth to converse with them.[24] The king, who was known in Whitehall as "Reader One," also gave her insight into the world of the red box, which contained top-secret letters, confidential state papers, and other vital documents that she would someday review, approve, and sign herself.[25] From the beginning he treated his daughter seriously and with respect, expecting and getting a similar response from his daughter.

As photographer Lisa Sheridan recalled, "I noticed that he drew Princess Elizabeth's attention to a document and explained matters to her very earnestly. Princess Margaret, meanwhile, sat silently...knitting." As the months ticked by, this bond of understanding between the king and the heiress presumptive matured. There was also a growing bond of affection. "When they went into the garden together, her arm went spontaneously around his waist and he pulled her towards him," recalled Sheridan. "They seemed to have their own little jokes together. Theirs was a special intimacy, more deep than perhaps was usual in an ordinary family."[26] The affecting closeness between father and daughter extended to the family quartet. Their happy affectionate state was observed by the girls' friend, Alathea Fitzalan Howard, who lived on the estate and regularly joined them for drawing and dancing lessons as well as other social events. In her wartime diary she described the royal family as "four people who mean everything to each other, whose lives form one spiritual whole, independently of the aid of all outsiders or even relations." In another entry she says of the sisters that "they are happier alone with their parents than with anyone else on earth."[27]

Yet within that loving family dynamic there were tensions. Margaret was rather envious of the increased attention her father showed to her teenage sister as they discussed current affairs and matters of state. In Margaret's eyes it disturbed the delicate balance of affection between "we four." In a childish attempt to assert her place as "daddy's little girl," she resorted to her two surefire methods of gaining her father's attention: behaving like a spoiled brat or making him laugh. Now aged eleven, she was far too old for tantrums, so she devised trickier ways to stand out. Sometimes, she would simply "disappear," sending her parents and staff in near panic until she appeared nonchalantly from her hiding place. Then, as she was being chided for her antics, she would make a joke, thus defusing the dressing-down. Once, her blue eyes shining innocently, she interrupted her father midway through a scolding: "Papa, do you sing 'God Save My Gracious Me'?"[28] On occasion she reduced him to fits of giggles, particularly when she mimicked some pompous visitor. For all of Margaret's naughtiness, the king, according to one observer, would still "look at Princess Margaret in sort of amazement that he had produced this object who found everything so easy and was a pretty little thing."[29] "The King spoiled Princess Margaret dreadfully," the daughter of one of his courtiers remembered. "She was his pet. She was always allowed to stay up to dinner at the age of 13 and to grow up too quickly. The courtiers didn't like her much—they found her amusing but she used to keep her parents and everyone waiting for dinner because she wanted to listen to the end of a programme on the radio."[30] Her antics, however, cut no ice with Queen Mary, who, like a number of royal courtiers, thought Margaret "spoilt."

Between the sisters, Elizabeth responded to Margaret's antics with exasperated tolerance, rolling her eyes at her attention-seeking behavior and reacting with horror when she pulled practical jokes, such as hiding workmen's or gardeners' tools and on at least one occasion sounding the air raid bell to rouse the guard. While Margaret rolled with laughter, Elizabeth went into hiding, cringing with embarrassment while grudgingly admiring her nerve—a sassiness she entirely lacked.

When Crawfie tried to separate the two, Elizabeth would express reluctance: "Oh, it's so much easier when Margaret's there—everybody laughs at what Margaret says."[31] The reserved older sister came to depend on her vivacious younger sister to act as a buffer and protect her from having to make conversation. Often her shy teenage interactions would stutter to an awkward silence. On those occasions she was glad of the chatty presence of her sister.

This was particularly the case when the sisters entertained some of the Grenadier Guards officers based at Windsor. Elizabeth would host teas and luncheons, while Margaret would serve as the comedienne, keeping "everyone in fits of laughter."[32] As one officer recalled, Margaret's end of the table was always crackling with energy: "The conversation never lapsed for a moment. She was amazingly self-assured, without being embarrassingly so."

There was, however, another side to these gatherings. What Margaret didn't yet appreciate, though Elizabeth did, was that these young men were going off to an uncertain future. Some did not return. The queen picked up on her daughter's sensitivity, noting how she worried about these young soldiers, especially given the early trauma of the sinking of the *Royal Oak*. She wrote to her brother David Bowes-Lyon, expressing her concerns. "Lilibet meets young Grenadiers at Windsor and then they get killed and it is horrid for someone so young. So many good ones have gone recently."[33]

❧

Apart from the military men, the war made for many transitory friendships. During the war the girls met with a wider cross section of teenagers and young adults than they would had they remained cloistered inside Buckingham Palace. Much of the credit was down to Crawfie, who suggested establishing a Girl Guide troop, on similar lines to the previous one at Buckingham Palace, and organizing a Christmas pantomime. The girls joined with the sons and daughters of the household staff who attended the nearby Royal School to rehearse for the seasonal event. Headmaster Hubert Tannar wrote the scripts and assigned the parts, while the king himself helped with costume design.

When the sisters began preparations in the winter of 1941, Margaret made it clear that she wanted the lead role of Cinderella while her sister was happy to be cast as Prince Florizel, donning a powdered wig, white satin jacket, and knee breeches. This inversion, Elizabeth deferring to her younger sister, was a significant indicator of their relationship, argues royal historian Kate Williams. "You expect in the royal hierarchy that the future queen would get to play the big role but no, it shows how Elizabeth thought that Margaret was the one who could shine."[34]

The performances, staged every year in the Waterloo Chamber at Windsor Castle, raised money for the Royal Household Wool Fund, which supplied yarn for comforters to give to soldiers fighting at the front. Before staging the first show, Elizabeth was concerned at the high entrance prices, saying to her sister, "No one will pay that to look at *us*." Margaret, much more savvy concerning their drawing power, replied, "Nonsense! They'll pay anything to see us!"[35] In spite of Elizabeth's misgivings, the shows were always a complete sellout.

During the rehearsals, Margaret was a bundle of creative energy, badgering Crawfie constantly with wild ideas for the show. Yet as much as she enjoyed being the center of attention, on the morning of the performance it was Elizabeth who was calm and cool, while Margaret had turned a delicate shade of pea green ten minutes before her appearance.[36] Fellow cast members included star pupil Cyril Woods, who appeared in all four wartime pantomimes and struck up a lifelong friendship with Princess Elizabeth. He could not help but notice that one princess was an extrovert and the other more introverted. Another member of the cast noted about Elizabeth: "She wasn't able to relax with me any more than I was with her. She seemed most comfortable being protective to her sister."[37] Margaret was an entirely different proposition. The cast member added: "I, for one, admired Princess Margaret. I thought her a very good actress. She was the best in our little company. The star, I guess you would say. It had nothing to do with being who she was. Princess Elizabeth was rather stiff. She was never bossy with the other children, but she was quick to correct her sister if she did not approve of her behavior. Princess Margaret liked doing little pranks—moving props, things like that, and she giggled a lot."

Silliness aside, the show was such a hit that it became a regular feature of Christmas at Windsor Castle. The following year they put on a production of *Sleeping Beauty*, which so impressed the king's private secretary Alan Lascelles that he opined that it would have done credit to Drury Lane, London's theater district. "The whole thing went with a slickness and confidence that amazed me," he noted in his diary.[38]

The princesses' interest in music and song was not confined to the festive season. They took weekly singing lessons with Dr. William H. Harris, the organist at St. George's chapel in Windsor Castle. At one of these sessions Margaret and Elizabeth discovered *My Ladye Nevells Booke*, a collection of sixteenth-century virginal music by William Byrd. Their exploration of this work expanded into a madrigal choir every week, when Harris would bring in Guards officers and boys from Eton. Given Elizabeth's interest in music, it was perhaps no surprise that, shortly after her seventeenth birthday, in May

1943, one of her first patronages—the system whereby she lent her name to an organization or charity—was to become the honorary president of the Royal College of Music.

Elizabeth was growing up, mixing with more people from different walks of life and in the process becoming less reserved and more confident. Over time she acquired a certain degree of charm, charisma, and empathy. Her mother, who was acutely aware of her daughter's inherent shyness—just like her father's—constantly urged her to be brave and launch herself into a gathering, whatever her reservations. She gave Elizabeth a piece of advice that the young princess truly took to heart: "When you walk into a room, walk through the middle of the door." What she meant, recalled her friend Lady Prudence Penn, was "Don't go in apologetically, walk like you're in charge."[39] It was a technique that came naturally to Margaret.

Though she had confidence to spare, Margaret would always be four years younger than her sister, and it mattered. In 1944, Elizabeth came of age, quietly celebrating her eighteenth birthday. During that year she achieved a series of firsts: downing her first stag with a perfectly placed shot; catching her first salmon, an eight-pounder; launching her first ship, HMS *Vanguard*; delivering her first speech as president of the National Society for the Prevention of Cruelty to Children; and attending her first official dinner at Buckingham Palace. At teas and formal luncheons honoring military men, she arranged the seating chart, offered food, and initiated the conversation. Though the palace flatly denied she was entering public life, she was in reality undertaking more and more official engagements. Margaret especially envied Elizabeth's appointment as counsellor of state, knowing that the usual age to acquire such promotions was twenty-one, not eighteen.

She had already been given a taste of what lay ahead for her when, aged fifteen, she was made the honorary colonel of the Grenadier Guards regiment. Accompanied by her father, she carried out her first military duty at Windsor Castle, where the king and heir inspected the Guards. A year later, she undertook her first solo troop inspection of the regiment on Salisbury Plain. It was a daunting experience for the painfully shy teenager. "What shall I do with my handbag during the march past?" she nervously asked the queen's lady-in-waiting, Lady Della Peel, who was there to show her the ropes. As they neared their destination, Elizabeth's trepidation was such that she went pale and was on the verge of fainting. Her companion gave her a chunk of barley sugar and told her to munch it slowly. The color returned to her cheeks, and she got out of the car, shook hands with the various military dignitaries, and inspected the guard as if she had been doing it for fifty years.

Queen Mary's early years of training paid off. Just as she had been taught as a child, she stood completely still, not fidgeting the slightest when the battalion marched past her.[40] On the way back to Windsor, Elizabeth asked if they could make a detour to see the iconic Stonehenge circle. Lady Peel immediately said no, telling her firmly that it was not on their timetable. It was a sign of her future.

There was also a much more solemn task required of her as regimental colonel: writing to the families of those men who never returned to tell them how fondly the soldiers were remembered for their time at Windsor Castle.

Yet she longed for more—in her own words, "to do as other girls of my age do."[41] Her father remained protective as he tried to prolong the illusion of "we four." She took a leaf out of her younger sister's playbook, wheedling and cajoling her parents so that they eventually agreed to allow her to participate in the war effort. In 1945, Elizabeth joined the women's Auxiliary

Territorial Service, an event that made her sister "madly cross."[42] As an ATS subaltern, the future queen engaged in hard, dirty, physical labor—fixing engines; changing tires, spark plugs, and oil; reading maps; and navigating in the dark. Soon she was assigned to drive a fifteen-ton Red Cross truck. For the first time in her life, as she later told Labour politician Barbara Castle, Elizabeth was able to test herself against women of her own age.

She usually didn't arrive back until seven in the evening, often too exhausted to relay her latest adventures. As Crawfie observed, "Margaret was much too young to join up, and as usual she was very cross at seeing Lilibet do something without her." Fed up with the situation, Margaret repeatedly lamented, "I was born too late!"[43] Her weary older sister simply told Crawfie, in a familiar refrain, "Margaret always wants what I've got."[44]

The ATS was the making of the princess. Elizabeth had always yearned to experience life outside the palace, and now that she was imbibing a full draft of that freedom, she grew much more confident and forceful. As Corporal Eileen Heron related at the time, "She talks much more now that she is used to us, and is not the least bit shy."[45] After she had settled in, the king, queen, and Margaret came to visit the unit and looked on with interest as they fixed and renovated various trucks and cars. Margaret scrutinized her older sister, seizing any opportunity to criticize and demean. At one point, during the investigation of a truck engine, she triumphantly spotted a case of weak compression that Elizabeth had overlooked. "It's missing," Margaret insisted. "How do you know?" asked Elizabeth. "Why shouldn't I know?" Margaret demanded, poking aggressively at the buttons on her sister's tunic.

However, the major change in the relationship between the sisters was not Elizabeth's work for the ATS but her love life. It seemed to those in her intimate circle that, though Elizabeth entertained various young men as possible suitors, she only truly had eyes for the young man who could eat a plate of shrimp—and then ask for more.

Those innocent days were long behind Prince Philip now, as he was at the forefront of the war effort. The prince was promoted to become one of the youngest lieutenants in the Navy. He was mentioned in dispatches and awarded the Greek War Cross of Valour at the Battle of Cape Matapan in March 1941, where he took charge of a searchlight to enable British destroyers to locate and shell Italian warships. During the Allied invasion of Sicily through July and August 1943, his quick thinking helped protect his ship, HMS *Wallace*, from aerial attack and almost certain sinking.

During this critical and dangerous time he had kept up an irregular correspondence with Princess Elizabeth. On shore leave in Cape Town, his cousin Alexandra asked to whom he was writing. When he replied, "Princess Elizabeth, in England," she responded quizzically, "But she's only a baby."[46] Yet the mature, serious Elizabeth was hardly a baby anymore. As her cousin Margaret Rhodes recalls, "I've got letters from her saying: 'It's so exciting. Mummy says that Philip can come and stay when he gets leave.' She never looked at anyone else. She was truly in love from the very beginning."[47] It was an assessment endorsed by Lilibet's wartime friend, Alathea Fitzalan Howard, who was taken into her confidence when she overheard the princess, then still fourteen, talking to Margaret about someone called Philip. When she asked who he was, the princess told her: "He's called Prince Philip of Greece." Then the sisters burst out laughing. She eventually confessed that Philip was her "boy." Alathea noted in her diary on April 3, 1941, that the princess cut out photos from the paper relating to the young prince.[48]

There was, of course, a degree of romantic calculation and family plotting about this possible royal match. As early as 1941, Princess Marina's mother, Princess Nicholas, told diarist Chips Channon at a cocktail party in Athens that Philip was to be Britain's prince consort. Though Channon conceded that he was "charming," with Britain's very survival still hanging by a thread, talk of a dynastic union was premature and highly optimistic.

In truth, as much as Elizabeth appreciated Philip's panache, energy, and understated heroism, he was not the only man to make her heart beat a little faster. She told her friend Alathea Fitzalan Howard, a kinswoman of the duke of Norfolk, that she "adored" the earl of Euston, the two teenagers both vying for his affections. Alathea admitted that she had the most "tremendous crush" on the popular Grenadier Guards officer. Unfortunately for them, in 1943 he was posted as the aide-de-camp to the Viceroy of India, Field Marshal Archibald Wavell.[49] He was not the only royal suitor. Alathea's mother also singled out David Mountbatten, the marquess of Milford Haven, who was to be Philip's best man, as possible royal husband material. For her part Elizabeth appreciated the gentle virtues of her first cousin Andrew Elphinstone and felt that he was just the sort of husband "any girl would love to have." In her eyes, it would, she wrote to her cousin Diana Bowes-Lyon, be difficult to find anyone nicer.[50] She rather regretted the fact that he was her first cousin as at the time the risk of birth defects of any offspring was considered, falsely, to be high. In some states in America, marriage between first cousins was banned, although this was not the case in Britain.

Although, as Alathea recalled, her friend Princess Elizabeth was hugely popular at dances with young men lining up to whisk her on to the floor, she worried about her romantic future. In June 1942, Alathea wrote in her diary: "She wondered if she'd ever marry, and I assured her she would, and she said if she really wanted to marry someone she'd run away, but I know she wouldn't really—her sense of duty is too strong, though she's suited to a simpler life."[51]

Alathea, who was two years older than Elizabeth, emerges from her diaries as snobbishly judgmental and high-strung— she would scratch herself on her arms with a knife after family arguments—yet perceptively observant. When Elizabeth described her "beau," Prince Philip, as very funny, Alathea begged to differ, commenting that the royal family had the boring habit of telling jokes they had heard on the wireless. She wrote, "No one else I know is in the least interested in those sort of silly jokes, but then the K [king] and Q [queen] and the princesses are v. simple people."[52] When she was finally introduced to the royal sailor, she found him "quite nice" but not her type.

Though he had his sights fixed on Elizabeth, the dashing and debonair Prince Philip had quite the flotilla of admirers himself. As Princess Alexandra of Greece recalled, "Blondes, brunettes and redhead charmers, Philip gallantly and I think quite impartially squired them all."[53] In December 1943, Philip was given long overdue leave to celebrate the festive season. He wrote to the queen, asking if he could spend Christmas at Windsor, and she accepted. Philip was thus present for the sisters' performance of *Aladdin*, with Elizabeth, for the first time, playing the starring role of Aladdin and Margaret as Princess Roxana. On opening night, Elizabeth could barely contain her excitement: "Who do you think is coming to see us act, Crawfie? Philip!"[54]

While staying at the castle, Philip ended up seeing all five shows and even assisted with props backstage. Elizabeth sparkled in the title role, making her grand entrance by leaping out of a laundry basket and performing an animated tap dance routine. It was clear to Crawfie that she was dancing to an audience of one.

In an intimate Christmas Day dinner with only nine people present—the king, the queen, the two princesses, Prince Philip, and four Grenadier Guards officers—everyone had the chance to scrutinize the Greek-born prince. With his impeccable manners, wartime heroics, and easy charm, he seemed to be the real deal. The next evening, a bigger group danced to the gramophone and played charades, which Margaret of course loved. However, Margaret was only allowed to dance with her father, while Elizabeth spent much of the evening with Philip and was judged by the company to be the belle of the ball.

After he left, Philip and Elizabeth continued to correspond, the princess carrying his picture with her wherever she went. Margaret was consumed with jealousy. It was so unfair, Margaret probably thought to herself. It may have seemed to her that Lilibet got everything and she had nothing. She had her father's undivided attention and now a sweetheart. Once again she must have felt that she had been demoted, from second best to third wheel. It hurt.

If that wasn't bad enough, she seethed at the news that her sister now had a lady-in-waiting and her own sitting room, decorated with attractive antique furniture and soft furnishings in her favored shades of peach and green. It was here where she undertook private lessons and read and answered the many letters she received. It marked a huge change in their relationship.

Doubtless it brought home to Margaret the realization that, though she was more talented and intelligent than her sister, she would always be in the shadows, the court jester, never the star of the show. The princess, according to friends, may have felt, even briefly, that she had the right personality to be monarch. As their friend Alathea Fitzalan Howard wrote in her diary, "Margaret is far and away more the type I would like for the future queen—she has that frivolity and irresponsibility that L [Lilibet] lacks, though one couldn't call either of them dull."[55] For all this speculation, throughout her adult life Margaret was loyalty personified.[56]

Conversely, as Elizabeth grappled with the arcane details of the constitution, learning to distinguish between different medals and insignia—a particular hobby of her father—and tried to absorb complex government papers, she would probably have told her little sister to try coping with all the hard work that comes with being heir presumptive before wishing for the crown. However, these were the musings of sisters struggling in their own way to accommodate their respective roles. Elizabeth knew that her sister was cleverer and wittier; even the stern Queen Mary was, in spite of herself, occasionally dazzled by Margaret. She found her "so outrageously amusing that one can't help encouraging her."[57] Elizabeth always had to work harder and be more responsible, more correct, and more grown-up than her precocious sister. Yet the very qualities her wartime friend Alathea identified—"very matter of fact, uncurious and above all untemperamental,"[58] as a dull counterpoint to her high-spirited sister—were ideally suited for the social and political marathon the monarch must run. Every day she was being judged, assessed, and weighed for a position she never dreamed of occupying. Above all, she did not want to let her parents down, not after her uncle David's behavior.

Deep down, she was perhaps afraid her parents would stop loving her if she failed to fulfill their outsized expectations.

She was temperamentally the responsible one, the head of the family for future generations. It was Elizabeth who was tasked with dealing with life-and-death issues should anything happen to her parents. Sudden death had become a familiar feature of wartime Britain, all the more so toward the end of the war, when the Nazis blitzed London and the surrounding counties with indiscriminate flying bombs or "doodlebugs." The queen feared these devilish devices more than Luftwaffe bombers, which at least had a recognized target in mind. On June 18, 1944, several days after the bombardment began, a flying bomb scored a direct hit on the Guards Chapel, close to Buckingham Palace, killing 121 civilians and military men, many known to the royal family or their household. The tragedy profoundly unnerved the queen, and with the king's brother, Prince George, duke of Kent, already lost in an air crash, she wanted to take no chances. She wrote Elizabeth a letter of encouragement in case she and the king should die. "Let's hope this won't be needed but I know that you will always do the right thing & remember to keep your temper & your word & be loving—sweet—Mummy."[59]

With these increasing psychological pressures, Elizabeth's work in the ATS was as much a release as it was a contribution to the war effort. She felt that she was at least doing something and helping to make a difference. Meanwhile, with her sister away during the day, Margaret began cultivating a relationship with her father's equerry, Group Captain Peter Townsend, a twenty-nine-year-old Royal Air Force pilot and war hero who had joined the household in 1944. Margaret was besotted by his outstanding war record, which included shooting down or damaging at least thirteen enemy planes during the Battle of Britain and continuing to lead his unit even after having a toe amputated as a result of a shrapnel wound. Margaret and her sister had long idolized fighter pilots and had memorized the characteristic sounds and silhouettes of every plane, whether German or British. On their family gramophone, they endlessly played the wartime hit "Comin' In on a Wing and a Prayer," about a missing plane returning home against all odds. Pride of place in the nursery was a Spitfire model, crafted by a Czech pilot from a scrap of a downed Dornier bomber and presented to them in April 1941.

Thus, for Margaret to get to know a decorated Spitfire pilot was a dream come true. That he had piercing gray-blue eyes and the chiseled features of a matinee idol (a "shy Gregory Peck," as one person described him)[60] didn't hurt, either. The king, knowing both of his daughters' excitement at the prospect of meeting a Battle of Britain acc, allowed them to travel to his office at Buckingham Palace on Townsend's first day as equerry. They deliberately met him in the corridor, and both girls left their encounter entirely captivated. Elizabeth is supposed to have whispered to her sister, "Bad luck, he's married."[61]

Townsend's early impressions of the princesses echoed the views of many. In his eyes Elizabeth had not yet "attained the full allure of an adult," while Margaret "was as unremarkable as one would expect of a 14-year-old girl." He did, however, note that her eyes resembled "a deep tropical sea" and her occasional "shattering wisecrack" would ensure that "all eyes were upon her."[62]

As equerry, Townsend essentially served as the monarch's aide, assisting with events, organizing logistics, and ensuring that visitors arrived punctually and were looked after. In short, he made sure everything ran like clockwork and did so in a way that was agreeable, inconspicuous, and tactful. Though, according to Tommy Lascelles, he was a "devilish bad equerry,"[63] he soon became an indispensable part of the palace setup as a calming, empathetic influence on those around him. The king in particular valued his low-key style and appreciated a man who thought before he spoke. It helped enormously that Townsend's own brother Philip had a severe stammer. As a result, Townsend knew precisely how to help the king overcome his agonies, to maintain his flow of words and even rein in his "gnashes." The king so esteemed Townsend's presence that he agreed to be godfather to his second son, Hugo George, who was born in June 1945. The king also gave Townsend and his wife, Rosemary, the use of Adelaide Cottage, a grace and favor residence on the edge of Windsor Home Park. When the Air Ministry asked Townsend to return to service, the king and queen both resisted, insisting, "Dear Peter, we can't lose him."[64] His wife, whom he married in 1941, was less enthusiastic, feeling that her husband was putting his devotion to the royal family before his marriage.

A regular visitor to Adelaide Cottage was Princess Margaret. Accompanied by either her mother or sister, Margaret would spend an hour or two in the garden with Townsend, his wife, and their two sons.[65] Townsend would ride together with both princesses, and it was noticeable that he was always ready to drop everything and ride with Margaret. For her part, she simply saw Townsend as a companion, a substitute brother, someone to distract her from feeling forgotten by her sister—or so she probably told herself. Others saw it differently. Eileen Parker, the former wife of equerry Michael Parker, observed caustically: "Rosemary had to stand aside while Princess Margaret, hardly out of ankle socks, entertained her husband."[66]

Margaret finally felt that she had someone she could talk

to on the same intellectual level, discussing books, art, and theater. Authors and playwrights like Shakespeare and Chaucer became part of their conversation. Townsend was also close enough now to the family that Margaret felt that she could trust him, and she realized she had found a confidant in whom she could, in Townsend's words, "let down her reserves, confessing some of the frustrations she suffered and some of the aspirations she nurtured."[67] With her sister spending more time with her father, working in the ATS, or waiting for the mail from overseas, Margaret found in Townsend an adult male figure available for guidance and consolation. A crumbling marriage, a lonely princess, and a handsome courtier—the stage was set for a sisterly drama.

After nearly six years of war, the king organized a small private party to celebrate the coming victory in Europe. He invited singer and "Forces Sweetheart" Vera Lynn, comedian Tommy Trinder, and several others to entertain the princesses. As Dame Vera Lynn subsequently recalled, "So of course I wasn't surprised when peace was declared; we had already had a pre-warning, as it were, that it was finishing."[68]

The official statement came several days later, when Churchill announced victory in Europe on May 8, 1945. The profound sense of relief was palpable, and thousands converged on the gates of Buckingham Palace to celebrate the coming of the peace. For the princesses, it was a day and a night never to be forgotten. Speaking on the fortieth anniversary of VE Day, Elizabeth recalled the excitement of that historic day: "My parents went out on the balcony in response to the huge crowds outside. I think we went on the balcony every hour—six times."[69] Naturally it was Margaret's idea to join the exultant multitude outside, and the princesses pleaded with their parents, who finally agreed.

Of course, they were not allowed to go alone. Among the escort party was Peter Townsend, who watched over the sisters as they mingled with the rejoicing crowds. Elizabeth was wearing her ATS uniform, meaning that Margaret was the only one in their small party in civvies. Nonetheless, they still managed to go unrecognized, wandering among the merrymakers and cheering each time their parents appeared on the balcony. Decades later, Margaret nostalgically recalled: "VE Day was a wonderful sunburst of glory. I don't think I'll ever forget it as long as I live."[70] The sisters linked arms, sang, joined conga lines, and danced with strangers, soaking up the unadulterated relief and happiness. The king, watching the good-humored mayhem from the palace balcony, said to the queen, "Poor darlings, they've never had any fun yet."[71]

After five years of being virtual prisoners inside Windsor Castle, the sisters were at last living their fantasy of anonymity. For that brief and thrilling instant, it felt as if Elizabeth and Margaret had set aside their adolescent differences, uniting with the people of England. Little did they know that the relationships that had been sparked during the war would strain their bond during the peace.

3

Love in a Warm Climate

In early 1944, when journalist Rebecca West visited Buckingham Palace to interview Princess Elizabeth for her eighteenth birthday, she met two princesses for the price of one. It was an intriguing encounter, with West confiding in her diary that Elizabeth was "sweetly dutiful, possibly with her father's obstinacy." In her younger sister she saw what she described as a "shrewd egotism." "When she grows up people will fall in love with her as if she were not royal. The other one is too good, too sexless."[1]

After years of wearing matching outfits, the sisters began to explore and expand their own wardrobes, defining themselves outwardly by what they wore. It was clear that Elizabeth—as well as her maid and eventual dresser Bobo MacDonald—had little interest in fashion, which was just as well given the wartime edict of make do and mend. In addition, the sisters had to conform to one of their father's first and strictest edicts—not to accept presents, however well meant. That applied, much to the girls' chagrin, particularly to nylon stockings. Margaret, who was more interested in style, particularly French fashion, than her sister, still had to wear hand-me-downs unless the vouchers in her ration book enabled her to purchase a new coat, dress, or hat. As soon as clothes rationing ended, her wardrobe expanded accordingly.

The end of hostilities also meant that the girls could stage a great escape and move back to the palace, once the bomb damage was repaired. With the smell of fresh paint still hanging in the air, both princesses acquired their own apartments inside Buckingham Palace and began unpacking boxes of crystal, china, and family pictures that had been stored away for safekeeping. As she decorated her rooms, Margaret sang in her self-described "village choir voice," polishing and placing her precious wares. After six years of relative safety and abbreviated country living, adjusting to war-ravaged London was a challenge. As Princess Margaret later recalled, "It was a nasty shock to live in a town again."[2]

The king softened the blow by hosting dances every fortnight in the Bow Room. Guards officers as well as young men like the duke of Rutland and Lord Euston, who was Lascelles's considered choice as husband material for Princess Elizabeth, were invited. At one dance the king, in unusually high spirits, led a conga line through the palace corridors, leaving the dance band playing to an empty room.

The princesses gradually spread their wings, going out for dinner and dancing at restaurants like Quaglino's, Mirabelle, and Ciro's or catching the latest Noël Coward play. Their quest for fun extended way beyond the capital, Elizabeth informing her cousin Diana Bowes-Lyon in a letter dated November 1945 that, during their stay in Scotland, they had learned a number of Scottish reels, which they had put to good use at Ghillies

Balls. The highlight of their stay had been the arrival of a six-foot-four Army captain named Roderick Cameron Robertson-Macleod, who had spent almost five years in a Nazi prisoner of war camp. In her gossipy letter she told her cousin how she and Princess Margaret had met "a devastatingly attractive young giant (with fair hair and blue eyes of course) from Skye called Roddy Macleod. He caused my Margaret's heart to flutter a bit, I think (mine too, a bit) and he was great fun."[3]

Meanwhile it would be nearly a year before Princess Elizabeth would see her sailor sweetheart, as the prince was still on active duty in the Far East and not due to return until early 1946. As amusing company as Roddy Macleod had been, there was no doubting where her affections lay. Margaret recalled how her sister had "danced round the room for joy" after receiving a photograph of Philip one Christmas.[4] Nonetheless, it was an achingly long gap, especially as their last meaningful meeting had been at Coppins, the home of the duchess of Kent, during Easter 1944, where Princess Marina played both chaperone and cupid. As the historian Sir Steven Runciman, a friend and confidant of both Princess Marina and the queen mother, later observed, "It was Princess Marina, not Mountbatten, who was the marriage broker between the Queen and Prince Philip." It was noticeable during these trysts in the country that if Philip complimented her on wearing a certain style and color of dress, she would ensure that she was wearing something similar the next time they met.

Even though her parents put plenty of eligible bachelors in her path, Elizabeth was steadfast. While the likes of Hugh Euston and Andrew Elphinstone had been charming diversions, she had never wavered from the main event, her love for Prince Philip. As one courtier observed, "There really was no one else she could possibly marry but Prince Philip," meaning that as he was genuinely blue-blooded with both parents of royal lineage, he fit the profile necessary as a future consort.[5] Once Philip was granted leave from his destroyer, HMS *Whelp*, he immediately asked for permission to see Elizabeth. A private dinner was arranged for them at Buckingham Palace, with Margaret present to act as chaperone and footman as she carried a table and chairs into her sitting room.

On the day of the dinner, the princess, clearly wanting to look her best, spent an uncharacteristic amount of time on her wardrobe and makeup. When she and Philip were finally reunited, it was clear that their devotion to one another remained true. During a brief tour of her apartment, the princess pointed out the photograph of Philip, suitably bearded and now out of date, that took pride of place on her mantelpiece.

There was a childish simplicity about their wooing. After dinner the trio played tag and chase along the palace corridors, and they also enjoyed a parlor game called Murder in the Dark, which, as the title suggests, meant hiding away in dark corners with the lights turned off. For his part, Philip enthusiastically embraced these juvenile activities. On one occasion, he jokingly removed the sign on the door that said NURSERY and replaced it with another one inscribed MAGGIE'S PLAYROOM.

The presence of Margaret kept the progress of their romance in check unless Crawfie interceded. "It was always a threesome, unless I took a hand and did something about it by removing Margaret on some pretext or other," she recalled.

Undoubtedly Margaret would have preferred to freeze time and continue as the "Three Musketeers," but the romance between Philip and Elizabeth continued to blossom. The noisy arrival at Buckingham Palace or Coppins of the prince's zippy black MG sports car, a gift for his twenty-sixth birthday, served as the starting gun for that day's or weekend's wooing.

As Philip's visits to see Elizabeth became more frequent, the outer royal family began taking notice. Queen Alexandra of Yugoslavia told Princess Marina, the duchess of Kent, "I only hope Philip isn't just flirting with her. He's so casual that he flirts without realizing it."

"I think his flirting days are over," replied the duchess. "He would be the one to be hurt now if it was all just a flirtation or if it is not to be. One thing I'm sure about, those two would never do anything to hurt each other."[6]

During his teenage years he proved that he was capable of grand passions, in the summer of 1938 falling madly in love with the beautiful actress and model Cobina Wright Jr., whom he first met at Harry's Bar in Venice. They were virtually pushed together by Cobina's ferociously ambitious mother, also named Cobina.

For the next three weeks the prince escorted Cobina, two months his junior, around Venice. They went dancing and drinking together—Philip has a reputation as an excellent dancer—and he took her for late-night gondola rides. He followed Cobina and her mother back to London, where they spent days walking the streets of London hand in hand. Before they sailed for New York, Philip gave Cobina a bracelet inscribed "I Love You" next to a Greek flag. Uncharacteristically, he cried as he kissed her goodbye. According to Cobina's friend Gant Gaither, he wrote regularly to her and even talked about marriage. Cobina though was not interested in a young man with a title but no money. She ended up marrying Palmer Beaudette, the millionaire heir to an automobile fortune. Years later she revealed that she kept photographs of the three loves of her life in her apartment—one of whom was Prince Philip.

Cobina Wright Sr. was not the only mother with dynastic ambitions for her daughter. The mother of Hélène Cordet, a supporter of the Greek royal family in exile, made no secret of her hope that her daughter and Philip would one day marry. Hélène had other ideas. Though they were close friends, as Philip often stayed at the Cordets' French country home, Hélène fell for an Oxford student instead. The couple married on April 29, 1938, and Philip not only was best man but gave the bride away. After her marriage failed she had two children out of wedlock. Prince Philip agreed to become their godfather and even helped with school fees. His generous gesture sparked rumors that he was the father of her children, gossip that she firmly dismissed, saying that her children's father was a French fighter pilot.[7]

Yet his reputation as a flirt preceded him. During the latter part of the war, he served in Australia and the Far East. His fellow officer and friend Mike Parker stated that Philip collected "armfuls of girls," a phrase he subsequently regretted. While on leave in Sydney and Melbourne, the two young officers had a few drinks and went dancing. "There were girls galore but there was no one special," insisted Parker. His Australian friend was probably being too loyal. As his romance with Elizabeth was long-distance and uncertain, he had every right to play the field. He had always had an eye for a pretty girl, and throughout his married life, when he walked into a room, the prince invariably made a beeline for the most attractive girl in the room and struck up a conversation.[8]

During his courtship of Princess Elizabeth, questions were raised inside the palace about whether this flirtatious first lieutenant would be faithful. The king's private secretary Tommy Lascelles thought not and may have been privy to the rumors that the royal sailor had bedded two women in Sydney while his ship, HMS *Whelp*, was being refitted. His friend and eventual equerry Michael Parker kept to the party line and argued that while Philip had met plenty of girls, there was never any-one special. In fact he was a "reserved" young man able to hold in his feelings.[9]

Though he had the support of his influential aunt and uncle, Dickie and Edwina Mountbatten, and his aunt, Princess Marina, as well as the unwavering devotion of the princess, Philip's acceptance as the future queen's husband and consort was by no means assured. There were skeptics, ranging from the king and queen; Queen Mary; Tommy Lascelles; members of the Bowes-Lyon family, especially the queen's brother David; and a group of High Tory earls, dukes, and lords, including Eldon, Salisbury, and Stanley. He was dubbed "Charlie Kraut" or "the hun," and they felt that he came from an impecunious royal lineage whose family married Nazis and that his father, Prince Andrew, was a person of dubious morality. Until Prince Andrew's death in 1944, he lived with his mistress, actress Andrée Godard, in the south of France. Ironically, in terms of blood lineage, Philip was more royal than the princess. He is related to the royal families of Russia, Prussia, Denmark, and Greece and able to call himself a great-great-grandson of Queen Victoria.

There was no family fortune, however. When his father died, Philip was bequeathed two suits, his ivory-handled shaving brush, and a signet ring. Moreover, his Navy salary would not support a princess and a family. During his shore leaves he stayed with titled relatives, managing to live well thanks to the largesse of others. Even his potentially brilliant Navy career was in jeopardy because he was technically Greek and would have to apply for British citizenship if he wished to continue as an officer. The admiralty considered that his retention in the service depended on his naturalization. In turn his natural-ization also hinged on the warring state of Greek politics. His decision to apply for British citizenship could be interpreted by the opposition as yet another Greek royalist heading for a safe haven abroad. Prime Minister Clement Attlee left the matter in abeyance until after the Greek plebiscite in September 1946, when the Greek people voted to restore the monarchy. In the end it needed Dickie Mountbatten's famous drive and contacts to jump through the remaining administrative hoops to secure his nephew's naturalization. It was noticeable, at least to newly minted Lieutenant Philip Mountbatten, that Dickie had had little help from the palace in solving this tricky issue.

As one of Elizabeth's ladies-in-waiting recalled, "They were bloody to him. They would have preferred the princess marry someone with a high position of his own, who would have slipped easily into Court circles—a rich, sporting English duke rather than a penniless foreign prince. The Greek royal family were regarded as being very much at the bottom of the royal heap."[10] In the eyes of Lascelles in particular, Philip was a "rough, ill-mannered, uneducated" upstart who did not show adequate respect for the court. Even though Philip's mother had been born in Windsor Castle, and he had been educated in Britain and served with distinction in the navy, he was not trusted as having the right stuff—that is to say, educated at Eton or Harrow rather than his alma mater of Gordonstoun, a nonconformist, politically radical school in the far north of Scotland run by a German Jew. Though the lovestruck Elizabeth was aware of this hostility toward Philip, her loyalty to him never wavered.

While Philip himself was keen to pursue the match, the opposition to him at times proved daunting. A senior clergyman who had known the prince for years explained: "In the early days of the courtship Philip certainly toyed more than once with throwing in the towel. He could already see that the restrictions being placed on him could be suffocating but he was dissuaded by Mountbatten."[11] In terms of court politics, Uncle Dickie's support was a mixed blessing. He was seen by many as pushy, meddling, and too influential. It was apparent that his main goal in life was to promote the house of Mountbatten, and by ensuring his nephew now carried his surname, he furthered his dynastic ambitions. As Philip soon appreciated, Mountbatten's support attracted the corresponding enmity of those, like Tommy Lascelles and Queen Mary, who sought to diminish his authority. Though Philip tried to be his own man, there were many at court who saw him as beholden to Mountbatten. So determined was Uncle Dickie to make the marital case for his nephew that the prince chided him for forcing him "to do the wooing by proxy."[12]

Meanwhile, the king's position was complex. He liked Philip, describing him to his mother as intelligent, with a good sense of humor, someone who thought about things the right way. At the same time, he remained possessive, intent on preserving "we four," the phrase symbolic of the close bonds between the royal quartet and a representation of all he had longed for during his own repressed childhood. Elizabeth was just twenty, had little experience of the world, and might well change her mind as she got to know the prince.

Queen Mary, though, was alert to the stalwart character of her granddaughter, telling her confidant Lady Airlie: "Elizabeth would always know her own mind. There's something very steadfast and determined about her."[13] For her part, the queen very much wanted her daughter to be happy but fretted that the self-confident, independent, and ambitious Philip would struggle to accept the junior role that would attend marriage to the future queen.

Margaret, meanwhile, apparently knew that her sister was

prepared to wait out the romance in order to placate her parents. As Crawfie observed, "There were no secrets between the sisters. Margaret came to my room one day, and fiddled around as she always did, picking up something and looking at it, and putting it down. Then she came and knelt down on the hearthrug beside me, and asked abruptly: 'Crawfie, do you like Philip?' 'Very much,' I said. Margaret replied: 'But he's not English. Would it make a difference?' 'He's lived here all his life,' I told her. For a long minute she said nothing at all. Then she said, very softly, 'Poor Lil, nothing of your own. Not even your love affair!' "[14] This exchange demonstrates that whatever jealousy and resentment Margaret felt toward her sister, she cared deeply about her future happiness.

The summer months spent at Balmoral that year changed everything. One day in September, Elizabeth patiently stalked and eventually brought down a twelve-point royal stag. It was perhaps symbolic. During that momentous summer, she had another royal stag in her sights, the princess waiting anxiously for an interview between Prince Philip and the king, which was due to take place in his study. At that historic meeting, Philip formally asked the king for his daughter's hand in marriage. The king had known what was coming, and after discussing the issue with the queen, he reluctantly agreed to the union. There were conditions, though. He pointed out that Elizabeth was very young to be taking such a momentous step and insisted that the couple wait "at least six months, and maybe more, before it could be made public."[15]

Philip took his sweetheart for a walk among the hills and the heather. Accompanied by the lonely call of a curlew, he asked her to marry him. She said yes. However, there were no plans for an announcement in spite of intense media interest. Such was the media hue and cry that later that month, in

September 1946, Buckingham Palace issued a formal state-ment denying an engagement.

Toward the end of the war the royal family had been invited to South Africa by the politically moderate government of prime minister Jan Smuts. The king, no doubt realizing that this would be the last hurrah of "we four," decided that the entire family should take part in the fourteen-week sailing and tour, which was scheduled for the winter of 1947. This historic visit was seen as a restorative for the ailing king and a thank-you to the South African people for their support during the war. Cour-tiers made clear to a crestfallen Princess Elizabeth that she was not being asked simply to make up numbers or to keep her and Philip dangling. It was impressed upon her that on or about her twenty-first birthday, which fell on April 21, 1947, shortly before the tour ended, she would be making one of the most impor-tant speeches of her life in Cape Town. The theme was one of dedication, both to the monarchy and the emerging Common-wealth. It was a marriage of sorts, but not one she had hoped for.

In what would prove to be the king's last overseas visit, the trip would give him one final opportunity to preserve his fantasy of perpetual togetherness before he had to publicly acknowledge his daughter's betrothal. As he admitted later to Princess Elizabeth, "I was so anxious for you to come to South Africa. Our family, us four, the 'Royal Family' must remain together."[16] Additionally, both the king and queen viewed the trip as a chance for Elizabeth to reflect on her romantic future without any pressure. As one courtier observed, "Undoubtedly there was hesitation on the part of her parents. They weren't saying 'You must or mustn't marry Prince Philip,' but rather, 'Do you think you should marry him?' It wasn't forced. The king and queen basically said: 'Come with us to South Africa and then decide.'"[17]

Once the family had digested the import of the visit to South Africa, it became clear to Elizabeth that the engagement would not be formally announced until their return in May. That was nine long months. This stonewalling by her father left Princess Elizabeth bewildered and uncharacteristically depressed. She felt resolute in her decision, feeling that it was her parents who remained indecisive and were using the South African tour as a means to test the couple's commitment. Even Margaret grew impatient, saying to Crawfie, "Lilibet's engagement keeps meandering on for ages."[18] But the couple had little choice except to agree to this timeline, especially as the prince still had to go through the process of naturalization.

Just two nights before departure and with royal engagement speculation at fever pitch, the family went for dinner at the Mountbattens' London home on Chester Street. The party, which of course included Prince Philip, was serenaded by Noël Coward. With Philip's naturalization to become Philip Mountbatten, RN, a matter of weeks away, it seemed the waiting would be over by the time Elizabeth returned.

King George VI made another crucial decision that summer, one with entirely unforeseen consequences. He decided that Peter Townsend would join the royal family as equerry on the South Africa trip. Understandably, Townsend's wife, Rosemary, left with two young boys in an isolated and barely heated cottage, was hardly thrilled at the prospect of spending what turned out to be a historically severe winter on her own. The diary he regularly sent her and the boys was scant consolation. As they shivered through another day, his description of warm climes, plentiful food, and rolling landscapes was unintentionally cruel.

While Elizabeth and Philip faced a period of imposed separation, Margaret and Townsend were gifted the rare chance of getting to know one another in ways that surprised themselves. Elizabeth treated the fourteen-week separation from Philip like a form of emotional torture, torn between duty and love. For Margaret, though, the idea of experiencing exotic places, enticing foods, and vibrant cultures—with a dashing British war hero tagging along—excited her immensely. For both sisters it was a breathtaking experience, all the more so as it was the first time they had been abroad. After more than seven years of rationing and make do and mend, it was as if they had sailed to some subtropical utopia, a land of endless skies, abundance, and warmth.

❦

On the day of their departure, the royal family gathered in the red and gold Bow Room at Buckingham Palace. Elizabeth appeared "sad" while Margaret seemed "very grown up in her pink coat and gay hat with its little feather."[19] Townsend escorted them to the car as snow fell, heralding the bleak days to come. Philip, meanwhile, was forbidden from seeing them off at either Waterloo Station or Portsmouth, from where HMS *Vanguard* would be departing.

It soon became clear that during the voyage and the tour, lovesick Elizabeth, for the first time in her life, was distracted and reluctant to fulfill her duties. Her head—and her heart— were clearly elsewhere. According to Bobo MacDonald, "Elizabeth was very eager for mail throughout the tour."[20] As Elizabeth moped, Margaret was overexcited and high-spirited, her exuberance difficult to rein in without Alah or Crawfie present. On board the warship there was growing concern about the king's health. Though they now were sailing into sunny climes, his health, never robust, deteriorated. His temper flared more frequently, his weight dropped, and his smoking and drinking were out of control. The queen, who was tending to her ailing husband, came to rely on Townsend to keep her daughters entertained. It was a job he clearly enjoyed.

Townsend had first properly noticed Margaret as a young woman the previous summer at Balmoral. At night after dinner, the guests would gather for charades while Margaret would sing and play the piano. Townsend recalled her lively performances: "Her repertoire was varied; she was brilliant as she sung, in her rich, supple voice, to the American musical hits."[21] At the time, Townsend was not only twice her age and married with two children, but also a commoner and member of the household. The two backgrounds would never mix. She was a flighty, flirty girl of school age, and though he was certainly fond of her, up until now, if he had ever entertained thoughts of romance in the past, he had quickly suppressed them.

On board HMS *Vanguard* and then traveling on the White Train, Margaret and Townsend were in a bubble of intimacy, constantly thrown together as the tour progressed. Years later, Margaret confessed to her lady-in-waiting Anne Glenconner that it was in South Africa, amid the undulating veldt and sweeping sandy bays, that she realized her attachment to Townsend was not merely platonic: "We rode together every morning in that wonderful country, in marvelous weather. That's when I really fell in love with him."[22] Memories of those halcyon days stayed with Townsend down the years. He echoed Margaret's sentiments in his romanticized memoir, *Time and Chance*, published three decades later in 1978: "We sped in the cool air, across the sands or across the veldt, those were the most glorious moments of the day."[23] These daily rituals—far away from home—marked the beginnings of an exhilarating and ultimately explosive love affair.

Those who witnessed the jaunty interaction between the king's equerry and the second in line to the throne dismissed Margaret's behavior as no more than a silly juvenile crush. The king, queen, and Elizabeth all felt that her coy interactions were merely a teenage extension of the flirtatious behavior they had witnessed Margo exhibit since she was young. Townsend had the ability of all good politicians—and courtiers—to make whomever they are addressing feel that they are the only object of their attention. Margaret, always complaining that she was second best to her sister, drank in his soothing ministrations. Even the king was lulled into easy confidences with the former fighter pilot. Once, Townsend recalled, he and the king were talking seriously in the car when suddenly he "shut up completely" as if saying to himself, "what am I doing speaking like this, I am the king."[24] It was perhaps a reflection of how he saw Townsend, an honorary member of the family, the son he never had. Apart from his immediate family, Townsend was the only person who could calm the king during his splenetic tirades, so frequent now that Prime Minister Smuts was concerned about his well-being.

Certainly he would never have dreamed that his youngest daughter and his equerry were on the brink of a secret romance—even though her high spirits and natural flirtatiousness had noticeably escalated with every additional teenage year. As one observer noted of Margaret, "She is the liveliest and most amusable person her family has produced for centuries, if not for all time."[25] As her function was to be the spare to the heir, as it were, she had way too much free time on her hands, especially as the royal party focused primarily on the king and the heir presumptive.

Elizabeth's upcoming speeches and her presence by her father's side aimed to project a reassuring image of change within continuity, with the princess being viewed as a competent young Queen Victoria figure waiting in the wings.

The high point of the tour was her twenty-first birthday speech, broadcast by radio on April 21 from Government House in Cape Town, where the princess announced her lifetime devotion and fealty to the crown. Her speech, heard by 200 million around the world, was the culmination of hours of rehearsal and rewriting of the original material, which the king thought "too pompous." She worked with BBC radio correspondent Frank Gillard before he finally judged her sufficiently "composed and confident."[26] On the big day, which Prime Minister Smuts proclaimed a public holiday, the princess began her seven-minute speech by making clear her dedication to a Commonwealth that would strive for racial inclusion. "I welcome the opportunity to speak to all the peoples of the British Commonwealth and Empire, wherever they may live, whatever race they come from and whatever language they speak." (Ironically, apartheid became the law of the land in South Africa just over a year after the end of the royal visit.) She pledged her personal commitment to the monarchy, reciting a moving, almost nun-like vow, totally dedicating her life to serving the crown and the people: "I declare before you all that my whole life, whether it be long or short, shall be devoted to your service and the service of our great imperial family to which we all belong. But I shall not have the strength to carry out this resolution alone unless you join in it with me, as I now invite you to do."

When she first read that paragraph, Elizabeth was moved to tears. It had the same effect on her parents when they listened to the broadcast. Even Queen Mary reached for a handkerchief, scribbling in her diary: "Of course I wept,"[27] as did that old romantic, Winston Churchill.

The speech especially moved Margaret, who sat with her sister at Government House while she made her broadcast. For the first time she sensed how important her sister's place in history truly was, and onlookers noticed that she appeared "visibly shaken" once the speech was delivered.[28]

On the morning of her twenty-first birthday, Elizabeth remained at Government House receiving messages and opening presents sent from around the world. There were a pair of Cartier ivy leaf brooches from her parents, a diamond brooch from the royal household, the Grenadier badge in diamonds from her regiment, and, perhaps most welcome, Philip's gift, which was believed to be a jeweled family Bible.

During the royal tour, students, civic dignitaries, and others had stood in traffic or on street corners shaking their collection boxes to raise money for a check to present to the princess on her birthday. In Johannesburg alone donations amounted to a whopping £140,000. At least these citizens had a choice in the matter. In Rhodesia, now Zimbabwe, more than forty-two thousand schoolchildren had to contribute their weekly pocket money, whether they wanted to or not, toward a platinum brooch set with three hundred diamonds, which was duly presented to the princess. Saddest of all was an earlier incident when a skinny barefoot African ran after the royal car while waving what seemed like a piece of paper. For his pains the queen mother hit him with her parasol, and then police wrestled him to the ground. The impoverished fellow was only trying to give the millionaire princess his own contribution to her birthday—a ten-shilling note, at the time worth around $2.

She was not the only member of her family gleefully accepting of the generosity of their hosts.

Not perhaps since the Delhi Durbar of 1911, when King George V and Queen Mary were given a cornucopia of gems from grateful Indian princes and maharajahs, had a royal tour returned home with such a shower of diamonds, rubies, and gold. The holds of *Vanguard* were swollen with tribute as well as gifts of fruit, sweets—and stockings. At a farewell lunch, the Union of South Africa presented the king with 399 specially cut diamonds to be made up into his Garter star, while the queen accepted a solid gold tea service plus a large 8.55-carat marquise diamond. Margaret and Elizabeth were presented with perfect 6.5-carat blue-white diamonds by De Beers. In total the royal family were given some 540 stones worth £200,000 ($10 million today). "Papa, Mummy and Margaret were all given diamonds on the last day, so we shall all be very grand when we come back," Princess Elizabeth wrote to her grandmother. "I think there are no more beautiful diamonds left in South Africa."[29]

The celebrations culminated in a ball, where Elizabeth wore a white tulle gown "sparkling with diamante and sequin embroidery." There, she was bestowed a gold key to the city and presented with a casket of twenty-one perfectly cut graduated diamonds by Prime Minister Smuts. When Elizabeth opened the casket, she gasped. The price she paid was having to dance with a nervous young man who trod on her toes and danced her into the fender in front of the ballroom mantelpiece. As guests departed they saw the royal sisters, their shoes off, rubbing their feet and giggling.

The jewels and money showered on Elizabeth—and the rest of the royal family—was seen as a physical manifestation of the love, affection, and loyalty felt by many South Africans toward the royal family. Townsend, rather romantically, sensed the love and adoration within the royal family and by the people toward this loving quartet. He observed: "A perpetual current of [affection] flows between them, between father and mother, between sister and sister, between parents and their daughters and back again. Then it radiated outwards to the ends of the world, touching thousands of millions of hearts who sent, rolling back, a massive wave of love to the royal family."[30] As Smuts's government was soon to be ousted and the cruel apartheid system legally introduced, this seems like so much self-delusion from a man dreaming of buying a farm on the Transvaal. He got short shrift from his wife when he returned home.

During the tour it was inevitable that Elizabeth, as the future queen, was the focus of attention. Margaret's role, noted Townsend, was "a relatively thankless one for, beside her sister, heir to the throne, she cut a less prominent figure."[31] As fashionable, effervescent, and lively as she was, the princess came to realize during this ten-week tour, the longest visit she would ever undertake with her sister and parents, that no matter what she said or did, she would play second fiddle to her sister. That was just the way it was and the way it was going to be. As she walked behind her parents and sister during the endless station stops on this South African adventure, she had the growing awareness that if she wanted to find adventure and fulfillment, she had better look outside her home country, a place where she was doomed to live in perpetual shadow.

While it might seem that all the gifts and attention lavished on Elizabeth would distance the sisters further, in reality they grew closer on this trip. For once there was something of a role reversal: Margaret was steady and optimistic, and Elizabeth became gloomy and doubtful. Margaret's growing maturity was noted by Tommy Lascelles, who described her as agreeable and good company, much less of the "palace brat" than

usual. With Elizabeth moping about Philip and eagerly awaiting his letters, Margaret was her ray of sunshine, continually
offering words of support and encouragement, especially when
Elizabeth expressed fears that their father would renege on his
permission for her to marry Philip.

Though Margaret was all bright smiles and mischief in
public—rolling her eyes at long-winded speeches, for instance—
she was masking the creeping awareness that, if all went to
plan, she would be losing her sister forever. This looming sense
of transition was exacerbated by the sudden death of Margaret's
nanny, Alah, who had shared her room for fifteen years. She
had been a daily part of her life, spending more time with Margaret than her own mother. This loss cut deep, and Margaret
was unable to do much more than send Alah's brother Harold
a long letter and flowers.

The girls had changed in other ways too. They had sailed
from Britain as newcomers to the royal road show but returned
as veterans, consummate professionals of the rope line or the
gala dinner. As Lascelles noted of the sisters, "There must have
been many moments in the tour that seemed intolerable to
both of them, but they behaved admirably."[32] He reserved his
highest praise for Elizabeth. "She has got all Princess Marg's
solid and endearing qualities plus . . . an astonishing solicitude
for other people's comfort; such unselfishness is not a normal
characteristic of that family."[33] In other words, the future queen
was thoughtful of others.

୶

The royal party returned to England in May 1947 to a nation
prostrated by the most catastrophic winter in memory. Millions faced widespread flooding, towering snowdrifts, trans-
port chaos, dwindling coal supplies, and food rationing even

more severe than in wartime. Though there had been muted reproach of the royal family for being away during the worst of the winter, the criticism quickly turned to concern as they saw newspaper pictures of the king upon his return. (Certainly there was no mention, even by radical Labour lawmakers, of the gems and other goodies presented to the royal family.)

His sunshine tour was supposed to help him regain his strength, but he came home seventeen pounds lighter, his face gaunt, his body weary. The queen immediately summoned the best medical care. From this point on, King George VI would undergo a series of increasingly serious and life-threatening operations followed by long periods of recuperation, rendering him more or less an invalid.

Elizabeth, who was seen to do a little jig on the foredeck of *Vanguard* as they sailed toward Portsmouth, was in much better spirits once she stepped ashore. Though Philip was not allowed to meet the royal party at the quayside, after two days he headed directly to Buckingham Palace during a break in his Naval Petty Officers' School course at Corsham in Wiltshire. He had an appointment with the king to discuss the engagement and to thank him for enabling him to become a naturalized citizen. During their conversation in his study, the king made an excuse about finding photographs of the South African visit and left him in his office alone. The next person through the door was Lilibet, glowing and excited to see her man.

Upon his return, the king made it clear to the loving couple that he was not prepared to announce their engagement quite yet. While Philip had become a naturalized citizen in February, what concerned the king, though he didn't spell it out at their meeting, was that a foreign prince with relatives who were married to Nazis was not going to be a popular choice with a war-weary public. His strategy was to make Philip, now plain Lieutenant Philip Mountbatten, RN, seem part of the royal furniture, not some exotic carpetbagger. The central thrust of that plan was to get the media on his side. Royal aides as well as Lieutenant Mountbatten and Lord Mountbatten himself approached the editors of the *Daily Express* and *Sunday Express* to emphasize Philip's English credentials and outstanding war record. Mountbatten also wrote to or met various lawmakers, including Labour member of Parliament Tom Driberg, stressing that Philip had spent barely three months in Greece in his entire life and did not even speak the language.

This careful strategy inevitably meant that the engagement announcement was delayed while the necessary groundwork was undertaken, which included inserting Philip's name regularly in the Court Circular. Elizabeth's father set the somewhat arbitrary date of July 15 for the engagement announcement. Whatever parental doubts the king and queen may still have harbored, the expression on their daughter's face told its own story. "She positively glowed," noted a family friend who was present at Royal Ascot week, where Philip and Elizabeth danced virtually every dance together at a ball held in the Red Drawing Room at Windsor Castle. "The smile that was once so diffident was now a declaration. Suddenly she was supremely feminine. She did become more appealing and somehow quite the young woman."[34] She had literally and figuratively come of age during her weeks away from home.

With Philip around, Elizabeth appeared "more delicate, and yet, curiously, less shy."[35] Philip was there to defend her, whether she knew it or not. Shortly before their engagement was announced, a friend of Philip's joked, "You've chosen the wrong girl. Margaret is much better-looking!" Philip tersely replied, "You wouldn't say that if you knew them. Elizabeth is sweet and kind, just like her mother."[36] In the meantime, he was rearranging furniture in his fiancée's apartment in Buckingham Palace. Over the coming months, the once rootless young man would demonstrate his unexpected instincts as a homemaker.

They were able to get to work sooner than they expected. When Philip's mother, Princess Andrew, wearing her distinctive gray nun's habit, was spotted going into the jeweler Philip Antrobus in central London, the game was up. She had gone to pick up the ring and bracelet, which had been fashioned from one of two tiaras still held by the family. The news spread, and the king, faced with a fait accompli, made the official announcement on July 9, to the utter delight of the young couple. For a nation on its knees, reeling from the demands of austerity, the announcement proved a welcome, albeit brief, tonic. The following day those lucky few who attended a garden party on the grounds of Buckingham Palace got the chance to see the happy couple and to glimpse the ring. The crowd spontaneously gave a cheer when they reached the tea pavilion.

When father and daughter came to discuss the wedding date, Elizabeth proposed a date before Christmas, while her father, dragging his feet as usual, suggested the spring or summer of 1948. The princess would have none of it, arguing that the couple had waited long enough to be betrothed, so they should marry promptly. For once her father accepted her argument, and the couple set the date as November 20.

Not unnaturally, the prince, for all his breezy confidence, harbored doubts about what was in store for him once he was set on the path of marrying the future queen. It was not his feelings for her or vice versa that concerned him but the unrelenting strictures of court life. He articulated those fears to his cousin Patricia Mountbatten at the second of two stag nights:

"I don't know whether I am being very brave or very stupid going ahead with this wedding."[37] His cousin, sensing that his question was rhetorical, replied, "I am quite sure you are being very brave." As she later recalled, "We were aware that he wasn't just taking on the immediate family. He was taking on all the outer aspects of court life. He was very well aware that there were going to be difficulties."[38]

He got a taste of those "difficulties" during his first Balmoral visit as a future member of the royal family. Many fellow guests, including the queen's brother David Bowes-Lyon, the Eldons, and the Salisburys, had opposed the match almost up to the day of the July announcement. Philip was aware of this hostility to the union and was on his best behavior shortly after the engagement announcement, when the betrothed couple traveled to Edinburgh on an official engagement. He made sure to stand dutifully two steps behind her while she delivered her speech. This physical and symbolic placing of duty before pride was noticed by everyone at court, who were carefully weighing and assessing the new arrival. It was a tricky first summer at Balmoral for Philip, the prince aware that he was under the microscope, scrutinized by both potential allies and enemies. He apparently annoyed the king when he dropped a mock curtsy to his future father-in-law while wearing a borrowed kilt that was a tad too short. He had not fully appreciated the king's punctilious attitude to correct dress and behavior. The incident perhaps symbolizes the prince's uneasy welcome into the world of "we four."

These doubts and misgivings were swept away in the national euphoria surrounding the wedding, the first royal pageant since the coronation of King George VI a decade earlier. The days leading up to the wedding were filled with rehearsals, parties, dinners, and dances. For some of the women, this formal socializing came at a price. Princess Elizabeth was not the only royal lady to sit throughout dinner with her tiara biting into her forehead. At the end of one evening, the princess sat on the grand staircase, removed her tiara, and gently rubbed her head. Before the big day, many of the 2,583 wedding gifts were displayed alongside the royal family's presents at St. James's Palace. Queen Mary gifted an entire chest of jewels, along with Georgian silver, an antique Chinese screen, several mahogany tables, linen, and even table lamps. The king and queen gave Elizabeth an assortment of necklaces and earrings, studded with glimmering sapphires, diamonds, and rubies. Margaret presented the most practical of gifts—a dozen engraved champagne glasses and a picnic case. Privately, she gave her sister a silver ink stand, perhaps in memory of the one she tipped over her head one day in the nursery so many years before.

On their wedding day, Philip was created a Royal Highness and made Baron Greenwich, earl of Merioneth and Duke of Edinburgh. (A day earlier, he had also been invested as a Knight of the Order of the Garter.) It was a great deal to give a man in one day, especially one whose worldly belongings filled only two suitcases and who went to his wedding wearing darned socks.

Surprisingly, amid all this controlled chaos, Margaret appeared content and grounded. Crawfie perceptively observed: "Margaret was sweet, happy in her sister's happiness. She was growing out of her onetime objection to Lilibet's doing anything she could not do, or having a train longer than hers."[39] Perhaps she had finally accepted, like her father, that time could not be paused to feed their fantasy of prolonged childhood. It would have been tempting, though, as Elizabeth spent the night before her wedding in her nursery bedroom, right next to her little sister.[40]

༈

On the day of the wedding, over 200 million tuned into the radio broadcast, while thousands more lined the streets outside Westminster Abbey. After eight long years of control and regulation, the spectacle was for many a welcome diversion from postwar austerity. There is an irony in the fact that the most radical government in British history—which founded the publicly funded National Health Service; nationalized the railways, gas, electric, and water supplies; and redistributed wealth through changes in the tax base—presided over a royal wedding at a time of unrelenting national hardship. The year 1947 was the nation's "annus horrendus," said the finance minister, Hugh Dalton. Besides the catastrophic winter freeze, there was a fuel crisis, which stopped factories and put millions out of work. This in turn precipitated a financial collapse, which halted reconstruction. A small group of Labour members of Parliament sent a letter to the chief whip complaining about the cost of the wedding, though finance minister Dalton, himself no fan of the monarchy, was able to confirm that monies from the king's Civil List funds had paid for the entire cost of the wedding apart from decorations outside the palace and along Whitehall. This was the only bill the taxpayer had picked up.

༈

It seemed then that as bread was in short supply, the circus would have to do. Royal wedding week was a colorful carnival that gave the British people and those of the empire the chance to renew their historic ties with this ancient institution, the wedding reminding them of the monarchy's place at the center of the nation. As one American observer wrote, the wedding functioned as "a movie premiere, an election, a World Series and Guy Fawkes Night all rolled into one."[41] Or as Churchill put it, the wedding was a "flash of colour on the hard road we have to travel."[42] By and large the man and woman in the street approved of an opportunity to enjoy a display of conspicuous consumption with 60 percent of those polled actively approving of the arrangements. While Mass Observation, a social research project aimed at uncovering grassroots opinion, found pockets of opposition to the event, mainly on cost grounds, the overwhelming majority were delighted to loosen their belts, if only briefly, after eight long years of stringent controls.

As anticipation built in the streets outside, drama unfolded backstage. Unlike the groom's modest preparations—he wore his workaday navy lieutenant's uniform—Elizabeth and her eight bridesmaids were being fussed over by famed couturier Norman Hartnell and his team. It took them a full two hours to fit the princess into her Botticelli-inspired ivory satin gown, embroidered with York roses, ears of wheat, and orange blossoms made of pearl and crystal. The historic creation had taken a team of 350 dressmakers seven weeks to construct. With its theme of rebirth and renewal, the dress had even been debated in the cabinet, as the Labour prime minister Clement Attlee expressed concern that the "Lyons silk" may have come from a country recently at war with Britain. Hartnell tartly pointed out that the silkworms belonged to Nationalist China. Princess Margaret and the seven other bridesmaids wore star-spangled ivory tulle—a politically neutral option.[43]

Inside the palace, just as Elizabeth was cautiously eased into her wedding dress, subdued panic spread through the staff. The bride's bouquet went missing, as did her favorite rope of pearls. Then, amid the controlled chaos, her sun-ray tiara snapped. After repairs performed by the crown jeweler, the tiara was refitted, and the pearls and the bouquet were found in the nick of time.

At last, with the bride ready, the royal guests gathered in the forecourt. At the head of the carriage procession were the queen and Princess Margaret, trailed by the carriages of foreign rulers, then the queen's suite and bridal coach. When the royal procession arrived at Westminster Abbey, Queen Mary took the lead, followed by the queen and foreign sovereigns. Inside Westminster Abbey, the largest gathering of royalty since before the outbreak of war in 1939 had assembled. As Margaret remembered, "It was a tremendous meeting place. People who had been starving in little garrets all over Europe suddenly reappeared."[44] Glaringly missing from the serried ranks, however, were the duke and duchess of Windsor and Philip's sisters. The Windsors were in exile, and Philip's family, because of their marital unions with Nazi aristocrats, were deemed too controversial to be invited—much to Philip's frustration, as he had always gotten on well with his four sisters.

After a thunderous blast of trumpets, the bride and her father entered the abbey. "I was so proud and thrilled at having you so close to me on our long walk in Westminster Abbey," the king wrote to his daughter afterward.[45] At the exact moment that the king and princess walked down the aisle, "a thin, watery sun shone through the stained-glass windows," giving the tableaux an ethereal atmosphere. Wearing hardly any makeup, Elizabeth looked pale and delicate, her veil accentuating her grace and resembling "a white cloud about her."[46] The rays streaming through the tall windows and light from the candelabra reflected off her dress, the bejeweled embroidery sparkling and twinkling in the half light.

Immediately behind the radiant bride and three steps ahead of the other bridesmaids was Margaret—alone. She stopped three times along the procession to straighten her older sister's extensive train.[47] It was a striking scene among many unforgettable moments, and the sight of the two sisters always together now embarking on their own journeys touched the hearts of many, especially their family and friends.

Inevitably the king was moved to tears when Elizabeth passed her parents as she and her husband prepared to leave the Abbey. Elizabeth curtsied first to her father, then her mother; it was a gesture the king had discouraged in his daughters, but at this moment it was Elizabeth's final show of gratitude. They then all returned to the palace for the wedding breakfast. After Philip delivered a short speech, the new bride expressed her sole wish that "Philip and I should be as happy as my father and mother have been."[48] Even the naysayers would have been surprised by the eloquent and touching letter Philip subsequently wrote to his mother-in-law, the queen. He was keen to reassure her that he would diligently care for her daughter: "Lilibet is the only 'thing' in the world which is absolutely real to me and my only ambition is to weld the two of us into a new combined existence that will not only be able to withstand the shocks directed at us but will also have a positive existence for the good."[49]

At the wedding breakfast, Margaret made sure to herd everyone together for photos, shouting, "Come along, everybody!" She appeared supremely happy that day, and Crawfie later reflected: "I hope that people were not too taken up with the bride to notice her younger sister. She moved with extraordinary dignity and grace. More than once the King and Queen exchanged a smile and a reassuring glance."[50] They could only hope that their younger daughter would find a partner as sensitive and dutiful as Philip was proving himself to be.

❧

The day was not yet over. Elizabeth and Philip changed into warm clothes for their honeymoon trip to the Mountbattens' country estate, Broadlands, and as they climbed into the open landau, a soft, cold rain began to fall. When the vehicle lurched forward, the king, the queen, Margaret, and other royal guests ran across the quadrangle, showering the newlyweds with white paper petals. Together, they watched the landau disappear into the darkening winter gloom.

That evening, as the newlyweds made their way to their country retreat, a thick fog descended on Buckingham Palace and a steady rain began to fall harder. Margaret headed to her room to change into her outfit for a private bridesmaids' party. As she proceeded down the corridor, she suddenly slowed while approaching the door to Elizabeth's now-former room. She paused a moment, then went quickly on her way.

It was a bittersweet moment. When the party was over, Margaret spoke emotionally to Crawfie about her deep sense of loss, which she had masked so well during the wedding day. She told her governess, "I can't imagine life here without her." Crawfie, who had her own sweetheart in Scotland, responded, "Never mind, you will be next."[51] Nevertheless, Margaret was once again the younger sister left behind at Buckingham Palace. This time, she felt more bereft than when Elizabeth joined the ATS or began a separate academic route. Her friend, playmate, counselor, companion, and adviser was gone. It was the end of an era and the beginning of a new life both for Margaret and Elizabeth.

4

The Long Goodbye

The first weekend of their honeymoon was, complained Princess Elizabeth, a "vulgar and disgraceful affair,"[1] owing to the constant presence of media and the curious crowds eager to catch a glimpse of them. When the honeymooners attended Sunday morning service at Romsey Abbey, those who could not wriggle inside mounted gravestones, carried chairs, or propped ladders against walls so they could spy through the church windows.

After a few days of being treated like animals in a zoo, the couple escaped to Birkhall in Scotland. They exchanged the cozy comforts of the Mountbattens' stately home for the spartan, snow-bound Scottish hideaway. They enjoyed privacy, albeit with Bobo MacDonald and Philip's valet, John Dean, within calling distance. When Philip's shivering turned into a heavy cold, his wife nursed him herself, writing to her family to let them know that in between snuffles and sneezes they were blissfully happy. Somewhat dolefully, the king responded: "When I handed your hand to the Archbishop I felt I had lost something very precious. Our family, us four, the 'Royal Family,' must remain together with additions of course at the suitable moments!" In closing, he confessed that "Your leaving us has left a great blank in our lives but do remember that your old home is still yours & do come back to it as much & as often as possible."[2]

The king's wishes were fulfilled much earlier than expected, when Elizabeth and Philip returned to London, escaping the bitter Scottish winter just in time for the king's fifty-second birthday. Without a place yet to call home, they moved back into Elizabeth's old rooms while the new couple's official residence at Clarence House, previously chosen by the king, underwent extensive renovations to become habitable. At one point, fifty-five men were working on the dilapidated pile.

There was, though, no avoiding the reality that "we four" had now become five. The king, used to ruling the herd, now faced a young, vigorous upstart at a time when his own health was failing. Philip burned off his excess energy with hard-fought games of squash and badminton, often with Peter Townsend. "These sporting affrays left me with the impression, which remains indelible, of the prince as a genial, intelligent and hard-hitting extrovert," Townsend recalled.[3] His rude health was in stark contrast to that of the king, who, though he was in his early fifties, was not the man he was before the voyage to South Africa. While the war had been over for two years, he still bore the physical and mental scars. His facial wrinkles were deeper, the dark shadows under his eyes more pronounced, the painful cramps in his legs barely tolerable. All this was compounded by the health consequences of decades of heavy smoking and drinking.

A new family dynamic was evolving. Elizabeth, always meek and accepting of her father's will, was gradually transitioning to a new role, as his nurse, careful of his health and his temper. At the same time, the queen and Margaret, who had a shared interest in art, music, and the theater, began to develop a closer relationship; the pair was known for their ability to add life and vim to any social gathering. While they enjoyed Balmoral and Sandringham, neither took part in the daily shooting parties or enjoyed stalking, though the queen was a regular with her rod and line on the river Dee.

It seemed, too, that Philip, since his elevation, had become rather more imperious than his sister-in-law cared for. When the couple's first choice of country house, Sunninghill on the Windsor Park estate, burned down shortly before their marriage, they found a second place, Windlesham Moor, for their use as a weekend retreat. Margaret was a regular visitor. However, she was not entirely appreciative of her navy officer host, who brought the terse orders and brisk language of the bridge to his social life.

On one occasion Philip forbade the staff from serving her breakfast in bed, her usual weekend habit. He also put his foot down when the trio went to a party together. Margaret insisted on staying longer, but Philip ordered that her coat be brought so they could all leave together. While Philip's treatment of her rankled, Margaret initially reacted as many teenagers turning eighteen would do—with casual indifference and a determination not to be intimidated.

But the sisters were as close as ever, and when in April 1948 Elizabeth privately revealed her first pregnancy, Margaret became even more solicitous of her sister, showing no trace of envy about being nudged down the line of succession. Everyone was thrilled that there was going to be a new addition to the family. The newlyweds had done their duty and the dynasty was secured. She had no intention of letting her pregnancy, which was known only to the family, prevent her from fulfilling her first foreign state visit to Paris in May. Not only did she feel confident in the language—all those years with Madame de Bellaigue were about to pay off—but she wanted the chance to wear the gorgeous Norman Hartnell gowns reserved for state occasions.

The visit, which was described as "the Norman Conquest in reverse,"[4] was a triumph, judging from the thousands who turned out to catch a glimpse of the princess and her dashing husband. When she returned home, she was somehow changed—more royal, majestic even. She was now seen as an independent ambassador for her country, no longer in the shadow of her father. The announcement of her pregnancy on Derby Day, June 4, ensured that with a November birth, 1948 was going to be the year of the princess.

This was as well, for the king was suffering. During the annual visit to Edinburgh in August, he complained to Townsend, "What's the matter with my blasted legs? They won't work properly." Normally a vigorous walker, he was now unable to climb the slope up Arthur's Seat, a prominent hill that overlooks Holyroodhouse. His pain was constant and at times excruciating, but the king kept his condition a secret from everyone except Townsend. He was with the royal party in August when the family celebrated Margaret's eighteenth birthday. Her most treasured present was the appointment of her first lady-in-waiting, Jennifer Bevan. The presence of the young aristocrat enabled the princess to go out and about without her sister, mother, or other staff—for Margaret, this was heavenly freedom.

Until then, Peter Townsend was on hand to accompany the princess on her first solo engagement. They flew to Belfast to launch the 28,700-ton liner *Edinburgh Castle* in October, a month before her sister's wedding, It has since been claimed that there was a request that Townsend be moved to an adjoining bedroom to the princess, who was staying at Hillsborough Castle. While there never was any suggestion of impropriety, if the story had emerged at the time of a married man sleeping in the next room to the queen's sister, it would have caused unnecessary scandal.[5]

~

The following September, her new lady-in-waiting, Jennifer Bevan, and Peter Townsend accompanied the princess to Amsterdam, where she represented the king at the inauguration of Queen Juliana of the Netherlands. Margaret, just over five feet tall, looked very young and rather lost amid the milling crowd. It was during this trip, without another senior courtier or member of the royal family present, that others got the first inkling of a definite chemistry between the king's equerry and the king's daughter. "They made eyes at one another, even on the most official of occasions," recalled one attendee.[6] She looked gorgeous, wearing a glittering tiara borrowed from her sister and dressed in a cream, pearl-beaded gown designed by Norman Hartnell. At the ball held at the International Cultural Centre that evening, she again looked "noticeably radiant" while dancing with the group captain. They did not leave until three in the morning. Rumors quickly circulated that she had gone so far as to "lean against" Townsend and "take his arm." His memory is rather different, complaining that the dance was stuffy, overcrowded, and far from enjoyable.

~

However, as Townsend himself would later admit, "Without realizing it, I was being carried a little further from home, a little nearer to the Princess."[7] He was increasingly seeing

Margaret not as his charge, an immature girl, but as an attractive and seductive woman. Townsend managed Margaret's entire visit, advising her on how she should conduct herself and even writing the short speeches she was scheduled to deliver. Margaret's biographer argued that this growing attraction still remained innocent and chaste—nothing more than an "easy, quite unselfconscious relationship based on liking, trust, shared tastes and interests, and admiration."[8] Crucially, however, it was at this juncture—as the relationship developed into a deeper bond of affection—that Townsend realized that he was trapped in a disintegrating marriage with a woman who no longer shared his ambitions. The South Africa trip had sparked a desire "for horizons beyond the narrow life at home."[9] Those horizons ironically began and ended at the office—Buckingham Palace. When he discovered that his wife, Rosemary, was having an affair with a Guards officer, that spelled the eventual end of his marriage.

For now, though, Margaret's embryonic romance was overshadowed by far more urgent matters. When they arrived back at Balmoral from Amsterdam they discovered that the king had finally told his doctors that he was suffering from debilitating leg pains. Not wanting to cause a fuss, he had been secretly treating his painful condition with homeopathic medicine and long walks among the heather. The delay almost killed him. His doctors, shocked by the seriousness of the issue, summoned an authority on vascular complaints, Professor James Learmouth, who traveled from Edinburgh to examine the king. The diagnosis was grave. He had Buerger's disease, or inflammation of the blood vessels. Gangrene had already begun developing, posing the dire possibility of amputation. His already dangerous condition was further exacerbated by cirrhosis of the liver and an unspecified lung ailment, possibly cancer.

The king insisted that the news be withheld from Elizabeth for the time being, as she was due to deliver her baby at any moment. Two days after the king's diagnosis, Elizabeth gave birth to a seven-pound, six-ounce son, Charles Philip Arthur George. Unrestrained celebrations took place outside Buckingham Palace, revelers cheering every vehicle coming in and going out of the palace. Margaret, who received the news while on an official visit to Sheffield, was apparently seen dancing around a celebratory bonfire and joking: "I suppose I'll now be known as Charlie's aunt."[10] Her offhand remark would follow her for the rest of her life.

Two days later, on November 16, the king accepted that a long-anticipated tour of Australia and New Zealand now had to be postponed. He gave permission to release a medical bulletin that stated that he was canceling all engagements for the foreseeable future. Margaret was both shocked and disappointed by her father's illness. She had been excited about accompanying her parents on the forthcoming tour and had spent many happy hours choosing her numerous and varied outfits. Now they would have to go back into the wardrobe. As the weeks passed, the king gradually recovered some strength, and the prospect of amputation receded. He was sufficiently well to attend the christening of Prince Charles in the white and gold Music Room at Buckingham Palace in December.

As a godparent, Margaret held the baby as he was baptized in the same robes of Honiton lace she and her sister had worn. After the christening, both sisters agreed to assume more official duties on behalf of their father, whose recovery continued to be slow. Both girls, but particularly the heir presumptive, were seen as the new generation, while the king was fading inexorably into the background. Within the family he became increasingly difficult to control. He had always been prone to outbursts of temper, but during his long, frustrating recovery he was even more irascible. From time to time he exploded with what one courtier called "the Hanoverian bark," the tendency of princes and kings to snap at members of staff for no particular reason. To an active man who loved being outdoors, this continued confinement to a bed or a chair was understandably frustrating. It was noticeable that during these episodes Margaret was the only one who could placate him. In March 1949, he underwent serious spinal surgery to restore the circulation in his leg. The procedure was deemed reasonably successful, though his recovery was painfully slow. At the Trooping of the Colour in June, it was his eldest daughter who rode sidesaddle—as her father predicted when he became king—at the head of the parade, while he was driven in an open carriage.

Though endlessly concerned about her father, Princess Elizabeth was beginning to lead the life of an independent married woman, a process that accelerated when the couple moved from Buckingham Palace to Clarence House that summer. In truth, away from the brooding palace, both sisters were having fun. American entertainer Danny Kaye was the life and soul at weekends spent at Windlesham Moor; Princess Elizabeth adored his semi-slapstick routine. She was such a fan that the American poet Delmore Schwartz wrote the lines "Vaudeville for a Princess," which was subtitled "Suggested by Princess Elizabeth's Admiration of Danny Kaye."

From time to time she and Prince Philip cut loose, going out for dinner and dancing in various London clubs. When the princess celebrated her twenty-third birthday, she went to the fashionable Café de Paris on Coventry Street before watching Laurence Olivier and Vivien Leigh in *The School for Scandal*. Then the glamorous thespians joined the royal party for an evening of tango, quickstep, and samba at a nightclub. At a ball held at Windsor Castle that summer the new royal parents stole the show, the couple admired for their smooth style on the dance floor.

In July 1949 they arrived in costume—Elizabeth as an Edwardian parlor maid and her husband as a waiter—for a summer ball hosted by the American ambassador Lewis W. Douglas, whose daughter Sharman had become a bosom buddy of Princess Margaret. Determined to make an impact, Margaret came as a Parisian can-can girl complete with lace knickers and black stockings. In her thank-you note, she told Douglas, "I was feeling so over-excited by the time our Can-Can was due that I could hardly breathe."[11] That didn't stop the "ecstatic" royal from putting on her costume and repeating her routine for her mother when she got home to Buckingham Palace. The following day the headlines read PRINCESS MARGARET HIGH-KICKS IT.

At this time of transition inside the family, the arrival of the girl known as Charmin' Sharman or Sass was just the tonic Margaret needed. With her sister focused on her own family, Sass replaced Elizabeth in Margaret's life, ensuring that Margaret's social life took an exhilarating and unexpected twist. The tall, animated, Vassar-educated blonde arrived in London in 1947 when her father was appointed American ambassador to London. The *Washington Post* described Sass as "an idealized version of a [college] homecoming queen."[12] The socialite met Margaret at an official embassy reception, and the two became fast friends—their fun-loving and audacious personalities meshing perfectly.

෴

Shortly after her arrival, Sharman lost little time in gathering together a circle of young companions who met informally at the ambassadorial residence, Winfield House in Regent's Park.

These animated gatherings soon became a regular feature of Margaret's social calendar, including one widely reported dinner party that continued until four the next morning. During the three years that Sharman spent in London, she and Margaret were frequently spied outside the embassy as well—on outings to fashionable nightspots such as the 400 Club, Café de Paris, and the Milroy in Park Lane, where they would dance the night away. The public salivated over stories about Margaret doing the samba, foxtrot, and Charleston with an array of eligible young aristocrats, including the Lords Blandford, Ogilvy, and Westmorland.[13]

Several times a week, a procession of private cars would arrive at Buckingham Palace filled with Margaret's new girlfriends, not just Sharman but also Judy Montagu, Lady Rosemary Spencer-Churchill, Rachel Brand, and many others—all of whom respectfully referred to Margaret as "Ma'am." Her closest confidants would call her "ma'am darling," a sobriquet that perfectly fitted her personality.

What became known as the Margaret Set was daily front-page fodder in the popular press. In drab, dreary Britain, in the midst of a long and painful reconstruction, the queen's youngest daughter and her American friend were a burst of color and ersatz controversy. In tabloid vernacular they were "top toff totty." Margaret, with her "large expressive blue eyes," porcelain skin and pouting lips, was the golden goose laying circulation eggs for newspapers and magazines. When a nightclub band struck up the refrain "Mean to Me," Margaret quipped, "That's a tune dedicated to some photographers."[14] Unlike her sister, who early on made a habit of not reading about herself, Margaret reveled in the speculation concerning her New Look fashions, her looks—and her love life. On one occasion, she turned to her dancing partner and said suggestively, "Do you know you are dancing with the owner of the most beautiful, seductive eyes in the world?"—a sarcastic reference to a recent article about herself.[15] She had what Cecil Beaton described as a "sex twinkle," a look that suggested a knowing naughtiness— with the hint of rebellion.

At the age of nineteen she was the first female royal to be seen smoking in public—the princess attached a cigarette to a long ivory cigarette holder after dinner in a West End restaurant. In an age when well-bred young ladies smoked in private, the move sparked controversy—and a trend. After Queen Mary objected, Margaret responded by making sure to be photographed with longer cigarette holders.

When Duff Cooper, former British ambassador to France, and his wife, Lady Diana Cooper, went for lunch with "we four" at Buckingham Palace in February 1948, Cooper, a noted admirer of the female form, was impressed by the lively quartet but was especially struck by Margaret. "Very sure of herself and full of humour," he noted in his diary. "She might get into trouble before she's finished."[16] Or as Chips Channon noted, "There is already a Marie Antoinette aroma about her,"[17] hinting that her exuberant lifestyle might end in tears.

She attracted critics and admirers alike. Her fans ogled her brightly colored Molyneux and Dior wardrobe, and the princess became a pin-up for the revolutionary New Look, with its cinched waists and full A-line skirts. Conservative critics attacked her lack of modesty and felt that she showed too much of her figure. Occasionally, that included her mother, who insisted that shoulder straps be added to at least one swooping evening dress. Her fans thought otherwise, and duplicates of her low-cut gowns, gold cigarette holders, and cherry-colored lipstick, named Margaret Rose-Red, flooded the market in Britain and America. On one occasion, during an official visit in

Italy, her hotel chambermaid was bribed to give the shade of her nail polish, type of perfume, and what book she was reading. One indiscreet fitter even disclosed her measurements: "a shade over five feet tall…a 23-inch waist and 34-inch bust."[18]

Though the princess was always at pains to point out that it was really Sharman's Set as most of the group were her friends, it was Margaret who was seen as the center of café society. As her cousin Margaret Rhodes observed: "During the postwar years, there were a lot of parties, and Princess Margaret was the star in the middle; a planet round which everyone revolved. She simply sparkled."[19] No event was considered truly "high society" unless the magnetic princess was present, and the media was intrigued by her sophistication, charisma, and beauty. However, the liveried footmen at Buckingham Palace who had to wait until the princess arrived back—usually with the milk bottles—would not have counted themselves in her appreciation society. Shortly before Crawfie left royal service, she complained about Margaret's exhaustion and irresponsibility. The queen simply responded, "We are only young once, Crawfie. We want her to have a good time. With Lilibet gone, it is lonely for her here."[20] Though there was talk that Margaret and Sharman enjoyed a romantic lesbian tryst, this seems doubtful if the many gossipy but decidedly platonic letters that passed between them are any indication. Whatever the truth, Sharman served as Margaret's surrogate sister and was a confidant she could trust.

Margaret was linked to an ever-growing list of possible male suitors. At one point, the gossip columns had her attached to no fewer than thirty-one eligible young bachelors.[21] Her eighteenth birthday was the starting gun for endless media speculation about "the one," and the latest suitor could change between newspaper editions. One evening, she was apparently driven home from dinner in a red sports car by Peter Ward, the son of the earl of Dudley. So for a short while he was "the one." The same week it was discovered that she had gone out with millionaire Billy Wallace after he arrived in London following a visit to New York. So he became the favorite to win her hand—at least as far as the media were concerned. Others who escorted her to the theater, ballet, and dinner included Dominic Elliot, younger son of the earl of Minto; Lord Porchester, heir to famed Egyptologist the earl of Carnarvon; and Lieutenant Mark Bonham Carter, who had made a daring escape from an Italian POW camp and first met the princesses at Windsor Castle during the war.

Bonham Carter, whose mother was daughter of Prime Minister Herbert Asquith, was an instant hit with the sisters, keeping them amused with a string of jokes and an ability to slide down banisters without using his hands. He recalls twice dancing with the teenage Princess Margaret and later reported that she was "full of character and very tart in her criticisms."[22] Among the other runners and riders in the royal marriage stakes were the joint favorites for her hand, Sunny Blandford, heir to the duke of Marlborough and with it Blenheim Palace, and Johnny Dalkeith, seven years older than the princess and heir to two Scottish dukedoms and the largest privately owned estate in the United Kingdom. While Margaret would never be the queen, if she married Dalkeith, she would at least be queen of all she surveyed, north, south, east, and west. There was even talk that she had caught the roving eye of Danny Kaye, who called her "Honey," much to her delight. It was also gleefully reported that, watched by her parents, she had entertained a minister of the church of Scotland with a raucous rendition of "I'm Just a Girl Who Can't Say No" from the sisters' favorite musical, Oklahoma!

Lurking in the shadows all the while was Group Captain Peter Townsend, the aviator always at her service wherever she went. In June 1949 he asked her if he could enter the King's Cup air race under her colors. As he was the king's equerry, it would have been more politic to ask his royal boss first if he wanted an aerial white knight to race through the skies on his behalf. Instead he asked Margaret, and, in his words, she "sportingly, but with no wild show of enthusiasm," agreed.[23]

More down-to-earth engagements beckoned. Townsend accompanied Margaret to a variety of official functions, inspecting hospitals, factories, and new housing developments, and giving short speeches, invariably written by Townsend. The king was convalescing at this point, and he undertook fewer appointments, leaving Townsend with plenty of time on his hands. As a result, it made sense for him to join her and her lady-in-waiting on official engagements. She also undertook a number of private, unpublicized visits to the House of Commons, the Law Courts, the Thomas Coram School, and similar institutions with the aim, she stated, of learning "about life."[24] "That was the beginning of it, I suspect," a royal aide later observed. "Poor dear Peter, if ever there was an inculpable man, it was him,"[25] suggesting that he undertook these engagements with no ulterior motive but as time went on gradually became romantically involved with the princess.

Those at court now started to notice the interactions between the couple. It was the little things, the knowing eye contact and the smiles that suggested more than teenage flirtation. Margaret's conversation, always droll, had a witty sheen when Townsend was around, as though she was trying to impress. In public he called her "ma'am"; in private it was "Margaret."

Though she also accompanied Elizabeth on several official

engagements, Margaret was now defined in the public mind as independent of her sister, and the days of the matching dresses were a distant memory.

In November 1949, Elizabeth flew to Malta to join her husband, who had previously reported for duty on board the 1,710-ton destroyer HMS *Chequers*. The six blissful if busy weeks she spent on the friendly and temperate island was a second honeymoon, the place where Princess Anne, her second child, was conceived. She lodged at Uncle Dickie's home, Villa Guardamangia, a gorgeous sandstone villa overlooking the bay with a substantial terrace and an orchard of orange and lemon trees.

Even though she was accompanied by Bobo, her lady-in-waiting, and a detective, Elizabeth managed to lead a more or less normal existence, despite the thousands who thronged the streets to greet her when she arrived. When not undertaking visits to hospitals, factories, and libraries, she filled her days with thoroughly conventional activities: shopping, sightseeing, and exploring the bays, coves, and inlets on a cruiser appropriately named *The Eden* with her sailor husband. To be safe, she would take a bag of Maltese *galletti*, a wafer biscuit, in case she felt seasick.

In the afternoons she hosted tea parties for officers' wives, attended gala dinners, and, on at least one occasion, went dancing on board his ship HMS *Chequers* at an officers' mess shindig. Their favorite night spot was the Phoenicia hotel, where the band leader religiously played her favorite tune, "People Will Say We're in Love" from the Rodgers and Hammerstein musical *Oklahoma!* Uncle Dickie, ever the social climber, was in seventh heaven. He discovered that not only did the future queen actually like him, but she enjoyed dancing with him.

He preened: "She dances quite divinely and always wants a samba when we dance together."[26]

For Elizabeth, this was a real taste of freedom. After all, it had only been four years since she and Margaret had to virtually beg their father to join the crowds on VE Day. Now she was driving her Daimler car on her own around the island. Bliss! As her confidant Lady Pamela Hicks noted: "It was the only place that she was able to live the life of a naval officer's wife, just like all the other wives."[27] For the first time in her life, she handled cash and got her hair done at regular salons. It was a refreshing taste of normalcy. The girl who would peer out from the palace or 145 Piccadilly to see what ordinary people were doing now had the opportunity to escape the cloistered world of the crown. Little wonder that she described her months in Malta as "the happiest days of my life."[28] As Edwina Mountbatten observed: "It's lovely seeing her so radiant and leading a more or less human and normal existence for once."[29]

Though the couple were able to spend Christmas together, at the end of December 1949 the princess waved farewell to her husband as his ship HMS *Chequers* was sent with six other warships to patrol the Red Sea, following tribal clashes in Eritrea. Shortly afterward the princess and her small entourage flew back to London on a Vickers Viking airplane. "Lilibeth has left with a tear in her eyes and a lump in her throat," Edwina told the Indian prime minister Jawaharlal Nehru, with whom she enjoyed a long, loving, and romantic relationship. "Putting her into the Viking when she left was I thought rather like putting a bird back into a very small cage and I felt sad and nearly tearful myself."[30]

Once back at Sandringham, Elizabeth settled into the comfortable rhythms of court life, and soon her time in Malta was like a distant dream. The king was delighted to have her home, and the familiar closeness between him and his heir was evident even to casual visitors. As Cynthia Gladwyn, the wife of a British diplomat who came for a "dine and sleep" at the Norfolk estate, observed, "Two of the most delightful sidelights I noticed on our visit were the real devotion and affection between the Princess and her husband and the Princess and the King. The father and daughter seemed happy in each other's company, and talked together eagerly and animatedly."

They were not in Britain long. Philip rejoined his ship and, a few weeks later, Elizabeth once again took up residence at Villa Guardamangia. She spent her twenty-fourth birthday there watching her husband and her uncle joust for bragging rights in their highly competitive games of polo. The princess turned a deaf ear to her husband's language, which, if the game was going badly, was of the industrial variety.

As the Mountbattens were leaving the island for another posting, Elizabeth and Philip rented Villa Guardamangia. She spent much of the summer relaxing on the island before flying back to London, where on August 15, a few days after her mother's fiftieth birthday, she gave birth to Princess Anne at Clarence House. There was cause for a double celebration, as Prince Philip was given command of his own baby, the frigate HMS *Magpie*, in September, shortly after being promoted to lieutenant commander. Only twenty-nine and now in command of a frigate, it was clear Philip's naval career was on a fast track.

Uncharacteristically, Elizabeth, who was known for her robust health, took some time to recover from the birth of her daughter. She had been expected to resume public engagements in October, but on doctor's orders, this was delayed for a month. Then in November there were further cancellations due to a "severe cold." This was perplexing, though her medical staff refused to elaborate. Nonetheless, after celebrating Prince Charles's second birthday in November, she flew to Malta to spend Christmas with her husband. Their two children were left behind at Sandringham, much to the delight of the doting grandparents and Aunt Margaret.

As ever, Peter Townsend was on hand to add entertainment and companionship during the short days and long winter evenings in Norfolk. He and Margaret talked and laughed as they rode "through the pinewoods and across the stubble at Sandringham."[31] The brief caress, the longing look, and the whispered comment—this was now their secret life, and it was a very thrilling but dangerous game. A friend of Margaret's described her mindset as she hovered on the brink of an affair with a married man: "One always felt the tremendous nervous energy, that the daring nature and cleverness was a kind of shield. That quizzical look in her eyes really reflected an inner confusion, a plea for better answers. I don't believe she envied her sister. Yet, she did so long for a purpose to her life. Marriage and children did appeal to her—but it seemed she wanted more. What that might be I don't think even she had the foggiest."[32]

As she struggled to find her way through the fog, her white leather Bible was her guide and consolation. The princess was not some frivolous fashion plate; she also held strong religious convictions, reading her Bible frequently. One night at dinner, she asked, "What *is* love? How can you define and recognize when it is real and when it is not?" This, onlookers concluded, was not some philosophical question but a dilemma the princess was facing in her personal life. If they had seen how she behaved while on a walk around the Scottish estate with her father that August of 1951, they would have been left in no doubt about who was the focus of her affections.

Following a picnic lunch, Townsend went for a snooze in the meadow, and when he awoke from his reverie, he discovered that Margaret was covering him with a coat. He recalled, "I opened one eye—to see Princess Margaret's lovely face, very close, looking into mine." Behind Margaret was the king, watching—not with anger or jealousy, but "kind, half-amused." Townsend murmured, "You know your father is watching us?" At which she laughed, took the king's arm, and walked away, "leaving [Peter] to [his] dreams."[33]

That summer others began to notice the undeniable chemistry between Townsend and the king's daughter. Indeed, it seems that the scarcely believable whispers about the couple began the previous year. Young socialite Lady Jane Vane-Tempest-Stewart returned from a week at Balmoral in August 1950 and told her mother that she was convinced that the princess and the recently promoted court official were in love. Her mother's response was that of stunned incredulity. "Don't be so romantic and ridiculous," she told her. "He's the king's servant. She can't be in love with the king's servant, that would be utterly wrong."[34]

At the time newspaper correspondents and indeed the king were focused on agreeable British aristocrats as possible husbands for the princess. As Margaret's friend Colin Tennant said years later, "If the King had lived, he would have made Princess Margaret marry Johnny Dalkeith."[35] In the House of Commons, lawmakers believed that Buckingham Palace had earmarked Dalkeith, who later became a much-respected Member of Parliament, for Princess Margaret. According to fellow lawmaker Tam Dalyell, his colleague Dalkeith "was a supremely eligible bachelor, [who] had tactfully but firmly resisted any entry into the royal family."[36] The story persisted, however, with Margaret telling her friend Sass in exasperation, "We have had a high old time here with the Press thinking I was going to marry Johnnie Dalkeith. I am not going to get engaged to him so yippee, and tell all your friends."[37]

In the summer of 1950 it wasn't Townsend who was concerning the royal family—that would come in good time—but the ex-king Edward VIII and their former governess, now retired, Marion Crawford. They were deeply unamused and angered to discover that both were writing or had written memoirs. The proposed publication in early 1951 of A King's Story, Edward VIII's memoir of the abdication, infuriated the queen mother, as she always believed that her husband's ill health was caused by his brother's decision to quit the throne. Now he was set to make several million dollars out of what amounted to a family calamity. As for Crawfie, the queen had written to her in April 1950, stating clearly that "people in positions of confidence with us must be utterly oyster."[38] Silence was the watchword. When Crawfie had disobeyed her edict and had gone ahead with her revelatory book, The Little Princesses, the sisters were united in their disapproval. Elizabeth said that the woman who shared her room, her thoughts, and her confidences had "snaked"—that is to say, betrayed her. As for Margaret, Crawfie's treachery made her "ill."

There was no chance of a reconciliation, which was much desired by Crawfie, even though the queen, Princesses Margaret and Elizabeth, Prince Philip, and various senior courtiers had previously given her the go-ahead to earn money by discussing domestic family secrets but only if her name was not used. This, as far as they were concerned, was vital as it would set a dangerous precedent and embolden other members of the household to spill the beans. For example, when Princess Elizabeth's private secretary Jock Colville had asked his royal employer if he could pen a memoir about his time working with her, he was given short shrift.

Instead, the family's preferred author was Mr. Reliable, Dermot Morrah. He was supposed to quietly collaborate with the former governess, but the plan backfired when Crawfie insisted on having her name on the book. Margaret subsequently left the royal journalist in no doubt as to her feelings. Morrah told publisher Bruce Gould that he was disturbed to discover that she and her sister were even more "bitter" than the queen. Crawfie discovered to her cost that, for all her dedication, once she had crossed the line, she was cast out of the family forever. Like Townsend, she too had a miserable Christmas, the former governess so guilt-ridden that in time she would make several suicide attempts.

～

In January 1951 Margaret, though, was determined that Crawfie's behavior would not dim her holiday with her sister on the island of Malta. Her excitement was palpable. In a hasty letter to her bosom friend Sass she said: "I am just rushing off to Malta to stay with Lilibet for a week, which sounds glorious and I fully expect to see the SUN!"[39] Not only did she find the sun, but she also found her sister ensuring that their world was sunny side up. She had recruited a loyal and dedicated staff to run the villa. Long after she had left Malta she maintained her friendships with them. Indeed, several children of staff members referred to her as "Auntie Liz."

As newspaper publisher and politician Mabel Strickland, who became a mentor and lifelong friend, later recalled, "(Elizabeth) feels very deeply and loves this island because she and Philip were happy here."[40] When he was not on board *Magpie*, Philip was racing his yacht *Coweslip* across the bay or honing his polo skills on a wooden practice horse. With the sun setting, he would walk down the cobbled streets to the sea for an evening dip—his butler in tow to carry his clothes and a towel. Elizabeth enjoyed the freedom of going for a drive, riding, visiting the wives of other Navy officers, or simply shopping for presents to take home.

Things revved up when Margaret arrived to join in the fun. She soon found the downstairs dance floor at the Phoenicia hotel, where they danced the samba and the rumba. It was a riotous few days of parties, late nights, and long dinners. Her stay on the island she called "dear Malta" gave Princess Elizabeth a lifetime's worth of memories. Every Christmas after she left the island, Mabel Strickland sent her a huge chest of avocados, tangerines, and other fruits from her gardens. During the 1950s and '60s, when such exotic fruits were in short supply, Mabel's gifts were much sought after by the royal family during the festive season.

Margaret was equally if not more ecstatic to receive a Christmas gift of nylons from her American friend Sass, who knew that they were in short supply in battered Britain. As Margaret looked out over drab, gray London, she was desperate for a longer taste of blue skies and warm climes than just the few days she spent in Malta. The lengthy correspondence with her friend Sharman, who had returned to America in 1950 and now worked as a showbiz press agent, reveals her frustrated longing to head west. "I am jealous of all your dinner parties and I will go to California when I go to America," she wrote. "Every day I get more and more invitations from kind people offering to show me the glories of North, South, East and West of the USA. I have been asked to go and see a film made here which has dear Mr [Gregory] Peck in it, so I'm rushing."[41]

Though she enjoyed hearing all the gossip about Holly-wood stars—complaining, for instance, that Elizabeth Taylor wore too much eyeliner—she was rather more prudish than her wild child image. In London, when she went to see a production of *Illuminations* created by Frederick Ashton, the famed British ballet choreographer, the princess was horrified by one scene of sexual intimacy. "It went a little near the knuckle I thought, and rather unnecessarily so. As for the rest of it—music, costumes, scenery were lovely and it seemed a pity to spoil the whole thing by one rather disgusting bit."[42] When she wasn't being scandalized by cutting-edge dance, she enjoyed watching musicals such as *Pal Joey* and American comedians like Bob Hope, Abbot and Costello, and of course Danny Kaye.

The movies and shows were a distraction from the worrying news at home. Her beloved papa was showing little sign of improvement. She had gone with him to the opening of the Festival of Britain exhibition in May 1951, which she described as "horrid" and "a shambles," but a bout of influenza caused the king to cancel a visit to Northern Ireland that same month. As he recuperated, the queen and Princesses Elizabeth and Margaret took on his duties, with his eldest daughter representing the king at Trooping the Colour in June. The king did travel to Balmoral, accompanied by the queen and Margaret, as well as Peter Townsend and lady-in-waiting Jennifer Bevan. It was a trying time all round. The king coughed a lot and was unable to walk a few steps without pausing. In his usual fashion he kept the doctors at bay for as long as possible. Finally, he gave in. The prognosis was, as he suspected, not good.

In September, seven doctors issued a short but dramatic bulletin saying that the condition of the king's lung gave cause for concern and he had been advised to go for an operation in the near future. Princess Elizabeth and Prince Philip delayed a five-week tour of North America so that they could be in London during the king's operation, which took place on September 23 in the Buhl Room at Buckingham Palace, which had been converted into an operating room. Prayers were offered throughout the country, and the royal family attended a service at Lambeth Palace conducted by the archbishop of Canterbury.

The doctors informed the queen and Princess Elizabeth that cancer had been found in the removed lung. This dire information was withheld from the king. As he made a slow recovery, he insisted that Elizabeth's tour of Canada and America go ahead. After a farewell lunch at Buckingham Palace on October 7, Elizabeth and Philip boarded a BOAC Stratocruiser for the seventeen-hour flight to Montreal, with Royal Navy ships stationed along the North Atlantic route in case of an emergency. It was the first time an heir to the throne had been allowed to make a long-distance flight. Among their baggage was a sealed envelope holding the draft Accession Declaration, should the worst happen and the king died.

They were welcomed by a crowd of fifteen thousand in Montreal, and the crush of photographers was such that glass from exploding flashbulbs covered Princess Elizabeth's fur coat. Ironically, Elizabeth had Crawfie to blame for her reception. Her book and its serialization in *Ladies' Home Journal* were a sensation, and the crowds came to gawk at the woman they had read about. Some were disappointed, complaining that the princess didn't smile enough, a sentiment that baffled the princess, who complained that her jaw was aching from constantly smiling. It was an early indication of how her impassive demeanor would be interpreted as unfeeling and aloof rather than a mask to contain her swirling emotions. This misreading would dog her throughout her reign.

Glamorous and sophisticated, Princesses Elizabeth and Margaret attend the Royal Variety Performance at The Coliseum, London, in November, 1949. Among the artists topping the bill were comedian Michael Bentine and French crooner Maurice Chevalier.

"We Four," as the king called himself, Queen Elizabeth, and his daughters Princesses Elizabeth and Margaret. Here the family pose for the official souvenir program to commemorate the king's coronation in May 1937.

King George VI and Queen Elizabeth with Princess Elizabeth and Princess Margaret in full regalia on the balcony of Buckingham Palace following their coronation ceremony on May 12, 1937. The king had special lightweight crowns made for his daughters. Margaret was jealous that her sister's train was longer than her own.

Queen Mary liked to take the princesses on improving visits to museums, art galleries, and other places of interest. On this occasion, in early May 1939, shortly before the outbreak of war, they toured St. Katherine docks in London.

The queen regularly dressed the princesses exactly alike, which had the effect of making Princess Elizabeth appear much younger. Here they are in June 1940, playing the piano together at Windsor Castle, where they lived for most of the war.

The princesses cuddle up for the official portrait to celebrate Princess Elizabeth's fourteenth birthday, on April 21, 1940. From this time on, Elizabeth was given special tutoring in constitutional history to prepare her for her future role as queen.

Princess Elizabeth gave her first radio broadcast from Windsor Castle on October 13, 1940. She extended her sympathies to the children who were evacuated from the cities and sent to the country or overseas, out of harm's way. Margaret joined her at the end of the broadcast to wish them all good night.

Princess Margaret in the title role of Cinderella and Princess Elizabeth as Prince Florizel during a rehearsal for their first pantomime production, which was staged at Windsor Castle on December 21, 1941, to raise money for a war charity.

Shortly after her eighteenth birthday, in 1944, Princess Elizabeth joined the Auxiliary Territorial Service (ATS), where she learned the basics of vehicle mechanics. During her training, the princess drove an army lorry through central London to Buckingham Palace.

Princess Elizabeth sounds the whistle of the famous White Train, which transported the royal party throughout South Africa during a historic visit in 1947.

George VI, Queen Elizabeth, and the princesses are escorted to Romsey Abbey, Hampshire, by Prince Philip of Greece, far right, for the wedding of Lord Brabourne and Patricia Mountbatten in October 1946. The princesses were bridesmaids, and when Philip helped Elizabeth off with her fur coat, his chivalry prompted speculation that they were dating.

Princess Elizabeth and Prince Philip on the balcony of Buckingham Palace following their wedding at Westminster Abbey, on November 20, 1947. Princess Margaret, who was chief bridesmaid, was forlorn at losing her sister.

Princess Elizabeth and Prince Philip spent many happy months as newlyweds in Malta. They stayed at Villa Guardamangia in Valetta, where the prince commanded his first ship, HMS *Magpie*.

King George VI, Queen Elizabeth, and Princess Margaret bid farewell to Princess Elizabeth and Prince Philip as they depart London Airport, now Heathrow, for Nairobi, Kenya, on the first leg of their six-month tour of Australia and New Zealand. This was the last time the future queen saw her father. He died six days later, on February 6, 1953.

United in grief, the newly proclaimed Queen Elizabeth II, Queen Mary, and the Queen Mother (*left to right*) stand shrouded in black during the funeral of King George VI, on February 15, 1953.

Queen Elizabeth II sits in the chair of state in front of the royal box, where the Queen Mother (*left*) and Princess Margaret encourage Prince Charles to stand for the coronation of his mother, on June 2, 1953.

Prince Charles, now four, looks thoroughly bored at the historic coronation ceremony of his mother, Queen Elizabeth ll, at Westminster Abbey. The coronation changed the relationship between the sisters forever, as a glum-faced Princess Margaret seems to acknowledge.

The newly crowned queen, wearing the Imperial State crown and carrying the orb and sceptre, smiles as she walks past a beaming Prince Philip shortly after her coronation.

Princess Margaret and her secret lover, Group Captain Peter Townsend, attend an RAF air display at Farnborough, Hampshire, UK, in July 1950. Their affair threatened to compromise the coronation celebrations.

A long-hidden, handwritten letter from Princess Margaret to Prime Minister Anthony Eden, detailing her plans regarding her relationship with Peter Townsend.

Princess Margaret and her rumoured beau, 1950s crooner and notorious womanizer Eddie Fisher, in deep discussion at a charity ball at the Dorchester hotel, London, in 1953. Fisher would go on to count actress Elizabeth Taylor among his five wives.

The queen gasps in concern as a mount slips during the dressage section of the equestrian Olympics at Stockholm, Sweden, on June 12, 1956. Her sister puffs nonchalantly on her cigarette in her trademark holder. Margaret was not as interested in equestrian pursuits as the queen.

Professional photographer Antony Armstrong-Jones grins at the waiting press as he and his fiancée, Princess Margaret, return to her London home, Clarence House, in March 1960 after attending a show. The couple married two months later, on May 6, at Westminster Abbey.

During the Swinging Sixties, Princess Margaret and Lord Snowdon were seen as the trendiest royals. Here they are greeting The Beatles at the world premiere of the band's film *Help*, in July 1965. John Lennon called Margaret "Princess Margarine."

The queen, flanked by President John F. Kennedy and First Lady Jackie Kennedy, and Prince Philip during the presidential visit to Buckingham Palace in June 1961. Jackie Kennedy was disappointed that she didn't meet Princess Margaret, then deemed the most glamorous royal, at the subsequent banquet.

For years, Princess Margaret and Elizabeth Taylor were the most photographed celebrities of the age. Here they are comparing notes at the 1967 royal film premiere of *The Taming of the Shrew*, which starred Taylor and Richard Burton, as well as Sir Michael Redgrave, seen behind them.

One of the traditions of Ascot Week is for members of the royal family to race along the track, usually early in the morning, before the crowds arrive. The queen and Princess Margaret, great rivals, are seen here trotting with the Duke of Kent in June 1968. Though she enjoyed riding, Princess Margaret preferred water skiing, and she is seen below practicing on the lake at Sunninghill Park. The queen would sometimes come to watch her sister go through her paces. She is pictured below helping Margaret into her wet suit.

During her Silver Jubilee tour of the Commonwealth in 1977, the queen and Prince Philip visited the private island of Mustique, in the Caribbean, where Princess Margaret had a home, Les Jolies Eaux. The queen went swimming and Philip snorkeled.

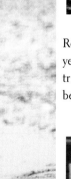

Roddy Llewellyn, Princess Margaret's partner for eight years, strolls along the beach wearing Union Jack bathing trunks during a stay in Mustique in March 1980, shortly before Margaret's fiftieth birthday.

Princess Margaret reclines barefoot on a sofa at her home, Les Jolies Eaux, on Mustique, in April 1976. Here she was the island queen.

The Queen Mother joins her daughters as they watch Princess Anne compete in the Badminton Horse Trials in 1973. They were a tightly knit trio who spoke to one another most days on the telephone, sometimes in French.

The queen and Princess Margaret get into the Christmas spirit after watching a performance of the classic ballet *The Nutcracker* at the Royal Opera house in 1991. It was not long before the queen needed support from her sister in a year that she called her *"annus horribilus,"* as royal marriages collapsed and Windsor Castle burned down.

The queen and her sister had a uniquely confiding relationship. Margaret was one of the few people the queen could trust absolutely. During the 1990s Margaret took on the role of enforcer inside the royal family, chastising Fergie and Diana for hitting the headlines for all the wrong reasons. At the Battle of Britain flypast at Buckingham Palace in 1990 (*below left*), the two young women look like they have just been ticked off. After Diana gave her infamous TV interview in 1995, Margaret wanted nothing more to do with her next-door neighbor at Kensington Palace.

The queen and the rest of the royal family pay their respects to Diana, Princess of Wales, as her funeral cortege passes Buckingham Palace on September 6, 1997. While the queen bowed her head, Princess Margaret barely acknowledged her passing. They had fallen out badly when Diana gave a wide-ranging interview about her life to the BBC show *Panorama*. The conflict between love and duty haunted the relationship within the triumvirate, in particular between the sisters.

The Queen Mother is flanked by her daughters as she waves to admirers from the balcony of Buckingham Palace to celebrate her hundredth birthday, on August 4, 2000. She was a royal of the old school in that she always put duty—or what she called *devoir*—first.

After years of ill health, Princess Margaret died on February 9, 2002, aged just seventy-one. She requested that she be cremated so that her ashes could be beside her beloved father, George Vl, at St. George's Chapel, Windsor. The queen, alongside Margaret's children and their spouses, look on as the princess' coffin is carried down the steps at the royal chapel. A few weeks later the queen suffered another blow when her mother, Queen Elizabeth, the Queen Mother, died on March 30. She was consoled by the many messages of support she received from members of the public.

When they returned home in November, the princess was relieved to see that her father had gained weight and was even talking about shooting, using a light gun. There were plans for him to travel to South Africa in March 1952 to enjoy the winter sunshine—Group Captain Townsend had been sent to South Africa for reconnaissance. Even though the king put a brave face on his condition, when he recorded his Christmas message he could only manage one exhausting sentence at a time.

In spite of his frail health, he was insistent that his eldest daughter and her husband take his place on the oft-postponed trip to Australia and New Zealand, breaking the journey in Kenya. When the time came for his daughter and son-in-law to leave, the king traveled from Sandringham to see her off. Their last evening together was at Theatre Royal Drury Lane, where they watched a performance of the Rodgers and Hammerstein musical *South Pacific*. Lilibet knew all the lyrics by heart.

The next day, January 31, against the advice of his doctors, the king stood for half an hour hatless on the wind-blown tarmac at London Airport (now Heathrow) to say goodbye to his beloved daughter. "He is like that," the princess later remarked, "he never thinks of himself."[43] Though the king and queen chatted with Churchill and other members of the official group, pictures showing George VI looking haggard and strained shocked and disturbed the nation. "I felt with foreboding that this would be the last time he was to see his daughter, and that he thought so himself,"[44] remarked the colonial secretary Oliver Lyttelton. He was not alone.

Princess Margaret, in a matching beige hat, coat, and gloves against the chill February wind, looked subdued as she waved off her sister and brother-in-law. She could barely raise a smile of farewell. It was Margaret and not her sister who was meant to sail Down Under with her parents and enjoy the sunshine, sea air, and adulation that accompanies a major state visit. It was an adventure she would have secretly shared with the man in her life, Peter Townsend. Then there was her new wardrobe, which looked accusingly at her every time she went into her palace apartment.

Instead she headed back to Sandringham—bone-chilling, bleak, and boring. At least she had the gramophone records sent by Sass to keep her amused. Fatefully, the number one single on the U.S. charts that month was "Cry" by Johnnie Ray and the Four Lads.

Tears would soon fall.

5

"Bad or Mad"

The children, Prince Charles and Princess Anne, lightened the mood. Charles kept his grandparents and aunt on their toes as he made an inedible "afternoon tea" for them on the train journey back to Sandringham after they had said their goodbyes to Elizabeth and Philip. That night, they heard Elizabeth's voice, crackly and reedy, on the international telephone line from Nairobi, the Kenyan capital where they had just landed on the first leg of their long journey to Australia. As thrilling as it was to hear her, it emphasized the distance that now existed between them.

Margaret was not in the mood for merriment, even though her father was in good spirits after a positive meeting with his doctors. She had previously written to her friend Sass, apologizing that she had not been her normal vibrant self as she was concerned about Papa: "I can't tell you how cheering up you were to talk to and have about, when things still were not going frightfully well with Papa. And I was going to ask you to forgive me if I didn't seem eager to come rushing out all the time, as somehow one didn't feel, after all the hell and worry and relief, like laughing like mad."[1]

Auntie Margaret and her mother took the children to Brancaster beach on February 5 and watched as Charles went paddling in the freezing North Sea. While the king was out shooting hares and rabbits on the twenty-thousand-acre estate on what was known as Keepers' Day, the queen and her daughter drove to the nearby village of Ludham to see the latest offerings of one of her favorite artists, the Norfolk-based painter Edward Seago. His landscapes and seascapes were so popular that people would stand in line to snap up his latest offerings. After going for a cruise on his boat, they returned to Sandringham, clutching several of Seago's new paintings to show the king. Before dinner, Margaret played the piano for her father while he did a crossword puzzle.

Over dinner he was in a merry mood, listening attentively to his racing manager, Charles Moore, as he described his adventures in Kenya at the Treetops Hotel in the Aberdare Forest, where at that very moment Elizabeth and Philip were sitting in a little cabin perched in a giant fig tree, watching elephants and rhino and other big game drinking from a water hole in the moonlight.

The king retired at 10:30 and the next morning, February 6, at 7:30 his undervalet James MacDonald took the king his tea but couldn't rouse him. After pulling back the curtain, MacDonald realized the king was dead. It was discovered later that he had suffered a coronary thrombosis, a blood clot that had reached his heart.

When the queen was told, she flew to the king's bedroom. Initially she thought that he was in a deep sleep. Then the truth dawned. As she wrote to Queen Mary, "he looked so peaceful—then I realized what had happened."[2] Before breaking the news to Margaret, she stood for a moment by his bedside and gently kissed the king on the forehead. Then she went to speak to Margaret. The princess was utterly stunned, saying plaintively, "He died as he was getting better." Years later, Margaret recalled that final evening: "There were jolly jokes and he went to bed early because he was convalescing. Then he wasn't there anymore."[3] In the midst of her misery, she wanted her sister home as soon as possible.

Meanwhile, Elizabeth was watching in silent wonder the almost mystical spectacle of an East African dawn. The sky was shimmering with a pale-blue light, and the whole atmosphere around the princess was vibrant and tinged with eerie magic. As she looked over the breathtaking, iridescent landscape, a magnificent fish eagle circled above her for some time, then dipped as though in salute and promptly disappeared.

Philip's equerry Mike Parker thought it an uncanny experience, which haunted him for a long time afterward. That silent early-morning encounter appeared to mark the end of one reign and the dawn of another. Eventually, the news reached Parker, who promptly told Philip, who suddenly looked as if the world had collapsed all around him. Once he regained his composure, he took Elizabeth for a walk in the garden, and there, in the dappled sunlight with the soothing sound of a rippling stream in the background, she learned of her father's death and that she was now queen. Hunter Jim Corbett, who had accompanied the Princess, recalled: "For the first time in the history of the world a young girl climbed into a tree one day a princess and the next day she climbed down from the tree a Queen."[4]

When Elizabeth returned to the lodge, her cousin and lady-in-waiting Pamela Mountbatten impulsively gave her a hug and asked, "What can one say?" Then she dropped a curtsy to her queen. Elizabeth shrugged and said blankly, "It's one of those things."[5] Over the next few hours, the new queen placed her emotions of loss and pain into a deep freeze, her years of royal training kicking into gear. As Edward Windley, the provincial commissioner for Nyeri district, later described, "She was very pale. She was like ice; just like ice." When asked how she received the news, Windley said, "She took it like a queen."[6]

At one point during the endless flight back to London, she anxiously asked her private secretary Martin Charteris, "What's going to happen when we get home?"[7] By the time they landed at London airport she was poised and calm, looking out of the passenger window at the waiting row of what she called "hearses," the royal fleet of Daimlers and Rolls-Royces. Waiting for the arrival of their new queen were senior politicians from all parties, led by Prime Minister Winston Churchill, who had sobbed when he was told of the king's death.

As the new queen and her entourage drove through the streets of London back to Clarence House, a different kind of blackout had descended. Throughout the capital, Elizabeth glimpsed countless men in black suits and women in black dresses while on Bond Street, a haberdasher even displayed black lingerie in his shop window. As George VI's biographer John Wheeler-Bennett recalled, "The people of England made no secret of the depth and sincerity of their sorrow. I saw many in tears."[8] But tears would not be permitted for Queen Elizabeth II, suddenly "the Most High, the Most Mighty and Most Excellent Monarch." While all those around her were dabbing their eyes, now more than ever, she needed to control her own feelings. Queen Mary showed how it was done. The dignified monarch, who had lived through three reigns and who had now lost another son, made the short journey from

Marlborough House to Clarence House, where the new queen was patiently waiting her arrival. Queen Mary took her hand, kissed it lightly, and said, "God Save the Queen." Then she added, "Lilibet, your skirts are much too short for mourning."[9] Her response may have provoked a wry smile from the new sovereign, who was facing the most daunting weeks of her life.

After three days of unrelenting sleet, the sun finally appeared on the morning of February 8, when Elizabeth was scheduled to hold her first Privy Council at St. James's Palace. In a clear but sorrowful voice, she made a Declaration of Accession to her privy councilors, acknowledging that she would now assume the responsibilities of sovereign: "My heart is too full for me to say more to you today than that I shall always work as my father did. I pray that God will help me to discharge worthily the heavy task that has been laid upon me so early in my life."[10] She then headed back to Clarence House, where she watched the announcement of her succession on television, the moment marked by a gun salute in nearby Hyde Park.

After that, she set off for Sandringham to say goodbye to her father and console her mother and sister. Though young Charles and Anne provided an innocent counterpoint to the grievous sense of loss, little could relieve the deep sorrow felt by the three women left behind. When she arrived at the Norfolk home, the queen's first act was to visit her father's ground-floor bedroom, where his body lay in a coffin crafted from a single oak, felled months before.

She silently promised that she would follow in his footsteps and make him proud. In spite of the years of training at her father's knee, the queen still felt unprepared for her sudden role. The new queen put those nagging doubts to one side—after all she was the same age, twenty-five, as the first Queen Elizabeth had been upon her accession, and she had had no father to guide and nurture her. Yet her reign was one of the most notable in British history. She knew she had to be the strong one, for both her family and the nation. The unceasing demands of her new office kept her busy and helped her cope with, or at least suppress, her personal pain. As she later acknowledged, "Mummy and Margaret have the biggest grief to bear for their future must seem very blank while I have a job and family to think of."[11]

In any case, given the endless details to be decided regarding the king's funeral there was little time for self-pity. On Monday February 11, five days after Elizabeth's accession, the royal mourners departed Sandringham for London, traveling by rail with the coffin to King's Cross station, and from there taken in procession to Westminster Hall, where the king's body lay in state. The image of the three queens, Queen Elizabeth, the queen mother, and Queen Mary, heavily veiled and dressed in black, standing together outside Westminster Hall, left a powerful impression.

From there, the coffin was taken in procession to Westminster Hall for the lying in state. Over the next four days, more than 300,000 mourners braved the chill winter winds to file past the casket. One witness described the sobering scene: "a feeling that the coffin also contained a sizable chunk of themselves—the dangerous thirties, the war, the disappointing peace. The death of the King, who stood for completely trustworthy good among unpredictable evils has given many people the sense that something important in their lives is over, too."[12] The people of Britain were in mourning for a man, a moment, and their own mortality.

When the cortege began its journey to Windsor for the funeral, the television cameras captured the black-veiled silhouette of Queen Mary standing in the enormous bay window of Marlborough House, somberly watching the procession—which included the queen, queen mother, and Princess Margaret in the Irish State Coach—passing directly below her. When the procession arrived at Paddington Station, the king's body and the funeral party were conveyed to Windsor by train. Once the cortege reached Windsor, the queen and queen mother stood side by side at the head of the coffin as the congregation was ushered inside. At the completion of the service inside St. George's chapel the queen stepped forward and sprinkled earth from a bowl as the coffin was lowered to the ground. Elizabeth left a white wreath of flowers which was inscribed, simply and lovingly, "To Papa, from Lilibet." Her sister's was equally modest: "Darling Papa from his ever loving Margaret." Churchill's wreath read "For Valour," the motto for the Victoria Cross, Britain's highest military award for bravery.

With King George VI's burial over, Queen Elizabeth II's standard was raised over Buckingham Palace. As Chips Channon proclaimed, "We shall be the new Elizabethans."

∽

Margaret and her mother couldn't believe the king was gone. As comforting as the hundreds of kind, thoughtful letters and messages of sympathy were, they couldn't assuage the profound and continuing sense of loss. "The bottom has really dropped out of their world,"[13] the new queen observed, knowing that she had the comfort of her husband, the distraction of her children, and the heavy responsibility of her exalted position. In the coming months, Elizabeth maintained a self-contained calm and composure, while her sister endured something close to an emotional breakdown.

During her father's illness, Margaret had taken it upon herself to lighten the gloom, singing or playing the piano for an audience of one—dear Papa. Her devotion drew them closer in his waning months, which made his departure all the harder to bear. As she wrote to Lady Astor, "You know what a truly wonderful person he was, the very heart and centre of our family and no one could have had a more loving and thoughtful father."[14] Utterly inconsolable, she could barely eat or sleep, depending on sedatives to numb her grief. Columnist John Gordon reported that she had been given bromides for four days in a row to calm her nerves.[15] The girl who was the life and soul of every party became reclusive and withdrawn, later confessing that "there was an awful sense of being in a black hole [and] feeling tunnel-visioned, and I didn't really notice things."[16]

Like so many who are trying to come to terms with primal loss and grief, Margaret turned to religion for solace and support. Contrary to her party girl public image, Margaret had been a committed Christian from an early age, inspired perhaps by the Bible stories her mother read to her and Elizabeth in the morning while she ate breakfast. When she was fourteen, she asked her parents if she could be confirmed, but was told to wait until her sixteenth birthday, the same age as her sister. Such was her interest in theological discussions that, according to her friend Janie Stevens, "clergy frequently were astonished by her ability to hold her own in any discussion."[17] Together with her close friend Marigold Bridgeman, Margaret searched for like-minded communities to discuss the mysteries of heaven, hell, and the Trinity, leaving the palace early in the morning to join in groups of mainly young people. She became a regular at St. Paul's Church, Knightsbridge, attending meetings and Lent lectures led by Reverend "Jock" Henderson and, later, the dean of Westminster, Eric Abbott.

In these seminars, Margaret would often hesitate to ask questions aloud, instead whispering them to her friend Marigold, who would then relay them to the group. She would also show up unannounced at post-confirmation classes at the vicarage, just "a black-clothed, sad little figure, inconspicuous in her pew."[18]

As she tried to come to terms with her father's death, she and her mother had to adapt to the new royal hierarchy. Both the queen mother and Margaret had to curtsy to the new queen, and Elizabeth now took priority at all official and private functions. In the early going there was an awkwardness about precedent, as the queen, sensitive to her mother's previous status, often allowed her to enter first at social and public events. Though Margaret was accustomed to playing second fiddle to her sister, the queen mother found her demotion difficult to cope with.

Just as difficult was the domestic reshuffle, in which the queen mother and Princess Margaret were assigned Clarence House while the new queen and her family moved into Buckingham Palace. These discussions proved especially emotional for the queen mother, who, on at least one occasion, burst into tears when the topic was raised. In a letter to her daughter in March 1952, she apologized for her behavior. "I have been feeling very unhappy all day, and I suppose that talking about leaving Buckingham Palace just finished me off."[19] Such uncharacteristic behavior indicated the emotional turmoil wrought by the death of the king.

Ironically, the biggest loser in this reshuffle was the latest recruit to the royal family, Prince Philip. Within a matter of weeks he lost his name, his career, and his home, the prince bruised and broken following his encounters with two political heavyweights, Prime Minister Winston Churchill and the queen's veteran private secretary Tommy Lascelles. In the early weeks of the reign he lobbied to stay at Clarence House, the first real home he had helped design and decorate himself. He and members of his staff argued that Buckingham Palace could be used as an office. Their lobbying was given short shrift by Churchill and Lascelles, who told the prince in no uncertain terms that as the queen's standard flew above Buckingham Palace, that is where she must live.

When he took them on about the family name, he fared no better. When it was pointed out by the editor of *Debrett's*, the bible of social standing, that since King George VI's death, the royal house was now technically the House of Mountbatten, Churchill, supported by Queen Mary, swung into action. Much to Philip's dismay, Churchill formally advised the queen, advice she was constitutionally obliged to take, to state that the royal house remained the House of Windsor. As a last-ditch rearguard action, the prince sent a position paper to the prime minister arguing that the royal house be called "Edinburgh-Mountbatten." Once again he was rebuffed. Queen Mary, who was queen consort when the name House of Windsor was formally proclaimed by her husband, George V, in 1917, was utterly dismissive of her grandson-in-law. "What the devil does that damned fool Edinburgh think that the family name has got to do with him?"[20] It remained a sore point, the prince protesting, correctly, that he was the only man in the kingdom not allowed to give his surname to his children.

Churchill's combative stance toward Philip set the tone for other courtiers inside Buckingham Palace who feared that the prince might try to do a "Prince Albert," the consort of Queen Victoria, who came to have considerable influence over day to day royal and political matters. Though Churchill wished Philip no ill, he told an aide that he neither liked nor trusted him and hoped he would not do harm to the country. As Philip's cousin Pamela Mountbatten recalled, "Prince Philip was unwelcome at Buckingham Palace. Courtiers closed ranks. Churchill made him feel apart from the whole thing. He never expected to be king but nor had he expected to be so brutally and cruelly sidelined."[21] Or as the prince pithily put it: "I am nothing but a bloody amoeba."[22] To cap it all, he contracted jaundice and was left staring at the walls of his new abode for the next three weeks.

There was one ray of sunshine in this gloomy landscape. The king's death prompted a reshuffle in the various royal households. Townsend was offered and accepted the post of comptroller of the queen mother's household, which meant that he would inevitably have increased professional and personal dealings with Princess Margaret, who came under her mother's organizational umbrella.

In his new capacity, Townsend oversaw the task of converting Clarence House into a suitable residence for both mother and daughter once the queen moved out, planned for May 1952. At Clarence House, the princess enjoyed her own commodious apartment, which included a sitting room on the ground floor and bedrooms on the second floor. It was constructed at the opposite end of the building to her mother so that Margaret could spend entire days without seeing her. She now enjoyed a more private life, certainly more cloistered than her days at Buckingham Palace. For the first time in her life she could entertain people with complete discretion—perfect for pursuing a love affair.

During the remodeling at Clarence House, Margaret's rooms on the second floor of Buckingham Palace were converted back to a nursery, while she was given a suite at the opposite end of the palace, above the visitors' entrance. The queen mother, so used to ruling her domain, found her reduced household and status difficult to accept. Nor was Prince Philip, now nominally the head of the family, easy to live with, especially during his battles with Churchill and senior courtiers like Lascelles who made it clear that he should keep his nose out of royal business. For all these reasons mother and daughter found it more restful to spend long weekends at Windsor Castle. As he lived nearby, Townsend would often accompany them on the fifteen-mile journey from central London.

The weeks in the spring sunshine at Windsor proved a real tonic for the queen mother. As Margaret wrote to her friend Sass, "The flowers and blossoms were magnificent and beautiful, and I think it did Mummy a lot of good. It was such a wonderful feeling of permanence and continuation—most soothing."[23] The queen mother even felt able to start answering the small mountain of correspondence, some of it mixed up with her daughter's mail. As Margaret noted, "Mama is cursing the day they named Lilibet Elizabeth."[24]

During this reflective period of Margaret's life, Townsend was one of the few people who recognized and appreciated her complex nature. She was not simply the hard-partying royal who loved fashion, singing, and dancing. Townsend saw at firsthand the other side to the princess: the sensitive, thoughtful churchgoer in search of a purpose in life, a young woman who was desperate to define herself independently of her sister.[25]

As far as Margaret was concerned, when she confided in Townsend it felt natural and healing. Here was a man who had been a dependable presence throughout so much of her family's and her own recent life. "Peter was always there for her," said a friend. "He was incredibly kind, sensitive, gentle, and understanding."[26] Like Margaret, he also was deeply religious and would often pepper his conversation with biblical references. A dreamer, too, his oft-stated ambition was to buy a farm and live in South Africa.

Discreet, loyal, and understanding, Townsend drew closer to her as his own marriage was in its death throes. He and his wife, Rosemary, tried to maintain the pretense for as long as they could, even inviting Elizabeth, Margaret, and Philip over for tea at their home in June 1952. It must have been one of the more socially tortuous events that any of them had taken part in. Peter and Rosemary were on the outs while the air ace and the princess were struggling to keep their romance secret. Indeed, as Rosemary left the cottage that winter and their decree nisi was granted in December, it is possible that the mechanism for their divorce was already in motion.

In an age when the Matrimonial Causes Act of 1937 would only allow divorce for adultery, cruelty, or desertion, the husband normally agreed to be the guilty party and admitted to an affair that was duly logged by a private detective. It was both significant and unusual that Rosemary accepted the role of guilty party. The brigadier's daughter did so, according to her sons, Hugo and Giles, so that Princess Margaret's name was kept out of divorce court proceedings. If she had been named as the mistress, the scandal would have not only stained her reputation but also clouded the first important months, perhaps years, of the new reign. According to her son Giles, a wine merchant, Rosemary Townsend never truly came to terms with her role as the scapegoat. He told writer Geoff Levy, "She agreed to be the guilty party only because someone had to be—and it wasn't going to be my father, as far as the Royal Family was concerned.

"My mother took all the blame, which was very unjust. She definitely got a raw deal." Fifty years later she felt the same way. As Giles observed, "She was hurt very much. Everyone knew that my father was seeing the Princess. The divorce action could just as easily have gone the other way."[27]

During this difficult period, however, neither party wasted much time in getting on with their lives. In December Townsend was not only granted a decree nisi, but, unusually, he was awarded custody of their two sons. Two months later, Rosemary married John de László, the youngest son of the notable society portrait painter Philip de László. Townsend later stated that Rosemary's actions gave him the closure he needed and that though his initial instinct was to "lose himself in his loneliness," instead he found himself "gravitat[ing] back into the atmosphere of that person who all along had shown me such generous sympathy and affection"[28]—that is to say, Princess Margaret.

His memoir, *Time and Chance*, published some twenty-five years after the event, places the beginning of his love affair with Margaret conveniently after his divorce. However, the contemporary account of private secretary Tommy Lascelles dates the romance from at least the summer of 1952, and other witnesses, such as Lady Jane Vane-Tempest-Stewart, claim it was years earlier. In fact Townsend and Margaret were the subject of common chatter at court and beyond months before his divorce. In September 1952, just a few weeks after the Adelaide Cottage tea party, Townsend was at Balmoral and went to see private secretary Tommy Lascelles on some routine matter. After they had resolved the business of the day, Lascelles, who had frequently entertained Peter and Rosemary Townsend at his home, told his colleague that he was the subject of gossip with regard to his relationship with Princess Margaret. Lascelles reminded him of the cardinal rule that no member of the Royal Household should give cause for such talk about the queen's sister, especially as he was a married man. Townsend left the room without making any reply.

In a world where Downstairs silently but implacably watches Upstairs, their attempts at secrecy had fooled no one. "At Balmoral, dressed in tartan skirt and green tweed jacket," Townsend remembered, "she would sometimes walk with me...a discreet but adequate distance from the rest of the party, so that we could talk *en tête-a-tête*. We talked while walking on the hill, among the heather, with the breeze in our faces; or riding in the Great Park at Windsor."[29]

She was an object of delirious desire. Townsend described her appearance and personality with a sensuality and affection that suggests that this was not a chaste love affair.

He found himself enamored with Margaret, admitting that she "gave me what I most lacked—joy."[30] Townsend tenderly described the princess as "a girl of unusual, intense beauty, confined as it was in her short, slender figure and centered about large purple-blue eyes, generous, sensitive lips, and a complexion as smooth as a peach. But what ultimately made Princess Margaret so attractive and lovable was that behind the dazzling façade, the apparent self-assurance, you could find if you look for it a rare softness and sincerity. She could make you bend double with laughing; she could also touch you deeply."

Were they lovers? Townsend is too much of a gentleman to kiss and tell. Yet, given they were about to embark on a high-profile relationship, it would seem unusual if they did not explore the physical side of their relationship. As writer Geoff Levy diplomatically observed, "In later years when Margaret fell in love she did so with a deep and almost reckless physical abandon."[31]

It was one quiet afternoon at Windsor Castle when,

according to Townsend's account, they made the mutual discovery of how much they meant to one another. He told her of his feelings; she reciprocated. "It was, to us both, an immensely gladdening disclosure but one which sorely troubled us."[32] They had fallen head over heels in love but realized that there were many hurdles to overcome. The issue of a divorcé either marrying in a church, which was at the time contrary to Church of England doctrine, or becoming a member of the royal family was an obvious obstacle from the start. This was a social milieu where divorce was not just frowned on but legislated against. Divorcées, for example, could not gain entry to the Royal Enclosure at Ascot.

☙

They knew without being told that the abdication in 1936, when Edward VIII forsook the throne so he could marry Wallis Simpson, a twice-divorced American with two husbands still living, would cloud any discussions regarding their own dilemma.

Sometime before Christmas in 1952, Princess Margaret made an appointment to see her sister in the Belgian Suite at Buckingham Palace to discuss this issue. No longer could Margaret casually walk into her room. These days a liveried footman ushered her in before she was formally announced. She essayed a brief curtsy before uttering, "Ma'am," which symbolized how much their relationship had changed since their father died. After exchanging these formalities, Margaret bravely broached the topic of her romance with Townsend. Though she did not mention the prospect of marriage, she confessed how deeply in love she was with the group captain, expressing the wish that he might be included in more family get-togethers to pave the way for others to view them as a suitable match. Margaret hinted to her sister that she would settle for these small allowances, rather than a full-fledged backing for marriage, though this topic could not, in the end, be avoided.

Elizabeth reacted to the not wholly surprising news with her usual calm and compassion, remembering how loyal Margaret had been in South Africa when she and Philip had been separated. She would never forget how her younger sister had helped ease her doubts during that trip, supported her decisions, and praised Philip in front of their parents whenever possible. Elizabeth had always liked Townsend, especially his ability to handle her often irascible father. As one courtier argued, "She was very fond of Peter in the old days. If she had been on her own, she wouldn't have minded about Princess Margaret's desire to marry him."[33] Though she was noncommittal, in her usual fashion, the queen was certainly not hostile, and Margaret left the audience feeling buoyantly optimistic that the constitutional and religious obstacles could be overcome. This positive belief was intensified when, a few days later, the queen invited his sister and Townsend to join her and Prince Philip for supper. It was, according to Townsend, an agreeable evening, with Philip making jokes about the predicament facing the couple. One unforgettable impression lingered, as Townsend recalled: "the Queen's movingly simple and sympathetic acceptance of the disturbing fact of her sister's love for me."[34]

Their rose-colored glasses were soon removed. Shortly after the royal dinner in December, Townsend went to see Tommy Lascelles again. This time he told the queen's private secretary that he and Princess Margaret were deeply in love and wished to marry. According to Townsend, a visibly shaken Lascelles expostulated, "You must be either mad or bad."[35]

Lascelles subsequently saw the queen, whereupon they discussed the matter and he outlined the provisions of the 1772 Royal Marriages Act, passed during the reign of George III. Under the act, Margaret could not marry without the sovereign's permission until she reached age twenty-five. In other words, as Margaret was twenty-two, her sister would have to consent to her marriage as she was directly in the line of succession, behind Prince Charles and Princess Anne.

If such consent was not given, the royal petitioner had to wait until he or she was twenty-five to alert the Privy Council to his or her intention. The marriage would thereafter only be legal if both Houses of Parliament did not raise any objections within twelve months. Elizabeth knew that the Privy Council and Commonwealth would likely advise against the marriage because Townsend was not just a commoner but a divorcé who would not be allowed to marry in church. It was also pointed out that besides these constitutional and ecclesiastical minefields, if Margaret proceeded with marriage, under the worst-case scenario, she would have to surrender her titles, her place in the succession and her Civil List allowance, the monies voted by parliament to pay for the upkeep of the royal family and the monarchy. At that time Margaret received £6,000 a year (approximately $400,000 today). Not only would she become plain Mrs. Peter Townsend, but the couple would be obliged to live abroad for a time.

Initially this bleak situation does not seem to have been as carefully explained to the anxious lovers as it should have been. Later on, Princess Margaret felt that if the hopelessness of the situation had been properly articulated, Townsend would have departed the scene and no major tragedy would have ensued. As it was, the couple were given the impression that they might—just might—be able to navigate a course through the many obstacles in their way. "It's not impossible," Tommy Lascelles had said.[36]

Shortly before Christmas the family left for Sandringham with these issues left hanging in the air. They were broached during conversations between the queen, Prince Philip, Princess Margaret, and Lascelles in the New Year. Ironically, during these talks, the royal family attended the January wedding in Edinburgh of Johnny Dalkeith, the future duke of Buccleuch, and Norman Hartnell model Jane McNeill. The princess, along with the queen and Prince Philip, were among the first to congratulate the happy couple. The wedding attracted a crowd of twenty thousand and newsreel coverage precisely because Dalkeith and the princess were once seen as a serious item. Instead, shortly after her return to Sandringham, Margaret finally informed her mother about the true identity of "the one."

The queen mother's response perfectly reflects the mixed signals the lovebirds were given. She listened, according to Townsend, "with characteristic understanding" and "without a sign that she felt angered or outraged."[37] Outwardly calm but inwardly devastated, she contacted Lascelles to discuss these "dreadful things." She wept when the topic was discussed and admitted that she was "quite shattered by the whole thing."[38] Yet, rather than inviting Townsend to resign and leave palace employ, she added to his duties and included him in family gatherings so that he and Margaret could spend more time together. It was a recipe for confusion.

The queen and the queen mother were mostly biding their time, expecting that the romance would run its course and fizzle out. As always, they reasoned that it would be preferable to placate Margaret rather than to alienate her, which could provoke her into making a rash decision. This cautious approach illustrated the family's longtime policy of "ostrich-ing," ignoring a potentially explosive situation until it became untenable.[39]

Nor did it help that Lascelles, nominally assigned the unen-viable position of holding the ring, was distrusted by Margaret, while he in turn felt that Townsend had let them down, breach-ing the unspoken but inviolable rule of becoming involved with his "betters." Margaret had, quite rightly, suspected that for his part Lascelles neither trusted nor respected her, and the princess blamed him for the calamity that was about to befall her and her lover. "There goes the man who ruined my life,"[40] she would say, the princess implying that neither she nor Townsend had any control over their lives. The reality was that his primary loyalty was to the queen and the monarchy, not to Princess Margaret and his colleague, who needed their own champion to argue their case and had mistakenly relied on Lascelles.

With the coronation in June looming ever larger, Lascelles insisted that Elizabeth could not afford a scandal before this momentous event, a pageant that would define the new reign. He proposed that Townsend be given an appointment abroad, preferably somewhere far away, like Singapore. It was not a notion that met with the sovereign's approval—yet. She did, though, ask for Margaret to wait until after the coronation to decide on a clearer path forward: "Under the circumstances, it isn't unreasonable for me to ask you to wait a year."[41] Given the fact that Townsend was still part of the household and had an apartment at Clarence House, the couple believed it wouldn't be so difficult to wait for two and a half years until Margaret was twenty-five.

Discussions were halted when Queen Mary was taken seri-ously ill with a recurrence of an existing stomach ailment.

After a short illness, she died on March 24, 1953. Elizabeth inherited a cornucopia of jewels—a chest filled with diamonds, pearls, and emeralds—as well as profound memories of her unswerving loyalty to the crown and a deeply felt conviction that country must always take precedence over self. As she prepared for the coronation, she accepted that the weight of that past was now placed squarely on her slim shoulders. Margaret saw her grandmother's death somewhat differently. Since Margaret was a child, Queen Mary had criticized her, initially for her weight, then her size, and finally her spoiled behavior. Queen Mary had little time for her granddaughter—and Margaret had less for her grandmother. She may have been quietly relieved that Queen Mary had passed on before she could add her critical voice to those who wanted to see the romance between herself and Townsend ended.

Before she died, Queen Mary insisted that nothing should affect the smooth buildup to the coronation. Court mourning, at her request, was kept to a minimum so that the court could focus on the royal event of the decade. Once the preparations began, they consumed the entire palace. Margaret had little time to worry about her own problems and was swept up in the organization. The ceremony was expected to be the most spectacular show in British history, a reign-defining ceremony that had to be pulled off "not just well but supremely well."[42]

Thousands were expected to line the route and millions to listen to the pageant on the radio. Initially, however, the queen was against the televising of the event, a position supported by her mother, Churchill, Lascelles, and the archbishop of Canterbury, Dr. Geoffrey Fisher, who worried that the queen's habit of licking her lips would look indecorous on such an august occasion. Elizabeth recognized the sacred import of the coronation, an ordinary mortal transformed into a powerful symbol, half human, half priest, in a solemn ritual dating back over a thousand years. At heart, she was a traditionalist who did not want such a holy occasion monitored by the unblinking stare of the television camera. It added another layer of stress to an already difficult occasion, and if there were a mishap, as there was at her father's coronation, it would be captured and repeated for all time. The young girl who insisted that her shoes were perfectly arranged under her bed was not going to risk placing her name, her family, and herself in jeopardy for the sake of a newfangled technological fad.

When her father had been asked about admitting television cameras into Westminster Abbey, he was staunchly opposed, so in addition to Elizabeth's own feelings in the matter, that settled it. What was good enough for her father was good enough for the queen. On this crucial decision she butted heads with her husband, who chaired the coronation committee. He wanted to let daylight in on the magic and believed that televising the ceremony would make the monarchy relevant to a new generation and herald a new, dynamic Elizabethan Age. The prince was overruled, and the government announced in October that the ceremony would only be broadcast on the radio. Within hours, politicians and newspaper editors, not to mention television manufacturers, were in an uproar.

"Truly astonishing," the *Daily Express* complained. "The people will be denied the climax of a wonderful and magnificent occasion in British history."[43] For once people power— with the eager support of the television manufacturers—won the day. Ministers and MPs were overwhelmed with an avalanche of mail protesting the decision to keep the cameras out of the abbey. Most lawmakers agreed with their constituents. In October ministers reconsidered their initial verdict. After a lengthy cabinet discussion, ministers decided that in the light of serious public disappointment, they would reverse their decision. The queen, too, seems to have had a change of heart, allowing the cameras in but kept away from sacred aspects of the ceremony.

With television cameras now an integral part of the historic ceremony, Elizabeth was determined that they did not catch the slightest gaffe. At Buckingham Palace, she spent hours in the White Drawing Room rehearsing her lines and walking down a makeshift aisle in between indicative posts and tape to signify each phase of the ceremony. She listened to recordings of her father's coronation on numerous occasions, paying particular attention to those segments that had caused difficulty. She even wore the cumbersome St. Edward's Crown—solid gold and studded with rubies and sapphires—while going about her daily tasks so that she was accustomed to having five pounds on her head.[44] On other occasions, she practiced with a bag of flour instead of the crown and, along with her attendants, had white sheets attached to her shoulders to substitute for robes. During one rehearsal she pulled aside the bishop of Durham and beseeched him to refrain from wiggling his eyebrows so that she didn't get an attack of the giggles.[45]

With her father's coronation, the sacred was in danger of becoming slapstick: The crown was placed on the king's head the wrong way around, a bishop stood on his robe so he couldn't move, the Bible was too heavy to carry, and, as a final insult, the archbishop of Canterbury put his thumb over the wording of the oath as the king was trying to read it. With this in mind, the queen paid attention to the tiniest details, requesting short pile for the carpet in Westminster Abbey so that her heels and train would not get stuck, placing two silver stars on the crown so that the Archbishop of Canterbury would know the front from the back, choosing the flowers, examining stamp designs, and, though she was not usually vain, scrutinizing dozens of photographs of herself to see which makeup and lipstick suited her best for her television close-up. Despite all the painstaking preparation, dressmaker Norman Hartnell sewed a tiny, sequined four-leaf clover in her gown for good luck.

Still, no token of good luck could stave off the ticking time bomb that was Princess Margaret and Group Captain Townsend. Their relationship had been the subject of gossip and discussion within court circles for a year now. Miraculously, it had not yet reached the wider public. Fearing that the story could break during the coronation and divert attention away from perhaps the most important moment of the queen's reign, Prince Philip suggested sacking Townsend. The queen would not hear of it, arguing that he was technically a member of her mother's household, not hers. Moreover, if the romance ran its course—as she and the queen mother anticipated—no further action would be required. Margaret was her sister, the one woman on earth who appreciated the constraints under which she could act, who could sympathize with the difficulties and pressures of her role and knew exactly which liberties she could take. She was a mirror into her own life, her own history.

❦

On the evening of the coronation, vast crowds, undeterred by pouring rain, began to gather around Buckingham Palace and along the festooned procession route. The gloomy weather could not dispel the pervasive sense of optimism that a new Elizabethan age was about to dawn. The queen herself managed to maintain a sunny disposition. At a luncheon with Commonwealth leaders the day before her coronation, she appeared relaxed and calm, admitting, "The extraordinary thing is I no longer feel anxious or worried. I don't know what it is but I have lost all timidity."[46] Perhaps she had been better trained than she thought.

On Coronation Day—June 2, 1953—Elizabeth and Philip traveled in the majestic Gold State Coach to Westminster Abbey. Ironically, in one of her final edicts before she died, Queen Mary felt that the queen should travel alone. She was overruled. With Philip by her side, the queen seemed serenely composed and confident. Earlier, when one of the milling throng asked if she was feeling nervous, she responded with a straight face, "Of course I am, but I really do think Aureole will win"—referring to her horse running in the Epsom Derby the following Saturday.[47] Her relaxed good humor continued. Before making her grand entrance, Elizabeth turned to her maids of honor and, with a wide smile on her face, asked, "Ready, girls?" With that, she fixed her gaze forward without the slightest hesitation.

Her sister had already entered the abbey—in suitably dramatic fashion. As designer Norman Hartnell recalled, "a shaft of silvery sunlight suddenly pierced the lofty stained-glass windows and splashed a pool of light" when Margaret appeared in a gorgeous white satin gown, sparkling with pearls, crystals, and silver thread.[48] Looking "like a snowdrop adrift from its stem," Margaret was seated in the front row of the Royal Gallery beside the queen mother.[49]

Then, Elizabeth stepped forth onto the carpet, as Brigadier Stanley Clark recalled, "a lovely picture in diadem and in a robe of crimson velvet trimmed with ermine and bordered with gold lace."[50] She maintained her impeccable poise throughout the entire ceremony. Even at its most intense moments, as Clark described, "not a quiver showed in her hand. While blood-stirring Hallelujahs lifted in a crescendo."

Her sister, however, appeared tense and emotional from the moment the queen and her attendants entered until the chants of "God save Queen Elizabeth" filled the ancient abbey. Like her sister's marriage to Prince Philip, the ceremony was taking Lilibet further and further away from familial shores.

While the arcane rituals conveyed an aura of tradition, the queen's youth and femininity promised dynamic new beginnings. As her sister later reflected, "The Coronation was like a phoenix-time. Everything was being raised from the ashes. There was this gorgeous-looking, lovely young lady, and nothing to stop anything getting better and better."[51]

It was a profoundly life-changing ceremony for the queen, as she pledged her life and her soul to the monarchy and the nation. "It is the most solemn thing that has ever happened in her life," Canon John Andrew later observed.[52] As the crown was lowered onto her head, the queen sensed that the figurative weight of monarchy—the legacy of her grandfather and father—had been transferred to her. According to the archbishop of Canterbury Dr. Geoffrey Fisher, that ethereal moment was one in which the "country and Commonwealth were not far from the Kingdom of Heaven."[53]

Most of the congregation now headed to Buckingham Palace, covering their ermine and furs from the relentless summer rain. The endless downpour did little to dampen spirits, however, as the new queen and her consort embarked on the Gold State Coach equivalent of a victory lap, waving and smiling to her new subjects soaked by the downpour. Huddling beneath umbrellas, they cheered with all their might when they saw their youthful new queen. As one of Elizabeth's maids of honor, Anne Glenconner, remembered, "The sound reached fever pitch, so loud it felt as if the whole nation was entering into one massive long cheer."[54]

As Elizabeth's procession clattered away from the abbey, a few still lingered in the Great Hall, awaiting their vehicles. Among them were Townsend and Margaret. The group captain looked dapper and distinguished in his sky-blue RAF uniform, while Margaret stood by his side, "looking superb, sparkling, ravishing."[55] They exchanged a few words, and then with her white-gloved hand, she brushed a bit of fluff off his uniform. It was an intimate moment, her action both familiar and tender, reminiscent of a similar unguarded action when Wallis Simpson's hand rested lightly on Edward VIII's bare arm during a yacht cruise along the Dalmatian coast.

It did not go unnoticed by eagle-eyed journalists. Years later, Townsend told columnist Jean Rook, "It didn't mean a thing to us at the time. It must have been a bit of fur coat I picked up from some dowager in the abbey. I never thought a thing about it, and neither did Margaret. We just laughed over it. But that little flick of her hand did it all right. After that, the storm broke."[56]

They still had a few days of untroubled waters. Though several New York and Continental newspapers made much of Margaret's gesture, the British media focused exclusively on the coronation, which was deemed a triumph for the new sovereign, ranking it "among the century's greatest full-colour spectaculars."[57] As for the television coverage, the fact that more than 27 million people in Britain alone, twice the BBC estimate, tuned in was undoubted proof of the popularity of this new medium—and a sign of things to come.

Elizabeth spent the rest of the night making numerous appearances on the palace balcony with her family before later delivering a short speech of thanks and dedication to her new subjects. The next morning, Elizabeth's first as crowned queen, was business as usual, with a medal ceremony, meetings, tours, and a state banquet. Throughout, the new queen seemed happy and accomplished, all those years of coaching and conditioning standing her in good stead. Her horse Aureole, however, despite plenty of coaching for the big day that Saturday, only managed to come second to the Derby winner.

When the queen congratulated the winning trainer, Norman Bertie, he graciously replied: "May I congratulate you, Your Majesty, on winning the world."[58]

Her relaxed demeanor belied the brooding storm back at the palace. After Lascelles informed her that the *People* newspaper was preparing an article on Margaret and Townsend for publication the following Sunday, she gave him permission to speak to Prime Minister Churchill. As long as the affair had remained private, she believed that it could be dealt with "in house." But that was no longer the case now, and while she was still a loving sister, she was also the crowned queen with constitutional obligations and duties. On this matter she had to take the formal advice of the prime minister and other Commonwealth leaders.

Lascelles, who by now wanted Townsend out of the country yesterday, was somewhat taken aback by Churchill's initial response. On June 13, he traveled to Chartwell, the prime minister's private home, and there, before Churchill; his wife, Clementine; and his private secretary, Jock Colville, proceeded to lay out the history behind this vexatious matter. Ever the romantic, Churchill opined that politicians should never intervene in matters of the heart. "What a delightful match!" he gushed. "A lovely young royal lady married to a gallant young airman, safe from the perils and horrors of war!"[59] Aghast, his wife retorted, "Winston, if you are going to begin the abdication all over again, I'm going to leave! I shall take a flat and go and live in Brighton."[60]

Of course, the comparison was far from accurate, as Margaret was the queen's sister and only third in line to the throne. Townsend was an English hero and a trusted insider, not a foreigner who was suspected of being a Nazi spy. Furthermore, attitudes toward divorce were changing. Not only had three senior members of the cabinet been divorced—foreign secretary Anthony Eden, minister of labor Walter Monckton, and president of the Board of Trade Peter Thorneycroft—but so too was Churchill's own son, Randolph.

According to Lascelles's memorandum, Churchill was seized more by the possible reaction of the Commonwealth than the almost certain disapproval of the Church of England. While Churchill offered to take soundings from senior cabinet colleagues, the queen demurred, believing it was still a family affair—even though the *People* was about to print its story. She still resisted Lascelles's view, which was now shared by Churchill, that Townsend should be sent abroad as soon as possible so as to avoid stoking the scandal. Instead, the queen's private secretary and her press secretary privately lobbied the prime minister to speak directly to her. He agreed to do so.

Meanwhile, the British public was enthralled with details of the secret romance between the beautiful bachelor princess and the handsome war hero who had flown over five hundred combat missions and had a chestful of medals to show for it. Just twelve days after the coronation, *People*, in time-honored Fleet Street fashion, backed into the story, dismissing the claims in the foreign media as outrageous while publishing every last jot and tittle of the affair. "This story is of course, utterly untrue," they thundered. "It is quite unthinkable that a royal princess, third in line of succession to the throne, should even contemplate a marriage with a man who has been through the divorce courts." They told their readers that if, in the unlikely event the story was *true*, the consequences would be explosive, as "a marriage between Princess Margaret and [Townsend] would fly in the face of Royal and Christian tradition."[61]

Churchill saw the queen and emphasized that as the story was now in the public domain, she should agree to send Townsend abroad forthwith. The danger was that the scandal could undermine the enthusiasm for the monarchy inspired by the unequivocal success of the coronation. He explained that the cabinet and the Commonwealth prime ministers unanimously opposed the marriage. The most sensible short-term solution was for Townsend and Margaret to stay apart for at least a year. Reluctantly, the queen took his advice, and Lascelles was deputed to inform the group captain that he was to go abroad immediately. Townsend was given the choice of three postings: Singapore, Johannesburg, or Brussels.

At first, Townsend thought Lascelles was joking, but soon enough the realization sank in that he was being exiled for the crime of falling in love with the queen's sister. He considered it an almost medieval punishment, especially as Lascelles knew full well that he had sole custody of his young boys. Harried by Lascelles to choose quickly, he picked Brussels, as it was the nearest to his sons' boarding school in Kent. The parting from them would be particularly harrowing.

The queen tried to soften the blow by delaying Townsend's separation until after July 17, when Margaret and the queen mother were due to return from a tour of Rhodesia, an official visit that Townsend had been due to accompany them on.

The night before Margaret departed for her overseas visit, the lovers exchanged heartfelt goodbyes, the queen mother tactfully giving them their desired privacy. As Townsend had been promised that he did not need to leave for Brussels until after July 17, they treated this as a brief farewell before they were once more united. As Townsend recalled, "The Princess was very calm for we felt certain of each other and, though it was hard to part, we were reassured by the promise...that my departure would be held over until her return on 17 July."[62]

On the same day as the princess and her mother left for Rhodesia, the queen asked Townsend to accompany her as equerry-in-waiting for a coronation tour of Belfast in Northern Ireland. Though Townsend viewed this move as a "most gracious and touching gesture," Elizabeth was advised to take this course of action to ensure that he was away from London in order to dampen media speculation. Upon his return from Belfast, he was coldly informed that his departure for Brussels had been brought forward two days to July 15, meaning that he would leave the country before Margaret returned. As one headline said baldly: QUEEN "EXILES" RAF ACE LINKED TO PRINCESS MEG.[63]

Princess Margaret was staying at the Leopard Rock hotel in Rhodesia's Bvumba Mountains when her mother broke the upsetting news. She was distraught and wracked with sobbing, and it was only Townsend on the other end of an international phone call who was able to calm her down and reassure her that all would be well. The distraught princess managed to pull herself together for the rest of the trip, though she missed several engagements, feigning illness. It was a wrenching time too for the queen, who took no pleasure from her sister's distress. Her policy of kicking the can down the road had palpably failed. She and her advisers had had six months to effect a discreet solution. Yet popular opinion was overwhelmingly in favor of allowing the lovers to marry, and the queen seemed out of step with her people on this issue. Little wonder that when she was entertained by Noël Coward the day before Princess Margaret's return, the queen, according to the playwright, "scowled through most of the performance."[64]

Once she returned to London, Margaret was immediately on the telephone to Townsend. They reassured one another that they would only be apart for a year and that after her twenty-fifth birthday they could finally marry. Their love was sweet and pure and could withstand any assault. It was indestructible.

Churchill and Lascelles had other ideas.

6

"My Dear Prime Minister"

In one of her first, and arguably most controversial, speeches, the young Princess Elizabeth, then only twenty-three, addressed a Mothers' Union rally of young wives at Central Hall, Westminster, where she denounced divorce and commended her audience's respect for the sanctity of marriage. Linking broken homes to broken children, Elizabeth declared: "We can have no doubt that divorce and separation are responsible for some of the darkest evils in our society today." Her traditionalist statement, made in 1949, stoked the controversy surrounding Britain's draconian divorce laws, and the then princess was condemned by those advocating the liberalization of existing legislation. "The harm to children can be greater in a home where both parents are at loggerheads than if divorce ensues," argued the chairman of the Marriage Law Reform committee.[1] In spite of this criticism, the king and queen totally agreed with their daughter's sentiments. A royal aide noted: "King George and Queen Elizabeth were completely satisfied that their daughter had been right, for their views on marriage and family life were the same."[2]

Three years later she was now the head of state, a state that allowed divorce though only under very specific circumstances, and she was also head of the church, which denounced it categorically. She was the living embodiment of this contradiction in that she was officially against divorce and yet mindful that she did not want to be responsible for denying her sister's happiness.

As a close friend of Margaret recalled, the queen "was absolutely determined that nobody should influence Princess Margaret over her decision, and that she should be free to make up her own mind."[3] Elizabeth thus did not exert any pressure either way. She knew that Margaret would, as a devout and committed Christian, be wrestling with the doctrinal implications of marriage to a divorcé. Could she truly countenance a civil ceremony rather than a church wedding? Margaret explored these doubts and dilemmas with her close friend, the Reverend Simon Phipps, who had got to know the princess well when his father was gentleman usher to the late king. Phipps, a gentle and kindly cleric, had accompanied her to hunt balls and other social events. During this period of waiting and uncertainty, her friend, who had been ordained chaplain of Trinity College, Cambridge, was her counselor and a listening ear. In addition she attended Bible study and weekly post-confirmation classes at St. Paul's vicarage in London conducted by the Reverend "Jock" Henderson.

The queen's practical decision to stand above the fray and let the romance take its course ensured at least the appearance of family unity. During Ascot week in the summer of 1953, the sisters, wearing jaunty headscarves, cheerfully raced each other along the Royal Mile, galloping at breakneck speed. Margaret surprisingly beat her sister.

The Balmoral summer holiday that year assumed greater significance, as in November the queen and Prince Philip embarked on the long-delayed visit to Australia and New Zealand; the royal couple would be leaving their children behind for six months, returning the following May.

It was not the happiest of holidays. The weather was miserable, Charles was confined to bed with an ear infection, and his sister had a fever. Princess Margaret, glum and missing her lover, was downcast and not in the mood for games of charades or attending shooting lunches. However, she did invite the Reverend Phipps to spend two weeks with her at the northern retreat.

In a letter to Sass Douglas, written from Balmoral on October 1, 1953, she vented her irritation at the media: "Thank you so much for your sympathy over the horrid Press being so beastly. It was rather agonizing, especially right after the glory of the Coronation and then having to be in S. Rhodesia. However I hope that your newspapers, at least, have quieted down. I was, of course, sent millions of clippings from unknown busybodies...the bore was that none of them were at all amusing, which is normally the saving grace of being written about!"

With talk of family rifts, the sisters had to negotiate a media minefield with every decision, big and small, now that Margaret's romance with Townsend was front-page news. That summer, for example, the queen ensured that her husband would be made regent should she die in the early years of her reign, superseding the existing arrangement whereby Margaret would assume the regent position until Prince Charles, then four years old, came of age.

In a confidential briefing memorandum to the Commonwealth heads of government at their meeting in London on June 19, she made clear that the move had nothing to do with any disunity between her and her sister. Nor was it a demotion for Margaret. In her note she stated: "The queen's wish in this matter was shared by other members of the Royal Family and in particular by Princess Margaret."[4] Nonetheless there was concern among government ministers that the decision would, quite falsely, be linked to Margaret's private life and thus give rise to controversy.

It seems that the prime minister's support for the change was lukewarm. He let it be known that he "sympathises" with "MPs from all sides" who had doubts about Philip in this influential position.[5]

In November, after navigating a tricky summer, Margaret appeared to be in a better state of mind. The two sisters exchanged teary goodbyes at London Airport, with Margaret promising to take care of Charles and Anne. With Elizabeth away for so long, Margaret felt, according to a friend, "utterly lost and lonely." She had no close family member with whom she could discuss her romantic quandary, because her mother, with whom she was barely on speaking terms, had adopted her familiar ostrich posture and was "completely unapproachable and remote."[6] Her sense of isolation and abandonment was only ameliorated by her conversations with Reverend Phipps. Her one consolation was the knowledge that once she turned twenty-five in two years' time, August 21, 1955, she would be able to marry without her sister's consent. Before he left for Brussels, Townsend had, according to at least one source, apparently proposed to Margaret. Biographer Anne Edwards, who became friendly with Townsend, recalled: "Margaret had accepted his proposal of marriage, which they both hoped could take place directly after August 21, 1955, when she would celebrate her twenty-fifth birthday."[7] In his detailed memoir, *Time and Chance*, Townsend remains coy about where and when he asked the princess to marry him or even if he gave her a ring or other sentimental memento to signify their eventual union. He downplayed the possibility, writing, "Marriage, at this moment, seemed the least likely solution; and anyway, at the prospect of my becoming a member of the Royal Family the imagination boggled, most of all my own. Neither the Princess nor I had the faintest idea how it might be possible for us to share our lives."[8]

Whether he liked it or not, Townsend was now the most famous air attaché in the world. It seemed that virtually every time he left his modest flat in Brussels, a clutch of photographers would be waiting outside for that day's picture of the lovesick airman. Without a hint of irony, he was dubbed "the loneliest man in Brussels" as the media followed him to the British embassy and back home again. To stave off boredom he carefully read his Bible, discussed theology with a Catholic friend, and took up amateur horse racing, losing weight from his already slender frame so that he could become a more competitive jockey. It was during a visit to a horse show in Brussels that he watched the talented teenager Marie-Luce Jamagne rattle around the course, only to fall, literally at his feet. Once she recovered, Townsend was introduced to her and her family. She was fourteen—the same age as when he first met Princess Margaret. With her luxuriant head of hair, intelligent forehead, and piercing eyes, she was the spitting image of the princess Townsend had left behind in London.

Apart from these excitements, the highlights of his days were the letters he received from his boys and Margaret. "Our own world," he lamented, "was a vacuum which had to be endured day in, day out, and during the yearning hours of the night."[9]

Rarely a week went by without a picture or story about the

couple appearing in the British and American media. The most hurtful tales concerned speculation about Townsend's latest "lover," who was invariably a beautiful European countess. Just as he had to be careful of his public demeanor lest an unflattering photograph be taken, so he had to be mindful of those to whom he spoke, however innocently. An offhand remark at a cocktail party or to a dinner companion could end up in the gossip columns or, heaven forbid, on the front pages. The constant speculation also obliged Margaret to rein in her public activities. She had been greatly looking forward to realizing her long-held dream of visiting the United States. Her friend Sharman Douglas had first piqued her interest, and now she was eager to see the country firsthand. However, following consultations with palace and Foreign Office officials, it was felt that, as the American press were noisier and more confrontational than the deferential British media, it would be best if the tour were postponed. Even though she was desperately disappointed, she had no desire to be subject to endless shouted questions about her romance.

In February 1954, while her sister was halfway through her Down Under tour, Margaret wrote to Sharman Douglas, telling her that her visit had been called off—much to her relief. "Everyone, including myself, felt it was better, just at the moment, not to come. I think it is wise, because it couldn't be anything but embarrassing to all of us—& specially me—if your delightful Press began asking questions. So there you are, and I'm sure you will understand or have an inkling what I might mean, and I would be most grateful if you didn't say anything even to your dear family."

Though she was sparing herself from an ordeal by the media, Margaret realized too that the sideshow of gossip and speculation if she went ahead would also overshadow her sister's historic visit to Australia. Her decision to think of her sister first and herself second was a sign of her growing maturity and awareness.

The queen's tour was grueling. She and Prince Philip traveled over 43,000 miles by sea, air, and train. During the visit the queen gave 102 speeches—Queen Mary by contrast only gave two speeches in her life—and was personally introduced to more than thirteen thousand people. These statistics alone vividly demonstrate how the monarchy had changed since the reign of King George V and Queen Mary, who would usually parade past their subjects in a horse-drawn landau. This distant relationship between sovereign and subject was drastically transformed during the brief reign of Edward VIII, who, as Prince of Wales, had exhausted himself meeting and greeting thousands of his future subjects during his many and varied empire tours. This more inclusive style of monarchy had continued in the postwar years, particularly with George VI's visit to South Africa.

As with the arrangements for the coronation, the six-month tour highlighted the queen's professionalism and steadiness, the monarch girded for a marathon not a sprint. She carried with her index cards listing the names, titles, occupations, and, where possible, even anecdotes involving the dignitaries she was scheduled to meet. Her record-breaking round of speeches, handshaking, troop inspections, receptions, banquets, Parliament openings, and cultural performances was unparalleled, leaving her exhausted from the constant demand of appearing human even as she was treated "as a waxwork, actually moving and speaking."[10]

Midway through the tour an Australian camera crew was scheduled to film her looking at wildlife during a weekend break at the O'Shannassy Reservoir in Victoria, where the queen and

Prince Philip had an executive chalet. When their chalet door opened, the cameraman started filming, expecting the queen and her husband to stroll into vision. Not this time. Out dashed Prince Philip, hotly pursued by his angry wife, who threw a tennis racquet and tennis shoes at the retreating figure. Eventually the queen dragged her husband back into the chalet, slamming the door behind her. It was sensational footage, revealing the fiery side of the royal marriage. Within minutes the queen's press secretary, Commander Richard Colville, appeared and demanded the senior cameraman, Loch Townsend, hand over the film. He duly obliged, and minutes later an apologetic monarch appeared. She told the crew, "I am sorry for that little interlude but, as you know, it happens in every marriage."[11] Not only did the incident open a window into the royal marriage, but it also revealed the deferential dynamic between the press and the palace. There was never any question that the film would ever be broadcast, and it was promptly destroyed.

Nothing could detract from the triumph of this historic visit, during which the queen matured into her role as sovereign and head of the Commonwealth before the eyes of the world. The royal couple were reunited with their children on board the new royal yacht *Britannia*, where Charles and Anne rather solemnly shook hands with their parents. In different times, this image would come to define the queen's cool and distant approach to motherhood.

After 174 days away, when she and Philip finally sailed through Tower Bridge on May 15, 1954, they were welcomed with undiluted affection and pageantry, with thousands braving the chill wind outside Buckingham Palace and along the Mall to greet them. There was general relief and delight that the young queen had arrived home. It seemed, at least according to one observer, "that she had returned from a voyage of six years, not six months, and that her land had been under foreign occupation in her absence."[12]

She found a full "in" tray waiting for her in her office in Buckingham Palace. The most pressing issue was how to deal with Margaret and Peter Townsend now that they had completed their first year apart, as requested. During this period Townsend had behaved impeccably and had not attempted to return even to see his two sons. It was time for the queen to give them some leeway. With her permission, in July 1954, the couple engaged in a secret cloak-and-dagger subterfuge so that they could enjoy a brief reunion. For once they totally outfoxed the ever-present media, as Townsend flew to London airport under the false name Mr. Carter. He was then ferried in a modest saloon car to the book department at Harrods, where he met Brigadier Sir Norman Gwatkin, veteran of Normandy and former equerry to the king. From there, he was taken to another vehicle, which transported him to Clarence House. There, after a full year of separation, the couple were reunited, spending two precious hours talking and laughing as if they had left off only the day before. Townsend later recalled: "Our joy at being together again was indescribable. The long year of waiting, of penance and solitude, seemed to have passed in the twinkling of an eye." Again, they reaffirmed their marriage plans, expecting that once Margaret turned twenty-five, they would be free to decide the next steps without having to worry about the queen's official veto. They were heartened to discover that their feelings for one another had not cooled, and the couple was steadfast in their love. According to Townsend, "Until then, there was nothing for it but to hold on and wait."[13] Before he returned to Brussels, he visited his sons at their boarding school.

Though the couple continued to write daily and to speak by

telephone at least once a week, Margaret still missed Townsend dearly. Her highly charged emotional state was obvious to her sister one "ghastly evening" at Balmoral when the family came together to celebrate Margaret's twenty-fourth birthday in August. Their mother wanted to maintain the tradition of dressing up and singing a specially composed song for her, just as they had done when the king was alive. One guest noted: "The Queen thought it might end in trouble but she didn't like to spoil her mother's enjoyment." Just as Elizabeth had predicted, the evening ended in disaster. A friend recalled: "The Queen Mother couldn't see what had upset Princess Margaret, the queen knowing this would happen and unable to stop it, and Princess Margaret in tears, partly because it reminded her of the times when the King and Peter were there."[14] She was inconsolable, the innocent party piece triggering her sense of loss and loneliness, emotions that were never far from the surface.

If her delicate state of mind was troubling, so too was her health, which, worryingly, seemed to echo ailments similar to those that affected her father. Over the New Year at damp and chilly Sandringham, Margaret came down with a nasty chest cough, which mutated into a bad case of influenza. After taking the advice of Margaret's doctor, the queen agreed that she could spend the whole of February on an official tour of the Commonwealth islands in the Caribbean on board the royal yacht *Britannia*. It was thought the warm climate would do her good. Though the decision irritated the media and not a few subjects as they shivered through another foggy, dank winter, it underscored the queen's confidence in her sister as her representative abroad. Her sister's faith was amply rewarded; the solo trip proved a surprising triumph, as thousands of people turned out in the intense heat for a glimpse of the calypso princess. The interest in Margaret was perhaps inevitable. Young, fashionable, and glamorous, she was the first princess to undertake overseas tours on her own. During the month-long visit, she never once mentioned Townsend's name, even to her lady-in-waiting. Yet his name was on everyone's lips. She returned to London in March 1955, tanned, fit, healthy, and ready for the media battles to come. Margaret accepted the public's interest in her love life with a bored weariness, finding the whole exercise the dreary part of her royal life.

⌒

With the August deadline mere months away, newspapers were eagerly printing stories about lonely Margaret and her air ace beau. Would she choose duty over love? Or would she follow her heart? It was a romantic dilemma that captured the public's imagination. Shortly after Margaret's return, the now defunct *Sunday Pictorial* published a front-page story suggesting that the chapel in St. James's Palace was being restored in time for the impending royal wedding. This tale was the starting gun that inspired a crowd of reporters and photographers to race to Townsend's front door in Brussels and demand that he make a statement. By his own admission, faced with this media scrum, Townsend needed some help from the palace. They, however, took the view that the best way of cooling the speculation was to remain silent and hope the frenzy would die down. It didn't. Townsend was left to his own devices. First the *New York Post* announced: "Meg flier will wed." Then Australian newspapers assured their readers that the "Romance was moving to its climax." It was Townsend himself, however, who upped the ante, giving a brief interview to the *Daily Sketch* shortly after Margaret's return in March. When asked about wedding plans, he responded enigmatically, "Wait and see."[15]

On April 5, 1955, wartime leader and international statesman Winston Churchill resigned as prime minister. On the
eve of his resignation he invited the queen and Prince Philip
for dinner at 10 Downing Street. The following day she sent
for his deputy, Anthony Eden, himself the innocent party of
a divorce, as Churchill's longtime successor. As Sir Michael
Adeane had replaced Tommy Lascelles as the queen's private
secretary, there was hope that a degree of flexibility would be
injected into the discussions about Princess Margaret's future
should she marry Townsend.

In November 1954, the day before she left for her tour
Down Under, the queen asked Lascelles to obtain a clear statement from the attorney general outlining the implications of
the Royal Marriages Act should a member of the royal family
wish to contract a marriage to which the sovereign was not
prepared to give approval. Attorney general Sir Lionel Heald
wrote the advice himself, and it was sent to the queen as well
as Princess Margaret together with a covering memorandum
from Lascelles, who pointed out the danger of "splitting the
Empire" if this issue was sent to various Commonwealth Parlia-
ments for approval and they took opposing points of view.[16] His
concern was based on the fact that the queen was not just the
head of state of England but also of numerous Commonwealth
nations, including Canada, Australia, and New Zealand.

His covering letter was in addition to his previous memorandum, which stated that Margaret would have to renounce
her title, all rights to the succession for herself and her heirs,
and her Civil List income and remain in exile for at least three
years so as not to damage the monarchy.

This was a harsh analysis based in part on the precedent
of the duke and duchess of Windsor, who went into voluntary
exile. The difference there was that the Windsors were paid a

substantial stipend by the king to stay out of Britain. If they had wished to return to Britain permanently, they would have had to give up the annual payment from the crown. Ultimately, it was their choice. It was very different for Princess Margaret and Group Captain Peter Townsend. She would be known as plain Mrs. Peter Townsend and receive nothing for her sacrifice.

Even though they spoke on the telephone most days, the queen and her sister avoided discussion about the Townsend affair. Both knew that the queen had to act on the advice of her prime minister and that advice would not be formally forthcoming until Margaret had reached her twenty-fifth birthday. Instead, they discussed innocuous topics like the day's schedule, their mother's health, and the children's latest milestones.[17]

When her much anticipated birthday finally arrived on August 21, 1955, Margaret spent the day not in her lover's arms, but rowing across Loch Muick on the Balmoral estate with some friends. She and the rest of the family were virtual prisoners on the forty-thousand-acre estate, the place surrounded by three hundred or so reporters and photographers who had arrived from around the world to see the dramatic conclusion of this fairytale romance. Would she sacrifice all, her position, her family, her faith, and her fortune, for love? Or would she conform to religious, government, and royal convention and remain a forlorn, lonely princess? The world held its breath, waiting for a decision. Or, as the *Daily Mirror* insisted: "Come on Margaret! Please make up your mind!"[18] Meanwhile, she quietly sat down at the Glas-allt-Shiel lodge on the Balmoral estate and searched her heart as she wrote down the reasons for and against their romance. "For: I couldn't live without him and Against: Because it does harm to the queen."

Days before her birthday, and following discussion with her sister, she decided as a matter of courtesy and polity to write to the prime minister to outline her future intentions. In the handwritten letter, dated August 15, she discussed her short-term plans, anticipated the response of the media and articulated her feelings for Townsend. Significantly, she made it clear that she already planned to see Townsend in October during his annual leave. Most telling of all was that these meetings were designed to see if the spark of love still remained after their two-year-long separation. In the highly sensitive letter, which only surfaced half a century after it was written, Margaret wrote: "My dear Prime Minister, I am writing to tell you, as far as I can of my personal plans during the next few months. During the last of August and all September I shall be here at Balmoral, and I have no doubt that during this time—especially on my birthday on August 21st—the press will encourage every sort of speculation about the possibility of my marrying Group Captain Peter Townsend. I am not going to see him during this time but in October I shall be returning to London, and he will then be taking his annual leave—I do certainly hope to see him while he is there.

"But it is only by seeing him in this way that I feel I can properly decide whether I can marry him or not. At the end of October or early November I very much hope to be in a position to tell you and the other Commonwealth Prime Ministers what I intend to do. The Queen of course knows I am writing to you about this, but of course no one else does, and as everything is so uncertain I know you will regard it certainly as a confidence."[19]

Her candor and her practical attitude gave the prime minister time to shape his own response to her predicament, politically and legally. Before he arrived at Balmoral in early

October for the traditional prime minister's weekend, he had sounded out legal aides regarding the 1772 Royal Marriages Act and the consequences for Margaret should she decide to marry Townsend.

Far from existing as two separate camps, the queen, prime minister, and Princess Margaret worked together to try to effectively resolve this vexatious matter to the satisfaction of all parties. When he subsequently arrived at Balmoral in early October, he came bearing welcome gifts, not reprimands. He had asked the lord chancellor Lord Kilmuir for his view on the 1772 Royal Marriages Act. In a scrawled response to Eden written on September 3 and marked "Top Secret and Personal," he stated that the act probably did not even apply to Princess Margaret because of its contradictory drafting. "This Act has no pride of ancestry, is badly drawn and uncertain and embarrassing in its effect," he wrote, adding that the act, which had always been unpopular, was no longer "appropriate to modern conditions." He concluded: "I think that at least 75 per cent of the electorate would be in favour of the marriage being somehow allowed."[20]

During his weekend at Balmoral, Eden recorded that after dinner on the first evening he saw the queen and discussed many topics, the Princess Margaret problem being the main item. After lunch the next day, he had another talk with the queen and Philip, followed by a conversation with Margaret. He explained the "limitations of [the] Royal Marriages Act," presumably paraphrasing Kilmuir's view, and went on to suggest that if she still wished to marry Townsend, the "best" approach would be "for her to write to the Queen on her own initiative saying so and renouncing her right of succession to the throne." Parliament could then legislate in compliance with her wishes.

"Princess Margaret accepted this," he recorded matter-of-factly, "and Michael [Sir Michael Adeane, the queen's private secretary] and Norman [Sir Norman Brook, the cabinet secretary] will now discuss form of letter, though Princess Margaret still seems uncertain or says she is."[21]

Far from being cast out, penniless, and shamed, she was informed that she would keep her title, her Civil List payment (which, upon marriage, would increase from £6,000 to £15,000 a year, the equivalent of $500,000 in 2020), her royal duties, and her appellation "Her Royal Highness." Moreover, at some point in the future, Townsend may have been given a title as well as his own official allowance. The only sacrifice she would have to make was to ask the queen to remove her and her children from the line of succession. As her chances of becoming queen were remote—she was third in line after Charles and Anne—it was no hardship. The other stipulation was that she would have to marry in a civil ceremony, which would be the case whether she was royal or commoner. As Paul Reynolds, a former BBC royal correspondent, observed, "Far from opposing her sister's marriage, the queen's attitude was summed up by Eden in a letter to Commonwealth prime ministers: "Her Majesty would not wish to stand in the way of her sister's happiness."[22]

Meanwhile Townsend, in anticipation of their reunion, worked on a plan to arrive in London unnoticed. He drove to Le Touquet in northern France and then crossed the Channel on the air ferry to Lydd in Kent. This way he hoped to outfox the media. Even though he had only mentioned his plan to a handful of friends, when he arrived at Lydd he was blinded by flashbulbs from the waiting press pack. He scrambled into his car and headed to London, followed by a media convoy. After arriving at 19 Lowndes Square in Belgravia, where he was due to stay, he was swarmed by photographers and reporters. He duly remained silent, avoiding answering any questions.

The next morning, October 13, Margaret returned from Balmoral to London by train. Before she left, the queen, who was fully appraised of her sister's intentions, asked that she continue with her official duties, that the lovers not be seen out in public, and that they meet either at Clarence House or at the homes of friends of the royal family. Margaret readily agreed.

Such was the melee when Margaret arrived at London's King's Cross station that she waited in her carriage for two hours before the crowds had sufficiently thinned for her to make her way back to Clarence House. Then she phoned Townsend to confirm their meeting that evening.

In this febrile atmosphere it was sensible that Townsend enter Clarence House through the back entrance to avoid the knot of curious onlookers. Once inside, Townsend followed a footman to Margaret's sitting room. After the servant had left, Margaret entered and they finally embraced after over a year apart. Townsend would later claim that their love persisted: "Time had not staled our accustomed sweet familiarity."[23]

For the sake of decorum, the queen's advisers asked that the couple spend just two hours together before Townsend was ushered out, returning to Lowndes Square for dinner alone. Just to add to the speculation, the queen's press secretary, Commander Colville, made a rare public statement, saying, "No announcement concerning Princess Margaret's future is at present contemplated." This was widely interpreted as *when* not *if* the princess was to marry Townsend and added to the sense of anticipation.

For their next meeting that weekend, the two headed to Allanbay Lodge, the home of Major John Lycett Wills and his wife, Jean, whose mother was the queen mother's sister, Lady Elphinstone. For a time helicopters and light aircraft circled above the Willses' Georgian mansion, while the streets surrounding the house were jammed with cars. Eventually, a squad of police and dogs were brought in to seal off the entire estate.

Once they were protected from the mayhem, the lovebirds were in a place ideally suited for romance. They seemed happy and comfortable with one another, a meeting of minds—and hearts. One friend later observed: "I had seen her in the company of several young escorts during her teens; and later, of course, Tony [Antony Armstrong-Jones, her future husband]. But she never was or would be so naturally suited to a man as she was to Peter. You simply could not doubt that this was that once-in-a-lifetime love that we all dream about. And the most marvelous thing was that it was so fully reciprocated. Peter adored her, it was in his voice as he spoke to her and in his eyes when he looked at her."[24]

This may have been so much wishful thinking on everyone's parts. As she previously made clear to Eden, Margaret was no longer entirely sure of her feelings. She needed to test the waters. In the two years since they were forced to part, Townsend had altered. The man she first knew—the dashing fighter pilot who became a confidant of her beloved father—was now forty, stuck, through no fault of his own, in a dead-end job and obsessed with his hobby as an amateur jockey. Indeed, he would later marry Marie-Luce Jamagne, whom he first met at a showjumping trial.

On the surface the couple seemed deliriously happy, sharing intimate candlelit dinners at the homes of respectable friends. But hurdles remained. As she once said, somewhat rhetorically, to her biographer Christopher Warwick, "How do you know after two years apart whether you do want to marry somebody?"[25]

Time though was wasting. Eden, whose primary aim in this affair was "to protect the position of the Queen,"[26] was increasingly concerned that the prolongation of uncertainty could do harm, though not fatal harm, to the monarchy. In October Eden expressed his worries to the queen's private secretary Sir Michael Adeane, who told him that "the queen had done all that was possible to bring a decision nearer." Shortly before his weekly audience with the queen at Buckingham Palace on October 18, an unsigned Downing Street memorandum stated: "I think the PM [prime minister] will consider mentioning to the Queen on Tuesday that harm will be done if there is much more delay and even possibly offering to see the Princess herself to say so." It was noticeable that his usual thirty-minute audience with the queen lasted for ninety minutes.

◦———◦

There were daily reminders for Margaret of what and who she represented, marriage or no marriage. On October 21 the princess, the queen mother, the prime minister, as well as representatives of the church and Commonwealth were present at the public unveiling of a bronze statue of King George VI in Carlton Gardens near Clarence House. If nothing else, the ceremony brought back vivid reminders of her father and her sacred duty as a member of the royal family. The queen's speech at the unveiling seemed to be a coded conversation with her sister. "Much was asked of my father in personal sacrifice and endeavor. He shirked no task, however difficult, and to the end he never faltered in his duty to his peoples."[27]

The speech came at a crucial turning point as the countdown for Margaret and Townsend had now begun. According to Townsend, "We were both exhausted, mentally, emotionally, physically. We felt mute and numbed at the center of this maelstrom."[28] On October 23, ten days after the reunion, Margaret joined her sister, mother, and brother-in-law at Windsor Castle for what turned out to be a difficult weekend. When the queen mother wailed about how Margaret would manage, Philip said laconically that she could buy a house. That was too much to take, and the queen mother stalked out of the room, slamming the door behind her. This exchange indicates that the queen mother seems to have been unaware of the soft landing being prepared for Margaret and Townsend by Eden should she wish to go ahead with the marriage. Townsend later recalled: "She did not say what had passed between herself and her sister and her brother-in-law, but doubtless, the stern truth was dawning on her."

There were many significant voices outside the palace gates who were eager to see the dawning of that stern truth. Besides senior churchmen, leading politicians like Bobbety Salisbury, Conservative leader in the House of Lords and friend of the queen mother, as well as newspaper editors felt that Margaret should do her duty and forsake her lover. As the princess wrestled with her conscience, an editorial in *The Times* was telling. It argued: "The Princess will be entering in a union which vast numbers of her sister's people, all sincerely anxious for her lifelong happiness cannot in all conscience regard as a marriage," and would, it concluded, "cause acute division among loyal subjects everywhere."[29]

⁓

On October 24, the day after Margaret's private meeting with her family, she and Townsend met once again feeling, in her own words, "thoroughly drained, thoroughly demoralized."[30] Just eleven days after they had first seen one another after their mutual exile, they decided that they could no longer continue. Townsend sat in his apartment and drafted a statement outlining why they should not marry. During his stay in London Townsend, according to contemporary press reports, had made just five short visits to Clarence House, attended four dinner parties, and enjoyed two country weekends. In that brief time they mutually decided that their love no longer burned as brightly as it had in the beginning.

When she read his draft she told him: "That's exactly how I feel." Townsend recalled, "We looked at each other; there was a wonderful tenderness in her eyes which reflected, I suppose, the look in mine. We had reached the end of the road."[31] At some point during this tumultuous period in their lives, it seems that they had made an informal pact that if they couldn't marry one another, they would marry no one.

Though there had been outside influences brought to bear, essentially the decision was theirs and theirs alone. During this entire saga the queen had been scrupulous in giving Margaret the opportunity to make her choice without undue pressure. Not only were government mandarins working assiduously to give Margaret everything that would allow her to follow her heart, but the queen sought to make it absolutely clear that she and Margaret formed a united front, sisters together. Behind the scenes, then, the true story was about the bond rather than the breakage between sisters, about a key moment when the queen was prepared to allow the crown to be stained, if not irreparably, in order to secure her sister's happiness.

As Paul Reynolds said, "The Queen and Prime Minister Eden were working to facilitate Margaret's romance with Townsend, not destroy it. The pervasive idea that Margaret was forced to give up her fighter pilot lover by the Queen and her advisers is a myth perpetuated in TV shows like *The Crown*."

As for Townsend, he labored under the assumption that Margaret had to give up everything—her titles, stipend, and royal rights—in order to marry him. He wrote in his memoir *Time and Chance*, based it seems on a detailed diary he kept during this period: "There would be nothing left—except me, and I hardly possessed the weight to compensate for the loss of her privy purse and prestige. It was too much to ask of her, too much for her to give. We should be left with nothing but our devotion to face the world."[32] From the evidence of his memoir it doesn't seem that Margaret was entirely forthcoming about the modest consequences they truly faced should they decide to marry. This perhaps explains why, for the rest of her life, she would always brush off questions about the crisis as something that happened a long time ago, most of which she had forgotten. Her official biographer, Christopher Warwick, observes: "Indeed, in light of what we now know, the most obvious conclusion to be drawn is that her love for him, and in all probability his love for her, was no longer as strong as it had once been and marriage was no longer an issue." Most likely, the intention of her renunciation, which would be accepted as fact for over half a century, was simply to save face. "After all the hype and international press coverage…it could scarcely be publicly admitted that they had simply fallen out of love."[33]

The public were kept in the dark for another week as Buckingham Palace and Downing Street worked on the exact wording of Margaret's statement. In the interim, the princess drove to Lambeth Palace to see the archbishop of Canterbury, Dr. Geoffrey Fisher. Upon entering his study, she asked him to put away the books he was reaching for and told him: "I am not going to marry Peter Townsend. I wanted you to know first." The archbishop's riposte was made with a beaming smile: "What a wonderful person the Holy Spirit is."[34] Then she returned to Clarence House and changed into a strapless pink satin gown and a diamond tiara to accompany her sister at the Royal Opera House, Covent Garden to watch a dazzling production of Smetana's *The Bartered Bride*, a comedy about the triumph of true love over scheming parents and a marriage broker.

With the final statement now agreed, on October 31, the pair drank a toast and exchanged their final farewells at Clarence House. "There remained only the glow, once shared, of tenderness, constancy and singleness of heart," Peter Townsend wistfully recalled.[35] He returned to Lowndes Square, packed his bags, and went to see his two boys at their boarding school.

As Townsend drove out of London, Princess Margaret's official statement was broadcast on the radio: "I would like it to be known that I have decided not to marry Group Captain Peter Townsend. I have been aware that, subject to my renouncing my rights of succession, it might have been possible for me to contract a civil marriage."

Her statement continued: "But mindful of the Church's teaching that Christian marriage is indissoluble and conscious of my duty to the Commonwealth I have resolved to put these considerations before others. I have reached this decision entirely alone, and in doing so I have been strengthened by the unfailing support and devotion of Group Captain Townsend."

What began as a constitutional and legal wrangle devolved and dissolved into a simple matter of conscience. She was a devout Christian, a practicing congregant of the Church of England. Once she turned twenty-five, this became an issue of church, not state. Indeed, the state bent over backward to facilitate Margaret's marriage. In the end she made a decision of faith, a choice she could have made when Peter and Rosemary Townsend first decided to divorce.

On the night that Margaret's statement was released, which was several days after her last meeting with Townsend, she spent the evening alone at Clarence House. Her mother, with whom she was barely on speaking terms, failed to say good night, but her sister dutifully called Margo for a brief conversation. Then Margaret put the phone back on its cradle and continued to watch boxing on television.[36] Her personal bout had gone the full fifteen rounds, but she knew that she had always had her sister in her corner.

What is striking about this dramatic romantic episode is how it parallels the theatrical contours of the abdication in 1936. There was, though, one important variation: This time around it was a woman, not a man, who was in control of the unfolding narrative. In the days leading up to the abdication, Wallis Simpson, like Peter Townsend, was left in the dark about the decisions and discussions taking place at Buckingham Palace and Downing Street. During the abdication drama, Wallis was in the south of France, staying with friends. Her only communication with the king was a daily phone call on a primitive international telephone link. Even though she shouted down the phone line: "Do not abdicate," warning that it would be "disastrous for you and destroy me," Edward VIII was deaf to her entreaties.[37]

Though Townsend and Margaret spoke on the telephone

and met in person during their romantic crisis, it seems the princess, like Edward VIII, withheld from Townsend important—nay, vital—information that would have affected his judgment about their possible future together, namely the soft landing crafted by the prime minister. Just as Wallis took no part in the discussions that would shape the rest of her life, so Townsend was kept out of the loop in regard to the meetings among the queen, the princess, and the prime minister. He said as much in his memoir, stating that he was "not in possession of any of the facts."[38]

If his memoir is an honest and fair recitation of their affair, it seems that Margaret, like Edward VIII almost two decades earlier, was withholding information from her lover. The princess was aware, following her meeting with prime minister Eden, that the penalties she and Townsend faced were modest and that she had the support and devotion of her sister, who was prepared to accept any decision she made. More than that, the queen was willing to countenance possible damage to the monarchy—a course of action that would have horrified her former private secretary Tommy Lascelles—if Margaret did decide to go ahead and marry Townsend.

Just as Edward excluded Wallis from information that would change her life, this time around it was the woman, Princess Margaret, who held the cards. The princess, with her sister's support, was the one who made the consequential decisions. Throughout the dramatic denouement, Townsend was on the outside looking in.

At the same time, neither party forced the pace. After two years apart, in August 1955, when Margaret turned twenty-five, they could easily have been reunited. Margaret was on holiday, while Townsend, too, had plenty of time on his hands. By his own admission, as an amateur jockey, he flew to racecourses all over Europe. Instead, he could have arranged to meet his beloved so that they could together address the looming question—Were they still in love?—a question to which Margaret alluded in her letter to the prime minister.

While the resolution of this issue lay at the emotional heart of their dilemma, in his memoir Townsend lamented the endless waiting: "And so the days passed, as I waited for the denouement of the Princess's and my problem."[39]

Nor is there mention of an engagement ring either before, during, or after his exile. This is all of a piece with his passive acceptance of events, waiting for something to transpire rather than taking his fate into his own hands. By contrast Margaret, with her sister's support, sought to control the narrative of her life—even though she was not completely honest with her lover about the secular consequences of her actions.

There is a further twist to this romantic drama. It seems that during their years apart, Margaret may have been two-timing the group captain with a man who bore a remarkable resemblance to her lover. With his chiseled features, compact mannequin body, and dreamy eyes, fifties crooner Eddie Fisher could have been Townsend's younger brother. He met the princess on numerous occasions during the early 1950s. At one midnight gala Margaret invited him to her table and asked him to sing or whisper his number one hit "Outside of Heaven" into her ear.[40] They met again at a charity ball at the Dorchester hotel in 1953, and the following August Fisher offered to delay his flight back to America if she wanted him to sing "Happy Birthday" to her—in person. Though she declined on that occasion, they were more intimate on others. His daughter and *Star Wars* actor Carrie Fisher revealed that the princess and her father, then married to *Singin' in the Rain* star Debbie Reynolds, were lovers. "They had a beautiful romance," she admitted.

She first talked about her father's affair at the royal premiere of *The Empire Strikes Back* in central London in 1980. As Princess Margaret walked along the receiving line, she whispered to her costars, Sir Alec Guinness, Harrison Ford, and Mark Hamill, "My father had sex with Princess Margaret. In a beautiful way they made love."[41] As soon as she blurted out this family secret, she said, "I'm going to get into a lot of trouble for this." According to Fisher, their tryst took place when he was twenty-four and she was twenty-two, which would date their meeting either in 1952, the year of her father's death, or in 1953, the year of the coronation, when the affair between Margaret and Townsend first became public. During that year the princess was photographed deep in conversation with Fisher during a ball at the Dorchester hotel.

Fisher, who had twenty-four top ten hits in the first six years of the decade, was as famous for his lovers as his LPs. Besides his five marriages, he had affairs with, among others, Joan Crawford, Édith Piaf, Kim Novak, Zsa Zsa Gabor, and Mia Farrow. If what Carrie Fisher was told is accurate, it would add a further question mark with regard to Margaret's long-term commitment to Townsend.

7

The Prince and the Showgirl

For once the queen rebelled. Since becoming monarch she had dutifully attended the annual Royal Command film performance held in a West End cinema. Before watching the film she first had to sit through a stage show and an interminable greeting line. The whole evening was a "long and garish ordeal," admitted Sir Frank Lee, permanent secretary to the Board of Trade, who was present at every performance. The choices set before the queen ranged from the "mediocre to the vulgar and distressing."[1] As far as the queen was concerned, the final straw was the screening of *Beau Brummell*, an overlong costume drama about the queen's ancestors, the Hanoverians. George III was played as a lunatic by corpulent actor Robert Morley in a "brief grotesque sequence," while the Prince of Wales was a fat, pleasure-loving wastrel. In its review of the movie, which starred Elizabeth Taylor and Stewart Granger, critic Bosley Crowther of the *New York Times* anticipated "some slight embarrassed fidgeting" by the royal party[2] as they watched..." He was dead on. The queen and the royal party threatened to boycott the event if the film choices were not improved, and she complained personally to the prime minister. The organizers took the hint. Their next choice was Hitchcock's *To Catch a Thief*, starring Grace Kelly and Cary Grant, which the queen and her entourage greatly enjoyed.

Nothing better exemplified the social divide between the queen and Princess Margaret than this annual ordeal. The queen had no choice but to attend, but Margaret could watch and enjoy whatever she wished. As she sat through another painful screen ordeal, the queen, though not prone to jealousy, may have been rather envious of her sister, now known, after her romance with Peter Townsend, as "the greatest catch in Britain." She could see what she wanted, when she wanted, and with whom she wanted. The princess and her American friend Sass Douglas watched the wildly successful *Cinerama Holiday* at least four times and *Kismet* five times. No complaints to the prime minister here.

❧

Music and musicals set her pulse racing. She and Sass attended a performance of the musical *The Pajama Game*, followed by a party that lasted until three in the morning while in December 1955 her lady-in-waiting Elizabeth Cavendish sat with her to watch the rehearsals of *Cranks*, a musical revue choreographed by South African-born dancer John Cranko and starring a young Anthony Newley. It was not uncommon for her and her other lady-in-waiting, Jennifer Bevan, to sing duets to tunes like "Baby, It's Cold Outside" on long car journeys to public engagements. The princess complained that her lady-in-waiting kept her waiting to hit the right note.

While Peter Townsend planned his solo round-the-world

tour to "mend his broken heart," the princess's heart was beating faster watching some of the jazz greats in performance. She caught stage shows by Lena Horne and Louis "Satchmo" Armstrong, who declared her "one hip chick" and gave her a shout-out before his rendition of "Mahogany Hall Stomp." She arrived unannounced at a Count Basie concert at Royal Festival Hall, stayed for two hours, left, then returned for the second two-hour showing.

She was a fixture at Quaglino's restaurant in Bury Street off Piccadilly, where her table was known as the "Royal Enclosure" and the princess and her party entered the restaurant by a side door. It was here that she first heard the legendary entertainer Leslie "Hutch" Hutchinson, a Grenadian-born singer who was strikingly handsome and exceptionally gifted. The popular crooner played a white grand piano as he sang hits like "A Nightingale Sang in Berkeley Square." The enraptured princess would then head to Berkeley Square, where Hutch, then fifty-six, performed in a late-night show at the Colony Room Club. His biographer Charlotte Breese quotes a friend as saying, "She would wait through his performance to dance and talk to him. They obviously loved each other's company. He was a big man but he danced like an angel."[3]

For a night to spend dining and dancing she chose the 400 Club, known as Les A, where on occasion bandleader Paul Adam encouraged her to join in at the piano and sing. When she went to the Café de Paris to see Noël Coward perform, the audience was cut to 350 from the 500 capacity to give her and her party room to dance. As she left the club, usually at around one in the morning after dining on lobster and steak, the Ambrose Orchestra would often play one of her favorite tunes, such as *Lizzie Borden*.

Then the dancing might continue in her apartment. Over

the years she had built up an extensive record collection, which included artists like Ella Fitzgerald, Josh White, Frank Sinatra, and Cleo Laine, who became a good friend. But rock and roll was banished from her kingdom. "I don't know about you," she wrote to Sass, "but I absolutely HATE rock & roll! I think it's the most irritating, dull, repetitive, boring music it's ever been my misfortune to come in contact with!"

Margaret continued: "Phew! I feel much better. The dancing looks amusing but it's beyond me and makes me feel OLD! Oh dear."[4]

Of course, every night she went out, the princess, who cultivated a rather raffishly glamorous image, was followed by the flashlights and cameras clicking hoping to spot "the one," the man who would mend Margaret's broken heart.

The favored aristocratic runners and riders were Dominic Elliot, son of the fifth earl of Minto; and the wealthy Billy Wallace, who had been a friend since childhood. Margaret did not simply ignore the speculation; she played with it. In May 1956, she showed up at the Red, White, and Blue Ball at the Dorchester hotel with no fewer than seven escorts. She continued her nights of carousing, usually in a party of six or eight, visiting theaters, restaurants, and nightclubs, all while smoking cigarettes through a trademark holder and drinking Famous Grouse whisky. During the previous years of waiting to resolve her romance with Peter Townsend, many of those who were members of the so-called Margaret Set had married, which left a diminished pool of suitable bachelors. With her sister married with two children and running a kingdom, Margaret must have felt the clock was ticking.

⤳

Though cursed with health problems—Billy Wallace had undergone so many kidney operations that he was left without a belly button—he was a witty and entertaining suitor, with an interest in theater and art—and gambling. The grandson of the illustrious architect Sir Edwin Lutyens, who designed and built much of New Delhi, Billy had come into a vast fortune, estimated at £2 million ($125 million in 2020) when his father, Captain Euan Wallace, the minister for transport, died suddenly in 1941.

His inherited wealth now placed him ahead of the chasing pack for Margaret's hand. It helped, too, that the queen mother liked him, particularly his eye for Post-Impressionist paintings—he collected artists like Walter Sickert and Matthew Smith. The lanky six-footer had been an early favorite of Fleet Street, when the Old Etonian made the front page of the *Daily Express* for his train ride to Balmoral in August 1951 to celebrate the princess's twenty-first birthday.

The story, headlined "Mr Wallace—And the cake—came on the 9.46," mistakenly claimed that he was the only non-family member heading to Margaret's "very private" twenty-first birthday party. When King George's polished silver Daimler arrived to pick him up from the railway station, a crowd of onlookers had already gathered: cameramen, villagers, tourists, station staff, an electrician, and a bus conductress, who eagerly asked, "Is that him?"[5]

⤳

The storm of speculation came and went, and Billy became a loyal friend, always ready for a game of charades or a sing-along

around the piano. To raise her spirits during her months of waiting to see Peter Townsend again, he involved her in an amateur
theatrical production of the Edgar Wallace novel *The Fellowship
of the Frog*. He was the lead, playing a detective; the princess,
after obtaining permission from her sister, was the play's associate
director. The production, though trashed by the critics, did raise
£10,000 ($300,000 in 2020) for a children's charity. Though
at six foot four he towered over the diminutive princess, he
was her regular "date," especially as so many eligible escorts
such as Colin Tennant and Jocelyn Stevens had married
during the Townsend interregnum. Just a couple of months
after the Townsend split, the gangling multimillionaire asked
the princess for her hand in marriage. Margaret, licking her
wounds after the departure of Townsend and worried about
being left on the shelf, accepted his proposal, although without
much passion. She later explained that it was better "to marry
somebody one at least liked" than to end up a lonely spinster
while everyone else her age had already paired up.[6] After the
Townsend imbroglio, Margaret gave Billy one condition—she
would marry him only with her sister's blessing. Until then it
remained an unofficial engagement. Certainly there was no
sign of an engagement ring.

Thinking it was a done deal, Billy, who was suffering another
bout of bad health, flew to the Bahamas to recuperate. Here he
was joined at an exclusive resort by a party of wealthy friends,
including magazine publisher Jocelyn Stevens and amateur
race car driver Tommy Sopwith. There he proceeded to have
a fling with a local girl.

Such was his overconfidence that when he returned, he
immediately confessed to Margaret, who summarily dumped
him, a sign not only of Margaret's disappointment in Billy but
also perhaps of her deeper reluctance to being tied down. It

was a suitably theatrical romantic cameo and was probably a way for both to back away from a commitment neither party truly wished to make. As a gambling man, Wallace should have realized that it was odds on that his confession would have had this result.

Yet, years afterward, Billy insisted that his and Margaret's love was far deeper than her affair with Townsend had been. "The thing with Townsend was a girlish nonsense that got out of hand," he said. "It was never the big thing on her part that people claim. I had my chance and blew it with my big mouth."[7] He added: "Most men didn't stand a chance of coping with Margaret, Townsend less than most. He might have been a war hero but he was too wimpish when it came to dealing with her. He had only her. She could choose virtually anyone she wanted."[8]

As Wallace was medically unfit for war service, to describe a much-decorated airman who had flown hundreds of sorties during the Battle of Britain as a "wimp" was wholly disrespectful. Indeed the fact that she wasn't able to marry Townsend rather contradicted Wallace's assertion that she could have anybody she wanted. In fact her royal status hobbled her search for a partner. When she visited Canada on a royal tour in 1958, there was much gossip that lawyer John Turner, who later became the prime minister of Canada, was "the one." Handsome, sporty, and highly intelligent, he was eminently eligible, but as a practicing Roman Catholic he was ruled out, as Catholics were legally barred under the 1701 Act of Settlement from marrying members of the royal family. As she reviewed the marital landscape, she realized that her search was limited to a wealthy, upper-class cadre of single men, of whom Wallace was a leading light.

Whatever Wallace may have thought, Townsend still held a significant place in her heart. On September 11, 1956, she secretly met him again at Clarence House when Townsend was invited just for lunch. Afterward he stayed chatting until about seven in the evening. It was their last meeting before he left on his eighteen-month solo journey around the globe by Land Rover, covering South America, Australia, Southeast Asia, and Africa. During his absence she kept his photograph near at hand.

In between the very public end of the Townsend affair and Margaret's dalliance with Billy Wallace, her sister was getting on with the serious business of being queen. In February 1956, as Margaret was contemplating Wallace, the queen was shaking hands with lepers in a colony during a three-week visit to Nigeria, an important exporter of oil and foodstuffs. Though she was wearing white gloves, it was a powerful gesture, her simple act helping to dispel the age-old prejudice and irrational taboos surrounding this disease. It wasn't the first time she had had contact with lepers—during the 1947 tour of South Africa, Princesses Elizabeth and Margaret had left the royal party at a Jamboree to talk to Girl Guides who were affected by the illness and were not allowed to take part in the festivities.

The queen's handshake foreshadowed a similar act by Princess Diana when she famously shook the hands of an AIDS patient in a London hospital in 1987. Both gestures, separated by a generation, vividly demonstrated the symbolic and actual reach of the monarchy. It remained, and remains, an institution able to change hearts and minds—a point she made after she returned from her coronation tour. She argued that the monarchy could be seen as "archaic and meaningless" but felt that her experiences during that tour were "visible and audible proof that it is real and living in the hearts of the people."[9]

Shaking the hands of a leper was a perfect illustration of how the monarchy continued to make a difference because the institution remained relevant.

While Elizabeth was away in Nigeria, Margaret and her mother spent time with Charles and Anne, ensuring that their schoolwork was up to snuff. Margaret took a special interest in the progress of her niece, reviewing the five-year-old's artwork, discussing her basic curriculum with her tutor, and reading picture books to her. What she considered to be her own inadequate education bothered her for the rest of her life, so she was determined that the next generation of royal women had more opportunity. Her lady-in-waiting Lady Jane Rayne-Lacey recalls: "She was intelligent but it was never put to any sort of good use. I think that's all that was expected of her; do good work, marry somebody and have lots of little princesses." Over the years Margaret and Anne built a strong bond, one often overlooked when describing the family dynamic. She took a continuing interest in Anne's education, quietly delighted that she was the first princess to be educated outside the palace at Benenden, an all-girls boarding school. As for Margaret, she rounded out her disappointing formal education by becoming a voracious reader and teaching herself. During one period she waded through a book of philosophy by novelist Iris Murdoch, an *Encyclopædia Britannica* by her side.

Margaret was with her sister in June 1956, her trademark cigarette holder incongruously in hand, at the cross-country horse-riding event at the summer equestrian section of the Olympic Games, which were held in Stockholm, Sweden. The queen and Prince Philip attended following their state visit. Philip took a special interest, as he was due to open the main Games in Melbourne later that year. The queen watched the action intently, gasping and putting her hands to her face in concern when a competitor's mount slipped. Margaret puffed away, unperturbed and seemingly indifferent. It seemed to symbolize the cultural difference between the sisters. Whereas the queen was at her heart a country woman who loved dogs and horses, her sister, though she loved her time at Balmoral and Sandringham, was essentially a metropolitan princess whose passion was for the ballet, theater, and the arts.

Ironically, their host, King Gustaf VI Adolf had romantic problems of his own to contend with. His twenty-one-year-old granddaughter, Princess Margaretha, had fallen for Scottish piano player and bon viveur Robin Douglas-Home, whose uncle became Britain's prime minister for a year during the 1960s. She was besotted; he spoke of marriage. Her mother, Princess Sibylla, appalled at the prospect, ordered her back to Sweden immediately. Douglas-Home subsequently wrote formally asking for her hand in marriage. It was refused. Queen Elizabeth sympathized, having only just finished helping her sister unpick her own romantic entanglement. A decade later Douglas-Home would be back to haunt the House of Windsor—this time Margaret was his love interest.

The appearance of the queen and Prince Philip at the equestrian Olympics was the prelude to the prince's solo voyage on board the royal yacht *Britannia* to sail to Melbourne, Australia, where he was to open the Olympic games in November. The four-month voyage also gave the prince a chance to visit inaccessible parts of the Commonwealth and beyond. The queen had encouraged this lengthy journey, as she saw how her energetic, progressive husband had been frustrated by the solemn pace of change at court. Moreover, during the yacht's planning stage, he had spent days discussing the overall design and interior layout with the ship's architect, Hugh Casson. With a visit to Antarctica as part of the itinerary, it was a unique chance to put the yacht through its paces. At the same time, the queen had watched with some satisfaction the way he had turned a corner in his royal career, embracing the institution as a way of promoting his own interests. His focus on design, science and youth, notably the duke of Edinburgh's award scheme to challenge young people mentally and physically, was a vivid manifestation of a man keen to harness his own energies to progressive causes.

Much to the queen's consternation, her magnanimous gesture backfired badly. Her decision to encourage her husband to travel the world on his own was interpreted as a royal marriage in trouble. Questions were asked at the time about why the prince had left the queen for four months on her own with two young children. It was not long before there were rumors in the gossip columns of wild parties on board the ship, which, given the fact that the 412-foot yacht had a crew of 240 plus a Royal Marine band, made the allegation somewhat implausible.

Nonetheless, the negative coverage persisted. It exploded after a story was published in the *Baltimore Sun* under the headline QUEEN, DUKE IN RIFT OVER PARTY GIRL. The story concerned Prince Philip's alleged friendship before the voyage with an unnamed woman whom he had met regularly at the central London apartment of a society photographer, presumed to be his friend Henry Nahum, who was known as Baron Nahum. It was widely thought that the party girl in question was musical star Pat Kirkwood. Their first meeting took place way back in October 1948, weeks before Princess Elizabeth gave birth to Prince Charles. They were introduced after her show by Baron, who was then dating her. The quartet, which included a naval equerry called "Basher" Watkin, then had dinner and went on to the Milroy nightclub—one of Princess Margaret's favorites—where the prince took the show-girl onto the dance floor, watched by fellow partygoers. Word quickly reached the palace, and Philip was given a dressing-down by an outraged George VI. Though for the rest of her life Kirkwood flatly denied an affair, she was always linked to the prince, the yarn in the *Baltimore Sun* the latest manifestation of a story that refused to go away.

For once the queen's press secretary, Commander Richard Colville—aka "The Abominable No Man"—was concerned at the rumors. As the state opening of Parliament approached in November, he reminded the queen that it would coincide with her husband opening the Olympic Games twelve thou-sand miles away. There would inevitably be further speculation about the queen performing the ritual without her husband by her side. He proposed that Margaret take Philip's place, a symbolic move that would also show the world that Margaret was very much in the royal fold following the Townsend split. It would, he hoped, show a family working in concert around the globe.

Margaret gladly agreed to the invitation. On a cold winter day, the sisters rode the gold Irish State Coach to Westminster, solemnly facing one another. Both wore white satin gowns and white ermine on their shoulders. They coordinated their waves, just as they had been taught to do when they were little girls. Once inside the Great Hall, the queen was fitted into her eighteen-foot-long velvet train, with Margaret dressed in a shorter train. This time no tantrum ensued.

Minutes later, the lights in the hall brightened as Elizabeth entered alone, four young pages of honor holding her heavy train. Margaret followed, head held high. Elizabeth stepped up to her throne, then Margaret approached the consort's smaller throne. "My Lords, pray be seated," the queen commanded. The two sisters settled down, one on the upper dais and the other on the lower, but still side by side as they had always been.

Margaret was publicly showing loyalty and solidarity to her sister at a time when rumors continued to swirl about the royal marriage. Even though the queen fondly, wistfully mentioned her husband's absence in her Christmas broadcast and the duke made a forty-minute documentary about his travels, the gossip persisted. "Last week," reported *Time* magazine on February 18, 1957, "the [rumor] mongering winds were howling louder around Buckingham Palace than they had since the day of Wallis Warfield Simpson and Edward VIII."[10]

As the yacht sailed on the final leg of the voyage, Philip's equerry, Mike Parker, tendered his resignation and left the yacht in Gibraltar. Some saw it as a sign he had led the prince astray and was now paying the price. In fact his wife, Eileen, had petitioned for divorce, and as Parker did not want to embarrass the prince, he resigned and disembarked. The prince was furious that he lost his friend and shipmate over what he considered to be a private matter. As Parker recalled, "The Duke was incandescent. He was very, very angry."[11] The prince's response to the gossip was characteristically blunt: "Those bloody lies that you people print to make money," he raged.[12] Parker's departure encouraged newspaper reporters to dig further into his background, and it wasn't long before Parker's and the prince's memberships at the all-male Thursday Club were revealed. Though senior journalists, actors like Peter Ustinov and David Niven, politicians, and literary figures were involved in the informal luncheon club, which met in a private room in a fish restaurant in Soho, central London, it was caricatured as a venue for wild behavior and schoolboy pranks.

Exasperated by the cascade of marital gossip and hearsay,

the queen authorized her press secretary to issue a statement, the first and last time Buckingham Palace commented on the state of the sovereign's marriage. "It is quite untrue that there is any rift between the Queen and the Duke" was the official palace line.[13] Although it was a bland statement, it said much about the queen's frustration and concern about the effect these stories were having on the monarchy.

Far from damping down speculation, the palace statement invited the media to legitimately discuss the state of the royal marriage. It seems that many in both the public and the media subscribed to the view of Tommy Lascelles, the queen's former private secretary, that Philip was unlikely to be faithful. It was a question of finding the one—if indeed she existed.

He was subsequently linked to the author Daphne du Maurier, whose husband, "Boy" Browning, was the treasurer in the prince's household, as well as fifties screen stars Merle Oberon and Anna Massey. Later there was Sacha, duchess of Abercorn, who was pictured with the prince in a swimming outfit. In 1987 she told writer Gyles Brandreth: "The queen gives Philip a lot of leeway." Then she added, "It was certainly not a full relationship. I did not go to bed with him. It probably looked like that to the world." She suggested that the prince "needed a playmate and someone to share his intellectual pursuits." Both had a fascination with the work of Swiss psychiatrist Carl Jung.[14]

Philip addressed the rumors head-on. He once told a brave female journalist who asked him about the continuing rumors of marital infidelity, "Have you ever stopped to think that for the past forty years I have never moved anywhere without a policeman accompanying me?"[15] Of course that did not stop his eldest son, who managed to conduct a long affair with Camilla Parker Bowles, detective in tow. Nor for that matter the disgraced former king of Spain, Juan Carlos, whose long-term mistress, Corinna zu Sayn-Wittgenstein-Sayn, accompanied him on royal engagements and holidays.

Respected royal biographer Sarah Bradford did grasp the marital nettle in 2004 and accused the prince of cheating on the queen. "The Duke of Edinburgh has had affairs, yes, full blown affairs and more than one."[16] Upon reflection, she felt she overstated the case. "I think perhaps I got it wrong over Prince Philip," she subsequently admitted. "I think he loves pretty women and likes to flirt but I am not sure how important actual sex is to him, put it that way."[17]

Once again Philip went on the attack, telling TV interrogator Jeremy Paxman, "As far as I am concerned, every time I talk to a woman they say I've been to bed with her—as if she had no say in the matter. Well, I'm bloody flattered at my age to think some girl is interested in me. It's absolutely cuckoo."[18]

What the queen found doubly frustrating about this endless media conjecture was that in reality, after ten years of marriage and now comfortable in the job, she was looking to increase her family—not that she would ever whisper a word to anyone and certainly not the media.

As Prince Philip's controversial cruise neared its end, more than 150 members of the media flew to Lisbon to witness the reunion between queen and consort before they undertook a state visit to Portugal, England's oldest ally. During the voyage the prince had grown a splendid full beard, which he had shaved off shortly before the end of the trip. When Philip went on board the royal plane, to his surprise the royal entourage, including his wife, were sporting false ginger whiskers. They apparently hadn't gotten the memo that he was now clean-shaven. But it broke the ice, a continuation of the practical jokes the couple played on one another.

Subsequently Margaret wrote to her friend Sass Douglas,

complaining about the behavior of the American media and extolling the virtues of her brother-in-law. "I see the fine old press in your country tried to make out the Queen wasn't getting on with my b-in-l [brother-in-law]. So of course the stinking Press here repeated it all sheep-like, like the nasty cowards they are. However, all is well and he's terribly well and full of fascinating stories of his journeys and it's very nice indeed to have him home again. The children are thrilled."[19]

Margaret's contemptuous response to the media coverage of her sister was little different from that of other members of the royal family, whose default position was instinctive disdain for the denizens of Fleet Street. She had suffered more than most. Not only had she been forced to abandon a proposed visit to the United States, but during the Townsend affair she and her lover had been at times prisoners or runaways in their own country. She knew that every time she left Clarence House, she would be fair game for photographers desperate to capture a shot of her with the new man in her life. Margaret was the first generation of royalty to do her courting in the new era of the paparazzi and the commercial long-distance lens.

As well as Margaret, the queen and Prince Philip had other admirers who noticed not a marital rift, but a couple who, after a decade of marriage, were a well-oiled double act. In April 1957, shortly after Philip's return, the couple undertook a state visit to France, where Cynthia Gladwyn, wife of the British ambassador, watched them in action. "Prince Philip is handsome and informal, creating an easy democratic atmosphere in the wake of the Queen," she noted. "This informality makes him very popular. He shines out as a breezy sailor who has known what it is like not to be royalty. He handles a difficult position in a remarkably successful way, and I cannot think that any other person, whom the Queen might have married, would have done as well."[20]

❧

It was perhaps no coincidence that these negative stories about Britain's First Family arose at a time of national crisis and humiliation, when the House of Windsor was a lightning rod for public dissatisfaction following the debacle of the Suez invasion in October and November 1956, when Britain, France, and Israel took military action after Egyptian president Gamal Abdel Nasser nationalized the vital waterway. Although US president Dwight D. Eisenhower, the Soviets, fellow Commonwealth nations, and the United Nations warned against conflict, the tripartite invasion went ahead, leading to a run on sterling, an abrupt military retreat, and the resignation of Prime Minister Eden. The brief conflict exposed Britain's much-reduced status in the world and perhaps emboldened the Soviets to crush the Hungarian uprising a few days later, in November. It also gave courage to critics nearer at home as the monarchy, a hitherto inviolate institution, came under intense questioning.

The talk of a new Elizabethan age was now a half-forgotten dream, and the monarchy was seen as a gilded mask that hid the pock-marked ancien régime from public scrutiny.

Playwright John Osborne, one of the so-called angry young men of the 1950s, described the monarchy as "a gold filling in a mouth full of decay." Loquacious TV personality and intellectual Malcolm Muggeridge dismissed the passion for the royal family as a kind of "substitute or ersatz religion." For his pains, he was banned by the BBC from appearing on their TV station.

It was, however, one of the queen's own, Lord Altrincham, who genuinely put the boot in, criticizing the "tweedy sort" who surrounded the queen. He described her speaking style as "a pain in the neck," her personality that of a "priggish school-girl," and her speeches as "prim little sermons." In the August 1957 issue of *National and English Review,* of which he was the editor, he complained: "Like her mother she [the queen] appears to be unable to string even a few sentences together without a written text."

In a note to *Ladies' Home Journal* publishers Bruce and Beatrice Gould, Altrincham, who years later gave up his peerage, wrote, "For the sake of the institution and for that matter of the Queen herself, changes are long overdue, and I hope the recent controversy may have helped to force the pace. Certainly I had given up all hope of achieving results by argument behind the scenes."[21]

What all three men—and others—were saying was that the monarchy was too backward looking, and that the queen was encircled by a coterie of men who did not remotely represent modern Britain. Though the religion of royalty had its critics, they were few in number. For all the contemporary and the subsequent historical focus on Altrincham and his ilk, when the queen overcame her innate shyness to give her first televised Christmas broadcast in December 1957, she attracted an eye-watering audience of 16.5 million. The royal family now embraced television as a means of reestablishing its popularity.

During this period of rancorous introspection Princess Margaret largely escaped criticism—at least for the time being. However, her embrace of the dramatic in her personal life meant that her reputation always preceded her. During the crisis in the Middle East, a German magazine published a cartoon of a desperate queen begging her sister, "Say, Margaret, couldn't you do something to distract the horrid world press from our Suez debacle?"

⁂

There were no such dramas during her so-called Blue Lagoon tour of Britain's imperial possessions in East Africa and the Indian Ocean. While in hindsight it was an object lesson in outdated colonial rule and imperial pretensions, at the time Margaret was the magical princess conferring largesse and fairy dust in smiles, handshakes, and pretty gowns. In September 1956, just weeks before the attack on Suez, she visited Kenya, Tanganyika, Mauritius, and Zanzibar (Tanganyika and Zanzibar united in 1964 and are now called Tanzania). The enthusiastic, colorfully clothed crowds, tribal dances, garden parties, and fireworks displays masked the underlying tensions as freedom fighters or terrorists, depending on perspective, such as the Mau Mau, led the struggle for independence. Her tour was, in retrospect, a swan song for British rule, Kenya and Zanzibar becoming independent in 1963, Tanzania in 1961. One of the last district commissioners was Peter Townsend's brother, Francis, who shook hands with the princess in a receiving line at Arusha in Tanganyika. Showing that she too was capable of impeccable control, Margaret greeted him with a polite smile before smoothly addressing the next person in line.[22] The program was grueling, and the princess was sent to bed on medical advice to rest during the Nairobi leg of the tour, though she managed not to faint at a snake-charming exhibition—no one had told the organizers that she had a snake phobia. During the visit, newspaper correspondents suggested that her presence was "just what was needed to reestablish more personal and solid relations with Kenya."[23] This was wishful thinking. When she visited the Rift Valley, her convoy drove near Mau

Mau fighters who were in hiding. In subsequent fighting, four were captured and three killed.

During this period Margaret was seen as bold, brave, and modern, the beauty who had sacrificed love for duty, while her sister was criticized for failing to evolve into a more assertive, articulate, and charismatic leader. When the queen did introduce changes, it seemed as if she was doing so under sufferance. Lord Altrincham severely criticized what he called the "embarrassing ritual" of the palace presentation of debutantes. He felt it should be discontinued to make way for a "classless" court. While the queen agreed with her advisers that the two-hundred-year-old custom had had its day, she refused to be bullied by Altrincham. Instead she waited for another year, until 1958, before the ceremony was quietly phased out—not a minute too soon, as far as Princess Margaret was concerned. "We had to put a stop to it, every tart in London was getting in,"[24] she commented acerbically. She had a point. The system itself was becoming open to abuse, as well-born ladies charged large fees to bring out girls whose credentials were not always of the highest. The most notorious of these "cash for curtsies" mavens was Lady St. John of Bletso, who would launch several debutantes at once. By 1958 the exclusivity of the season was eroded.

That same year the queen introduced garden parties, which reflected more of a cross section of society, and lunches, where she invited people she would not normally meet, such as bank managers, novelists, businessmen, actors, and sports personalities. On these occasions, Margaret was in her element—witty, chatty, and interested.

Margaret seemed to be on a roll, and her sister took full advantage, penciling her in for a trip to the Caribbean in April 1958 where she represented the crown at the inaugural Parliament of the newly formed Federation of the West Indies. She approached her duty conscientiously, studying Foreign Office documents, meeting key political figures, and listening closely to the undersecretary of state for the colonies, John Profumo. Wearing a beaded, gold-embroidered satin dress and a tiara, she read the queen's speech from a throne set on a dais in the Legislative Chamber in Port of Spain, Trinidad. The princess, now hailed as "Britain's ambassadress," was spoken of as a future governor-general of the West Indies. She was further put through her paces on official visits to British Columbia, Rome, and Portugal.

Of course it couldn't last. Her impeccable behavior combined with a radiant appeal was too much of a good thing. She damaged her reputation during a visit to Paris in April 1959. Cynthia Gladwyn, the wife of the ambassador, had given the queen and Prince Philip top marks for their enthusiasm and professionalism during an earlier state visit. Not so Margaret. In her eyes, the princess displayed unforgivingly impolite behavior: "She wishes to convey that she is very much the Princess, but at the same time she is not prepared to stick to the rules if they bore or annoy her."[25]

The first sign of trouble ahead was when she was enraged that the audience at a theater remained seated upon her entrance into the venue. Several hours later, in a bid to avoid a boring lunch party, she cooked up a last-minute excuse, coughing loudly and saying that she had a cold.[26] She then proceeded to get her hair done by the famous Alexandre and her dress fitted by Dior. Margaret was beginning to show signs of what would become a perpetual problem—as Gladwyn observed, she wanted to be treated like a princess without taking on the responsibilities.

She had always been late—even during an air raid—capricious, and willful, though her charm and high spirits had always compensated. Not anymore. Tommy Lascelles, who was no fan, noted that ever since the affair with Townsend ended, she had "become selfish, hard and wild."[27]

Her behavior toward her sister was a study in contrasts. She was the loyal Pretorian guard, protecting her from outside attacks and testing the waters for her before she jumped in. "My task in life is to help the queen," she often said. For example, when American Evangelical pastor Billy Graham held huge rallies following the coronation in London, the queen was intrigued, but it was Princess Margaret and the queen mother who invited him for coffee at Clarence House, to see if he was a suitable candidate to meet the monarch. He duly preached at Windsor Castle, where the sovereign and he found common ground in their uniquely isolated positions.

The flip side of Margaret's relationship betrayed a resentment and indifference that seemed almost ill-mannered. She could and would say things to the queen and, for that matter, the queen mother that had even long-serving courtiers shaking their heads. In turn her sister and mother rarely reacted with anything other than calm equanimity. They had seen and heard it all before—and then some. It was part of the intimate family dynamic. At a state banquet in 1957, the queen was complimented by a government minister on her evening dress. Margaret casually remarked, "Darling, that does show your bosom too much." As for her throwing a wet dishcloth at the queen's face during a barbecue at Balmoral, her sister simply ducked and got on with clearing up. She had learned not to show too much concern, as it merely pandered to Margaret's dramatic nature. This practiced indifference was exemplified the night the queen, the queen mother, and Princess Margaret dined together. The pièce de résistance was crêpes Suzette flambéed at the table. Unfortunately, a hapless young footman caught his foot on Princess Margaret's evening dress. The silver tray holding the crêpes Suzette dipped briefly, and a miniature waterfall of flaming brandy cascaded down her dress. The queen watched this extraordinary scene with a quizzical expression and then, in a voice of calm glee, said to the queen mother, "Oh look Mummy, Margo is on fire." Though a napkin or two was lost in the mopping-up process, the princess and dress emerged unscathed.[28]

Less amusing was Margaret's behavior on the tenth anniversary celebrations of the queen and Prince Philip's marriage. Not only was it a milestone anniversary, but it came during a year when the queen's marriage was under intense public scrutiny. But the princess did not turn up for the intimate dinner at Buckingham Palace, instead going with friends to watch the musical Bells Are Ringing, followed by dinner at the Savoy. She arrived at Buckingham Palace after midnight when the party was nearly over. There was no apology, present, or even a card. She joined the dancing for less than an hour and then left. This was not the first time she had failed to appear at functions she would normally be expected to attend. The princess did not accompany the queen and Prince Philip to the Royal Variety Show or the Royal Film Performance, even though she later saw the same film with friends. Her discourteous behavior was seen as a show of resentment toward her sister. The queen had the glittering prizes—a kingdom, a happy home, and two adorable children—while Margaret had been cajoled into giving up the one man who made her heart beat faster. In the swirl of emotions, she may well have felt that if her sister had never become queen, she would be happy.

It seems that there were times when Margaret was inflamed by a primal jealousy. During a visit to Windsor Castle, prime minister Harold Macmillan was startled when Princess

Margaret, clad in a dressing gown, entered the queen's sitting room and yelled, "No-one would talk to you if you weren't the Queen," before gathering up her gown and stalking out. A shocked PM felt that he had been witness to a domestic drama he had no right or wish to see.[29]

At the same time Elizabeth forgave her sister much. She had always felt responsible for her sister, and time had not changed that sentiment. Certainly no one else in the kingdom could have gotten away with such insulting behavior toward the sovereign.

The queen, meanwhile, took the rudeness with her usual stoicism, as indulging Margaret was something of a family tradition. Her mother was equally equable. No matter how provocative her daughter's behavior, she sailed on like a Spanish galleon, magnificently indifferent. Margaret's needling had little effect. "Why do you dress in those ridiculous clothes?" she would demand of her mother, who was still in the prime of her life. After she visited the queen mother's beloved Scottish retreat, Castle of Mey, the place that had inspired her spiritual recovery after the death of George VI, Margaret was dismissive. "I can't think why you have such a horrible place," she sneered. The queen mother replied, "Well, darling you needn't come again." And she didn't.

At Royal Lodge, where the family had such happy memories, the princess would switch the TV channel without warning when she did not enjoy what her mother was watching. When the queen mother's friend, Prudence Penn, objected to this behavior, the queen mother soothed her: "You mustn't worry. I'm quite used to it."[30] Though at times the family dynamic was one that might pique the interest of the playwright Tennessee Williams, the queen mother never rose to the bait to rebuke her daughter. "You will see that this tiresome incident will have

no effect on [the queen mother] at all," a lady-in-waiting said
to a guest. "She will enjoy her day as much as though it has
never happened. Nothing will disturb her happiness."[31] The
queen and queen mother had lived with Margaret's dramatic,
somewhat histrionic, behavior ever since she was a little girl.
She was a performer, and for all her faults, they knew that
at heart she was a loving and loyal sister and daughter. They
forgave her much, almost anything.

❧

Though Margaret was seen as more progressive and "with it"
than her older sister, the irony was that the queen, as a working mother with two children, juggling a household and a
demanding executive job, fit the mold of the new breed of
modern women. While the queen was up and about at eight
in the morning, Margaret, who often returned to Clarence
House with the milk bottles, did not even think about getting
out of bed until eleven, when her devoted maid and dresser
Ruby MacDonald brought her a tray of tea and orange juice
or fruit. If she had no public engagements, her day would
revolve around a lunch, her afternoon a fitting at Victor Stiebel
or Dior, or in the summer a quiet hour of sunbathing in the
secluded garden. While she was deciding what to wear for an
evening event—Margaret was an immaculate dresser—her sister could be hosting a gathering of diplomats or charity workers
or holding a weekly audience for the prime minister.

After an evening at the theater or ballet or dining and dancing, she might invite friends back for supper, serenading the
throng with songs as she played at her grand piano. In her
novel *Palm Beach*, author Pat Booth gave a description of the
late-night performance: "The voice was deep and throaty, the
legacy of too many cigarettes, the hint perhaps of the odd late

night. She wrapped her full, ripe lips indulgently round the syllables, milking them of their humour, as she rolled her eyes towards the ceiling." Guests who were in the know would make their excuses and leave promptly; otherwise they were in for a long night as the princess entertained her guests on the piano.

⁓

She was loath to go to bed, which meant that her servants were often on duty for eighteen hours a day. The queen's page Ernest Bennett, who was called Henry by the queen, once told his boss: "She keeps everyone up so late, ma'am. She doesn't go to bed until three and they can't go before she gives her permission. Then they do have to get up at seven, ma'am."[32] After Bennett spoke to the queen about Margaret's high life, she quietly intervened, and the royal night owl brought down the curtain a little earlier.

By contrast, the queen was predictable. Everyone knew what was expected of them, from the chef to the private secretary. She was an administrator's dream, quick, decisive, no-nonsense, and even tempered. Unlike her sister, she was rarely prone to last-minute changes of plans. As one staff member recalled, "I always found from my very young days, that if anything was wrong it was far better to go and say so to her. I always felt I could tell the queen anything and she would be understanding."[33]

Nonetheless, royal staff soon learned that for both sisters there was an invisible line that prevented people from getting too up close and personal. Cross it, and you were liable to encounter "the Windsor glare," a look that said, "Don't overstep the mark." Overfamiliarity was discouraged with a chilly look or glance.

Princess Margaret resorted to a frosty countenance whenever

she wanted to insist on her position, to remind people, in the words of her cousin Lord Lichfield, "Don't forget who I am."[34] Former Labour lawmaker Woodrow Wyatt observed: "Suddenly you may feel her psychologically draw herself up with the unspoken 'I am the sister of the Queen,' which is instantly crushing."[35]

Her renowned tendency to quickly switch from amiable to aloof with the arching of an eyebrow perhaps reflected the contradictory behavior of the princess: one moment kind, generous, and spontaneous; the next dismissive, self-absorbed, and exacting. The wife of a courtier observed that Margaret's mercurial behavior, her ability to shift from nice to nasty in seconds, was at times bewildering. She recalled, "She was the only one who would come up to you at a party and really talk to you but the next day she'd cut you."[36]

While Margaret was more volatile and extroverted than her sister, the queen, though blessed with a steady temperament, was from her youth very royal when she wished. "She was capable of giving you a very old-fashioned kind of look— nothing snobbish or pompous about it—that said she was a princess, and was going to be queen" said a long-serving aide.[37] Prince Charles's former valet Stephen Barry was more direct: "Nobody takes liberties with the queen. And if someone does she has a look that would freeze the sun."[38]

Meanwhile, no sooner had Peter Townsend arrived back in Brussels after his around-the-world adventure than he telephoned Margaret. Not that he had ever been that far away—he kept in regular contact with the princess by letter and radio telephone. Five days later, in March 1958, he was back in London, eager to see her before she left for a two-day visit to Germany. The problem was that the queen and Prince Philip were on a state visit to Holland. As soon as the media got wind of his arrival, the queen's tour was consigned to the inside pages and Townsend and Margaret got the headlines.

The London *Evening Standard* proclaimed, "They're Together Again."[39] After that initial sighting, reporters began taking eight-hour shifts to track his every move, day and night.

The queen was furious that his visit had overshadowed her tour, and for once Margaret regretted stealing her sister's thunder. She canceled their next meeting until the queen had returned to London. That did not stop Margaret from carrying one of the four dozen red roses Townsend sent to her before she boarded her plane to Germany. In a belated attempt to tamp down the media temperature, Townsend issued a statement through his lawyers stating that even though he had seen Margaret, there were no grounds for supposing that the situation, which was initially declared in 1955, had changed in any way, meaning that the reasons for not marrying still held true.

Margaret later recalled: "We had an understanding that if Peter was here he should come in. But it soon became obvious that that would never work."[40] When she returned to London from her German tour in early April, she called Townsend and told him that she had been "persuaded" not to see him again during his present stay in England. She was anxious that there should be no appearance of a rift between herself and the queen.

Yet the attraction still remained. She took the initiative to speak to him in May, shortly before her Caribbean tour, tracking him down to his sister's home in Somerset. They arranged to meet again once she had returned, "confident that the present excitement would blow over."[41] It was a forlorn hope. He saw her at Clarence House on May 14 and 15 for two and a half hours and then for three hours on May 26, when they were joined for cocktails by the queen mother. It seemed clear that they had a strong bond of friendship, if not love. As nothing had changed while Townsend was away, his presence at Clarence House could be seen as an unnecessary diversion that merely encouraged media speculation.

Inevitably, the media reported that Townsend and Margaret would shortly be engaged. While the palace would usually not respond to such reports, after the queen visited her sister at Clarence House, an official statement was issued denying any such engagement. This move was made in order to cool the rapidly rising media temperature. Shortly after that, Townsend left for the Continent, and it was accepted by all concerned that his continued presence and further meetings could only cause her public embarrassment. That Christmas she told her sister that she had decided not to see Peter Townsend anymore.

But they needn't have worried, because Townsend had already met the woman he would marry the following year, Marie-Luce Jamagne. Though she did not know it yet, Margaret had also met the man who would change her life: photographer Antony Armstrong-Jones.

8

"Sex, Sex, Sex"

The Black Lubyanka, the nickname for the unusual black and chromium Art Deco building on Fleet Street, was for many years the home of Express newspapers, publishers of the *Daily Express* and *Sunday Express*. New arrivals were always impressed by the imposing lobby with its silver and gold panels that stated EMPIRE and BRITAIN, the magnificent pendant lamp, and the unusual oval staircase. It was reminiscent of some of the more imposing office entrances in midtown Manhattan. The flamboyant grandeur of the lobby masked the easy callousness, vulgarity, and raucous philistinism of the day-to-day workings of a daily and Sunday newspaper, not to mention the culture of daytime drinking that, for some, made the impressive oval stairs difficult to navigate.

In this sub-Dickensian milieu, photographer Tony Armstrong-Jones was frequently seen in the smoke-stained cream corridors, camera slung over his shoulder, hurrying to a briefing from the magazine's picture editor. He was a regular if, at around five foot seven, diminutive presence, cigarette in hand, twinkle in his blue eyes. Like photographers the world over he was chatty, professionally charming, smiley but tough—able to use his elbows effectively in a media scrum.

෴

Known for his versatility as a photographer, Tony had already established himself as a rising star of the social, fashion, and theater worlds by the time he met Margaret. Only five months older than she, he was born at home in Belgravia, central London, on March 7, 1930. His father, Ronald, was a barrister; his mother was Anne Messel, whose brother, Oliver, was a celebrated stage designer. Growing up in the small village of Bontnewydd, North Wales, the teenage Tony contracted a serious case of polio, which confined him to a wheelchair for a long, lonely year and left him with one leg shorter than the other. His experience toughened him and later informed his groundbreaking work on behalf of the disabled.

Like his father, he went to Eton but proved an indifferent scholar. "Maybe he is interested in some subject, but it isn't a subject we teach here," said one end-of-term report.[1] Nonetheless he was admitted into Cambridge, where, after failing his second-year exams, he turned to photography as a career, swapping a microscope given to him by his father for a camera.

Thanks to the connections of his actress stepmother, Carol Coombe, he snagged a three-year apprenticeship with portrait photographer Henry "Baron" Nahum, who was a friend of Prince Philip's. After only six months, Tony set up his own studio in a former ironmonger's shop at 20 Pimlico Road and hosted numerous parties for a mainly bohemian crowd.

While he started his career taking party pictures for glossy magazines like *Tatler*, *Vogue*, and *Queen*, his reputation as a portrait photographer grew apace. In 1956 he was invited to take the twenty-first birthday pictures of the duke of Kent. The following year he photographed the duke's sister, Princess Alexandra, and soon afterward he was commissioned to photograph the queen and Philip together with Prince Charles and Princess Anne. His success rankled with rivals. The king of royal portraiture, Cecil Beaton, complained, "I don't think A.A. Jones' pictures are all that interesting, but his publicity value is terrific. It pays to be new in a field."[2]

On February 20, 1958, he was one of the guests at a dinner party in Chelsea organized by Lady Elizabeth Cavendish, Margaret's lady-in-waiting. Tony and Margaret did not seem to have any obvious chemistry, though they were seated beside one another and shared an engaging conversation throughout the meal.[3] Afterward, Margaret never once asked after the society photographer. She had initially assumed he was gay, and her instincts weren't far off, as it was later revealed that he was bisexual. They only met again because her longtime friend and sometime boyfriend the Honorable Dominic Elliot, the youngest son of the earl of Minto and such a familiar figure in the Margaret set that she called him "Dom-Dom," asked the princess if she would sit for some new pictures for her twenty-ninth birthday. Elliot told her that he knew of this up-and-coming photographer who was perfect for the job.

Margaret trusted his judgment and agreed to pose for Armstrong-Jones. When she arrived at his studio, he somewhat cheekily asked the princess to change her clothes and jewelry and then pose, all the while making jokey asides, gossiping about mutual friends, and relating tales about theatrical stars.[4] Few men had ever treated her in this way, and Margaret was used to calling the tune. She was intrigued, later recalling: "He understood my job and pushed me to do things. In a way he introduced me to a new world." Quite fortuitously she had

found a man, she said, who was "daring" and different, someone who encouraged her rebellious, bohemian side.[5]

The princess and the photographer had more in common
than anyone thought. Like Margaret, Tony was a man of con-
tradictions, as talented and charming as he was impetuous
and unpredictable, and occasionally cruel. Lady Cavendish
described him as having "a great zest for life," adding, "he
was great company and a brilliant mimic; always whizzing
somewhere on his motorbike."[6] His good friend Carl Toms, a
designer, saw him as a modern eccentric determined to have
his own way. This quality could "goad people to the brink
of assassination only held back by a charm that could halt a
ravening beast in its track."[7]

◦∽◦

She had learned one painful lesson from the Townsend debacle: If she wanted to truly explore a romance, it had to remain
secret. No more picking fluff off RAF uniforms. If the relationship started to go somewhere, only then would she tell her sister. Tony played along expertly, the secrecy of their encounters
only serving to heighten their passion. Even close friends were
kept out of the loop. In the autumn of 1958, Lady Penn asked
Tony for dinner, he accepted at first, only to back out when he
learned that Princess Margaret was attending, too—he didn't
want to give away any clues to the rest of the party. A few weeks
later, on November 11, 1958, Margaret insisted he attend a
luncheon party at Clarence House. Even though they sat side
by side, everyone assumed he was the hired photographer and
thought nothing of his presence. It was the perfect cover.

The subterfuge they practiced ensured that their romance
had the excitement of a cheap spy novel. Margaret's car would
drop her off on a road near his Pimlico studio. Then, after

checking that the coast was clear, she could sneak down the alley connected to the back entrance and then into her lover's arms. For once, she would dress as anonymously as possible: dark spectacles, tweed skirt, sweater, and headscarf.

Aside from his Pimlico flat, there was another secret romantic hideaway where Tony and Margaret could meet unobserved. This was a ground-floor room in a former East End pub at 59 Rotherhithe Street, Bermondsey, overlooking the river Thames.

For Margaret, these rendezvous offered her a glimpse into the world of the ordinary. She could eat shepherd's pie cooked by Tony, drink cheap wine, even wash dishes in the sink. Just as she and her sister had always desired, she could be "normal"—if only for a few fleeting hours. "It had the most marvelous view," she remembered nostalgically. "One walked into the room and there was the river straight in front. At high tide swans looked in. And because it was on a bend you looked towards the Tower and Tower Bridge with the dome of St. Paul's behind them to the left, and the docks to the right."[8]

In the early days Tony knew how to strike the correct balance between daring and deference. He always made sure to address Princess Margaret as "Ma'am," even as he enticed her into his unorthodox and nonconformist life. The ghost of her father hovered over the burgeoning relationship. Like George VI, Tony was fascinated by fashion, eagerly designing her dresses and dictating her overall look.

For the most part, though, it was a one-dimensional relationship. As one of Tony's friends recalled, "What he had foremost in common with Princess Margaret could be put in three words: sex, sex, sex. Theirs was a terribly physical relationship, they couldn't keep their hands off each other, even with other people present. He was very well made and obviously that had a lot to do with it."[9] The secrecy surrounding their relationship as well as the princess's mythical aura only intensified their lust. In spite of himself, Tony was impressed that even for a simple weekend visit, guests' names and dossiers had to first be submitted to Margaret's lady-in-waiting. Margaret was always served first at mealtimes, and no one could speak unless first addressed by her. If she did not eat a certain food, no one else could. For Tony, this air of exclusivity made Margaret an even more alluring catch, far more exotic than his many models, actresses, and debutantes.

By early summer 1959, the queen and queen mother were finally allowed into Margaret's secret affair. They already suspected that something was brewing, because Margaret had been lighter and happier than they had seen her for some time. He was invited to Clarence House for a "viewing" by the queen mother, who expressed herself thoroughly enchanted by this charming, easygoing, and eminently talented young man. Though the ghost of George VI would have been disappointed that Tony was a commoner rather than a landowning earl or duke, the queen was also welcoming, intrigued by the man who could manage her mercurial sister. In October, she invited him to join the family at Balmoral, a stay that is always regarded as a testing ground for any potential suitor. He came armed with a few cameras, and no one—aside from the queen and queen mother—attached any significance to Tony's presence, assuming he was there solely to fulfill professional obligations.

His visit was fated. During the time they spent together, Margaret received a letter from Peter Townsend telling her that he was going to marry the nineteen-year-old Belgian heiress Marie-Luce Jamagne. Stunned, the princess saw Townsend's engagement as a betrayal of their shared "understanding"[10] that, as they couldn't marry one another, they would marry no one. After she had regained her composure, she went for a walk with Tony and told him about the letter. During their walk in the October sunshine, the princess, anticipating that at some point during his stay at Balmoral Tony was going to propose, asked him to wait. She was too agitated to think clearly. Margaret was clearly surprised at how strongly she still felt about her former lover, and it disconcerted her in her response to her current beau. Later she recalled: "He eventually did but in a roundabout way. It was very cleverly worded."[11]

Reflecting on that episode some time later, during a holiday in Barbados, she told Conservative lawmaker Jonathan Aitken: "I received a letter from Peter in the morning and that evening I decided to marry Tony. It was no coincidence. I didn't really want to marry at all. Why did I? Because he asked me! Really, though, he was such a nice person in those days."[12]

She had time to reflect on her future with Tony, as she didn't formally accept his proposal for another two months. In December 1959, the couple became privately engaged during a weekend at their regular "safe house," Widcombe Manor in Bath, the home of his best friends, inventor and engineer Jeremy Fry and his wife, Camilla. Tony presented her with a ruby and diamond engagement ring in the shape of a flower. The queen mother, who had taken to Tony from their first meeting, was delighted with the news, though the photographer counseled caution as he had not yet asked for the queen's formal permission. In anticipation of a betrothal, in October the queen mother held a dance at Clarence House ostensibly to celebrate young Princess Alexandra's return from Australia following a successful visit in August and September. Most of the 250 guests had no idea that there was an ulterior motive behind the occasion: to welcome the dashing photographer into the royal family at some point in the future.

Even though the queen was six months pregnant, she, her mother, and Margaret danced until three in the morning, capping off the celebration with a riotous conga line along the corridor and down the stairs. It was led, at the queen mother's bidding, by her youngest daughter and Antony Armstrong-Jones. Only the very sharp-eyed would have noticed that the couple could barely take their hands off one another—as the queen mother beamed her approval.[13]

The queen mother did still more to support her daughter's unconventional romance. She knew that the two lovers had been spending every open weekend at Royal Lodge, and she had made fewer visits in order to give them privacy. Certainly no prude, she had noticed the growing physicality of their relationship, particularly their love of skinny-dipping at midnight in the pool at Windsor.

The queen's relationship with the couple was more distant. In the early days of their romance, if the queen ever visited Royal Lodge during one of these weekends, Tony would hide himself away in his bedroom. As one guest revealed, "Whenever the queen dropped into the Lodge for a drink with her sister, the main guest in the lodge would hide quietly away in his bedroom, coming down only when he saw the queen and the royal party move off down the drive."[14]

For all their discretion, that New Year Tony had to run the gauntlet of media who surrounded Sandringham during the festive season in the hope of capturing pictures and stories about the off-duty royals. He drove to the Norfolk retreat in January on the pretext of providing the queen with a replacement pergola to house a statue of Buddha. In order to maintain the pretense, he brought with him a perfect scale model to show the monarch. The queen greeted him and then retired to work for an hour or so. At last she rang for her page and asked for Mr. Armstrong-Jones to bring in his model. Once the doors were closed he asked the queen for permission to marry her sister. Shortly afterward, Princess Margaret, Prince Philip, and the queen mother were asked to join them while other guests in the main house remained perplexed by the merriment caused by the unveiling of a model pergola.

The queen, who was now eight months pregnant, requested one courtesy: to refrain from announcing their engagement until after the birth of her child. At the end of January, the royal party returned to Buckingham Palace, and the queen gave birth to a baby boy, Prince Andrew, a few weeks later, on February 19, 1960.

On February 26, 1960, a week after Andrew's arrival, the engagement of Margaret and Tony was formally announced, not in a front-page newspaper exclusive but in the venerable Court Circular, the official record of royal engagements. "To say that Fleet Street and the world were alike thunderstruck by the news is not to exaggerate," recalled former *Daily Express* reporter Dennis Bardens. "Nobody had the least hint that a romance was burgeoning and blooming between the fairytale princess and him."[15] Margaret was making history, the first daughter of a king in more than 450 years to marry a commoner. Not since 1503 when lowly squire Thomas Kymbe married Cecily the daughter of Edward IV and the most beautiful of the York sisters, had a royal princess married a commoner. Thomas and Cecily paid a high price for their love match, which was contracted without the permission of King Henry VII. Her first marriage was annulled by the king, while her second husband predeceased her. Both marriages were contracted after the king gave his approval. Now a widow, Cecily felt that she could marry the man she wanted without asking for the king's permission. Not so. Henry confiscated all their lands and banned the princess from court. She and her lowborn husband lived out their days on the Isle of Wight, dependent on the charity of other family members.

Historically, royal marriages were contracted to form alliances or gain territory; princes invariably married princesses. In England, where the 1772 Royal Marriages Act held sway, the sovereign alone could grant permission for members of the royal family to marry. During Queen Victoria's reign, the general rule was that German princes married English princesses or vice versa. This changed during the First World War, when George V proclaimed in 1917 that the new name of the royal House was Windsor. At the same time, English princes were encouraged to marry English aristocrats, the first being Elizabeth Bowes-Lyon, the daughter of the earl of Strathmore and Kinghorne.

Antony Armstrong-Jones wasn't just a commoner; he was working at the creative cutting edge of Swinging London. Fellow photographers, commissioning editors, and royal diarists were shocked and surprised by his choice of bride. Biographer Kenneth Rose, his former teacher at Eton, thought the engagement "staggering." "He seems to belong to a world of dress designers, photographers and interior designers. Seems to mark a tremendous revolution in development of Royal Family." He had a point. Though the photographer was the first commoner to join the royal family, it was the start of a new wave. Apart from Lady Diana Spencer, the daughter of an earl, every new entrant to the House of Windsor has been a commoner.

❧

Magazine owner and friend Jocelyn Stevens, who frequently commissioned Tony, sent him a sour cable saying: "Never was there a more ill-fated assignment."[16] What he and many others, including Tony's father, believed was that the energetic and talented photographer would never fit into the formal rhythms of the royal world. Many within the royal houses of Europe opposed the engagement too, shocked that Margaret had chosen to marry a commoner rather than one of their own. During lunch with Marina, duchess of Kent, and Princess Alexandra, Noël Coward observed, "They are not pleased over Princess Margaret's engagement. There was a distinct *froideur* when I mentioned it."[17] This was not especially surprising, as Princess Marina believed strongly that pedigree and rank mattered. So too it seemed did the royal houses of Europe. One by one, virtually all the wedding invitations were turned down by Europe's royal families for a variety of contrived reasons, normally bogus diary clashes. The sole acceptance came from Queen Ingrid of Denmark, whose mother had been a British princess.[18]

The man and woman in the street thought differently. They approved of this intelligent and creative fiancé. His professional skills were an answer to critics who complained that the court was out of touch, especially in the world of art and fashion. In March, when the newly engaged couple went to the opera with the queen mother, the whole audience stood up and cheered. The queen and queen mother welcomed the news rather differently. According to a friend, they "liked [Tony] a lot" and were more than a little surprised that Margaret had found a man willing to put up with her querulous behavior.[19] Tony was exceedingly charming, with good manners, a sunny disposition, and deep and abiding respect for royal protocol. He showed extreme devotion to the royal family, particularly the queen, who always appreciated his tact and loyalty. If the radio ever played the national anthem, he would, according to his friend and onetime lover Victoria Charlton, stop whatever he was doing and stand to attention. She recalled: "He thought the queen was the most wonderful woman in the world. Surprisingly he had a decent relationship with Philip as well."[20]

His unquestioning loyalty went hand in hand with his secret and rather rackety lifestyle. The queen and his fiancée would have been utterly mortified if they had discovered that in the months before the wedding of the year, Camilla Fry, the wife of his best man, was carrying Tony's child. From the beginning, Tony was betraying his future wife's trust, enjoying a three-way affair with his bisexual best friend, Jeremy Fry, and his liberated wife, Camilla. It was during one drug- and alcohol-fueled weekend that Camilla's daughter Polly was conceived. Tony was ultimately proven to be the father. As one intimate laconically observed, "It was a pretty good free for all."[21]

While this episode was kept to fewer than a handful of confidants—the photographer denied he was the father until a DNA test taken in 2004 proved his paternity—Fry's 1952 conviction and fine for importuning a man for "immoral purposes" reached a rather wider audience. He stood down from his position as intended best man, publicly citing a recurrence of jaundice, which left him too ill to take on his duties. In the search for a last-minute replacement, the name of the Devon lawmaker and future leader of the Liberal Party, Jeremy Thorpe, came briefly into the frame. The local police were asked to undertake a discreet background check, and Devon chief constable, Lieutenant Colonel Ranulph "Streaky" Bacon, reported that Thorpe was homosexual.

In fact, Thorpe cherished the ambition, as he wrote on a House of Commons postcard to a friend, of marrying the princess and seducing the husband.[22] Instead, another friend, Dr. Roger Gilliatt, took over best man duties on short notice. (Years later Thorpe appeared at the Old Bailey court on charges of conspiracy and incitement to murder relating to an earlier relationship with model Norman Scott. He and his codefendants were acquitted.)

With the big day only weeks away, the pre-wedding celebratory dinners began in earnest. One gathering was hosted by a former boyfriend and escort, Colin Tennant, later Lord Glenconner, and his wife, Lady Anne Tennant, whose wedding Tony had photographed four years earlier. Then he had been sent to eat with the servants at the society bash, which was held at the palatial Holkham Hall. When Margaret mentioned they were sailing to the Caribbean on their honeymoon, the Tennants invited them to visit Mustique, then a primitive, flyblown island near St. Vincent that Tennant had bought for £45,000 several years earlier. Little did anyone know that this distant plot of land, just three miles long and one and a half miles wide, would have enormous repercussions for the newly engaged couple—and the monarchy.

◦↜

The wedding, which took place at Westminster Abbey on May 6, 1960, was the first to be televised, attracting a worldwide audience of 300 million. Some 500,000 lined the streets to see with their own eyes the legendary princess in the glass coach make her way to the abbey.

In another break with royal tradition, Margaret chose to wear an unadorned dress, a suggestion and design sketched by Tony and fashioned by couturier Norman Hartnell, who created a plain, V-necked, tight-waisted dress with an enormous skirt—three layers of organza over tulle. The only glitter came from the princess's magnificent diamond Poltimore tiara. Her wedding ring came from the same Welsh gold as the queen's own ring.

During the ceremony, Noël Coward watched the queen closely and noticed her "scowl a good deal"—another sighting of the "Windsor glare." While some might have interpreted that stern expression as a sign of ill temper, those who knew her understood that she scowled when straining to control strong emotions. According to Labour politician Richard Crossman, "When she is deeply moved and tries to control it she looks like an angry thunder-cloud."[23] Perhaps she was touched by the prospect that her mischievous, contrary little sister had finally found happiness—or so it seemed.

The two thousand guests included the three wives of the bridegroom's father, Tony's former lovers Jacqui Chan and Gina Ward, and celebrities from the world of art and entertainment, including actresses Margaret Leighton and Joyce Grenfell, and writers Jean Cocteau and John Betjeman.[24] Tony even invited his housekeeper and the postman from his father's village in Wales. By contrast, Margaret did not welcome any of the Clarence House staff, who had served her so loyally. As the princess passed by Lord Adam Gordon, the comptroller of the household, he bowed and said, "Goodbye, Your Royal Highness." As her glass coach pulled away, the queen mother's page William Tallon heard him say, "And we hope forever."[25] It summed up the frustration some of her staff felt about her often inconsiderate behavior. That said, when she had her own staff at Kensington Palace, they were loyal and long serving.

This, though, was finally her moment to take a very public bow as she stood on the balcony at Buckingham Palace, acknowledging the enthusiastic crowds below.

After the traditional wedding breakfast, the couple climbed into an open-topped Rolls-Royce while the queen and other guests flung rose petals at them—a reversal of roles thirteen years after her own wedding. Then they drove to Battle Bridge

Pier in the Pool of London where they boarded the royal yacht *Britannia* for their sunshine honeymoon.

☙

On the evening of May 26, 1960, the Tennants were gazing at the sea outside their primitive Mustique home when the *Britannia* came into view. Margaret and Tony had reached the halfway mark of their six-week Caribbean honeymoon. A boat was lowered, and then a young officer came ashore to ask if the Tennants would like to join them for dinner. They were given a fully equipped guest cabin and enjoyed the luxury of electricity and a shower before joining the royal couple.

Every morning for the next few days, sailors from the *Britannia* would stake out a different white-sand beach, pitch a tent, and arrange a rustic picnic for the couple. In the evenings, they met the Tennants for cocktails and conversation. During one of those gatherings, Colin offered the princess a tantalizing choice for her wedding present: "Would you like something from Asprey's wrapped up in a box or a piece of land?" Without hesitation, the princess replied, "A piece of land."[26] She eventually picked a ten-acre plot on a bluff overlooking the breathtaking blue waters of Gelliceaux Bay.

Thus began the association between Margaret and Mustique, then simply 1,400 acres of tropical scrubland, occupied by a tiny community of fishermen, cotton growers, wild cows, and millions of mosquitoes—hence the name. Several decades would pass before the Mustique of popular imagination, with its luxury villas, jet-set crowd, and louche reputation came into being.

Margaret was already smitten, seduced by the prospect of sand, sea, and privacy during the long winter months. She couldn't wait to stake out the property, borrowing one of Tony's old shirts to make her way through the dense brush to her chosen acres. However, Tony hated the place, which he called "Mustake." The princess had badly misread her man. For such a restless spirit who needed to work like an addict needs drugs, the notion of being cooped up on a tiny island for weeks on end was Tony's idea of hell, not paradise. He was also livid that Margaret's former boyfriend had offered the land to the princess alone rather than the two of them, a fact Tennant later denied. Forevermore Tony would refer to him, in conversation and in print, as "that shit." Ironically the house she later built on the island, Les Jolies Eaux, or bright waters, was designed by Oliver Messel, Tony's uncle.

When they returned from their honeymoon in June 1960, the newlyweds, who moved into number 10 Kensington Palace, got a taste of the criticism to come. Inevitably it focused on money, the cost to the taxpayer of the wedding and the six-week honeymoon on board the royal yacht *Britannia* being the primary points of contention. When the queen subsequently allocated them 1a Clock Court at Kensington Palace as their official grace and favor home—that is, a home owned by the crown and allocated to members of the royal family and long-serving retainers by the queen—criticism was not long in coming. The estimated cost of renovation—the building had been hit by incendiary bombs during the war—was an easy target for lawmakers and media commentators even though the queen contributed £20,000 out of her own pocket or what is known as the Privy Purse (the queen's private funds derived in part from the ancient Duchy of Lancaster estates), toward the £85,000 ($1.9 million in 2020) worth of work.

Tony described the building as "bombed, falling down,

empty and totally uninhabitable" and offered to show journalists around the wreck. The minister of works refused his request. In order to keep down costs, Margaret telephoned her sister and mother for help in furnishing the place. The queen mother donated cupboards, while the princess and her husband veneered the doors, and Tony obtained the slate for the floors from a Welsh quarry from his godfather for nothing.

It counted for little. The criticism about the cost of renovation came from both ends of the political spectrum. Monarchist MP Sir Martin Lindsay described the costs as "madness."[27]

Though Margaret had faced criticism throughout her adult life, it was a new experience for her husband, who was, like most people, used to making decisions without partisan scrutiny. He found the comment wholly unfair and pointed out that the overwhelming majority of the restoration was the obligation of the Ministry of Works, as Kensington Palace was a publicly owned historic building.

There were other shocks to the system for the new arrival. While Tony found the queen, queen mother, and Prince Philip welcoming, others were not so friendly. Indeed, his induction into the royal world was effectively Philip 2.0. Like his royal brother-in-law, who tolerated the queen's dresser, Bobo MacDonald, through gritted teeth, Tony had his own experience with Bobo's younger sister, Ruby Gordon. She had worked for Margaret all her life—she called her charge "Margaret"—and made plain her displeasure at the arrival of the cocky photographer. Every morning she would deliver a calling tray, a pot of Earl Grey tea, and a glass of orange juice to the couple's bedroom. That practice continued after her marriage—still with only one cup and one glass. Tony got the hint. In the inevitable battle of wills, Ruby found herself fired and replaced by Isobel Mathieson. Ruby discovered that behind the casual smiles and easy charm, Armstrong-Jones was one tough cookie.

Again like Prince Philip, he experienced the same *froideur* with some of the stuffier courtiers who thought him way below the salt. They took to calling him "Tony Snapshot." He later recalled: "The most difficult aspect about being married into the royal family were some of the courtiers. Some of them were pretty awful. They thought that because I was a photographer I came from the slums. Which I didn't... quite."[28] Several weeks after they returned from their honeymoon, they joined the rest of the royal family at Balmoral. This was another test—one that Tony passed with aplomb. He brought a selection of cameras and snapped away happily, some of his pictures still hanging in the guest bedrooms today.

Philip had his own brisk way of inducting Tony into the joys of the great outdoors during the Balmoral break. He handed him a rod and line and told him to sit on a stool in the middle of the lawn and practice casting. When they went shooting, Philip, knowing that Tony had a leg shortened by polio, thoughtfully ensured that there was a Land Rover on hand to take him up the hill to the butts. The first time out, he proudly carried a pair of engraved Purdey guns, which were a personal wedding present from the queen. She later gave him one of her prize-winning black Labrador gundogs, a signal honor in that world and a genuine sign of her affection toward her brother-in-law. Determined and competitive, as befitting a man who led the winning 1950 Cambridge University crew, he had practiced at a clay pigeon shooting range in west London so that he didn't embarrass himself. In any case, as a photographer he had fast hand-eye coordination, and his prowess earned him the grudging admiration of his fellow guns.

However, it was the unspoken interactions that were more telling, as the photographer smoothly insinuated himself into the intimate royal circle and in time recalibrated the family dynamic between the queen, her mother, and her sister. For instance, when Princess Margaret tried to beg off a royal function, it would be her husband who would remedy the problem rather than her mother or sister. In short, he was a soothing, thoughtful presence.

He proved to be the emollient between the two sisters and their mother, who used Tony as an intermediary or referee in domestic squabbles. Issues that Philip ignored or dismissed, Tony took seriously, or at least seemed to take seriously. The silky interpersonal skills that served him well as a top photographer also helped integrate him into the fabric of the family. As Marjorie Wallace, campaigner, journalist, and former girlfriend, recalled, "He really relished his role as a mediator between Princess Margaret, the Queen and the Queen Mother. It is probably why he remained in royal favour to the end. He took Margaret off their hands."

Though, like Prince Philip, he had a caustic, sardonic wit, he masked this behind a charming and solicitous façade. What his brother-in-law may have said out loud, Tony merely thought. After the wedding he wrote gratefully to the queen mother, thanking her for the "wonderful feeling of warmth and welcome"[29] he had experienced now that he was part of the family.

During his induction into the arcane royal world, he learned early on that Philip was always right, so it was best to let him win an argument. He was impatient, certainly, but, like Tony, he was a man of energy and creativity. While they were hardly pals, they had mutual respect for each other. Philip in particular warmed to Tony because he was a man of utter discretion—as he had proved during his courtship.

As for the queen, he was more than a little in love with her, constantly having to be reminded to call her "Lilibet" rather than "ma'am." When asked if he was in love with both sisters, he said, "No." Then he revealed: "Both sisters were very sexy and attractive and I still think the Queen is now. She has the most brilliant sense of humour in private and the most lovely giggle. She makes jokes and she likes to be amused. Both sisters were very attractive compelling women to me."

In public Tony proved to be a fast study, quickly learning how to play the royal game, walking steadily two or more paces behind his wife, hands behind his back, smiling and attentive. He applauded performances with his hands raised, cut his hair, changed to English cigarettes, and upgraded his wardrobe. In the beginning they did everything together, from writing speeches to water skiing on the lake at Sunninghill Park, on the edge of the Windsor estate. From time to time the queen would come and watch their antics, bringing Andrew along in his Silver Cross pram. On one occasion Prince Charles joined his aunt and uncle and water-skied on a chair attached to a door.

For Tony, it took some getting used to. After all, he now found himself out of a job, and while it was fun to watch the Wimbledon tennis final from the royal box, the day-to-day grind of royal engagements, visiting factories, schools, and colleges, was a world away from what he was used to. Nonetheless, he proved a supportive and discreet partner, and Margaret appreciated that he was there to share the burden of, in her sister's words, meeting endless ranks of "boring, boring, boring" people.

No longer the odd one out, Margaret enjoyed a happy marriage like her sister's and, in the spring of 1961, was able to inform her that she was expecting her first child. Though they led busy, independent lives, the sisters spoke most days on the telephone and often saw each other at the private church at Windsor and for drinks and lunch at Royal Lodge.

Arguably, these brief years in the early 1960s were a time of contentment and happiness not just for Margaret and Tony but between the two sisters and their mother. While drama was never far away, this was a rare period of calm for the House of Windsor. Their mother had come through the gloom following the death of her husband, King George VI. She had embraced with enthusiasm her role as queen mother, and the family matriarch was still relevant and much appreciated on the international scene. She entertained foreign leaders, like her friend French president Charles De Gaulle, and undertook numerous overseas visits at a time when Britain, wounded after the Suez debacle, needed to project a positive image to the world.

The queen had resolved a long-standing matter in her own marriage, the issue of the family surname. Prince Philip had complained for years that he was the only father in the kingdom not able to give his own children his surname after then-prime minister Winston Churchill, Queen Mary, and others had argued that the royal house remain Windsor rather than take Philip's surname of Mountbatten. It had been the cause of much resentment and anger, and at a time when Philip was already feeling sidelined. After the birth of Prince Andrew, it was proclaimed, after much back and forth between Downing Street and Buckingham Palace, that in the future all male line descendants of the queen and Prince Philip would take the surname Mountbatten-Windsor when a surname was required. The royal House remained Windsor. Knowing the importance this matter had assumed to the queen, the decision, agreed to by the Privy Council, a formal body of advisers, usually senior politicians, took a "great load" off the monarch's mind.

In November 1961 the queen had also pulled off something of a personal political coup. She had been fiercely determined to visit Ghana, now independent from the British Empire, in spite of the hesitation of Prime Minister Macmillan and even Winston Churchill, who worried that she faced genuine physical danger in the unstable nation. With president Kwame Nkrumah being wooed by the Soviets, the queen saw it as her mission to ensure that the newly independent nation would remain in the Commonwealth. Her undertaking succeeded, symbolized by pictures of the queen and the African leader dancing together during a ball in the nation's capital, Accra. The queen's stalwart decision to go ahead with the visit, in spite of the many doubters, was much admired and a tribute to her acute political instincts and sound judgment.

A few weeks before she left, the queen expressed her confidence in the newest member of the family when on October 3, 1961, she conferred upon him the title the earl of Snowdon and the courtesy title of Viscount Linley of Nymans, while Margaret became HRH Princess Margaret, countess of Snowdon. Tony had declined the queen's initial offer of a title upon marriage but later accepted an honor so that their children would not be commoners. As he told diarist Kenneth Rose, "I do hope that people do not think that I wanted the title myself. The Queen wished me to have it, and it would have been arrogant of me to have refused."[30] Their happiness was complete when exactly a month later, on November 3, Margaret gave birth to a son, David Linley, by cesarean section. After seeing the baby, Princess Alice of Athlone remarked, "Almost anyone could be that boy's mother—he's so like his father." Tony was absolutely "thrilled and delighted" by the boy's birth and photographed him constantly.[31]

꽃

His son's birth also marked something of a turning point for the ambitious photographer. After twenty months of meaningless small talk and encounters with public officials—"All town clerks are the same," his wife once observed—Snowdon hankered to return to his previous profession. Both the queen and his wife had encouraged him to take up his old job again, and he had been the one to resist. But that was about to change.

꽃

One day, when the Snowdons were visiting their friends Jeremy and Camilla Fry, royal photographer Cecil Beaton dropped by for a drink. Beaton congratulated Margaret on her marriage, adding, "May I thank you, ma'am, for removing my most dangerous rival?" Poker faced, Margaret replied, "What makes you think Tony is going to give up work?" Early in 1962, after discreet lobbying by Princess Margaret, Tony accepted the job of artistic adviser of the *Sunday Times* color magazine—with the queen's blessing. The job came with plenty of time off so that Snowdon could perform and assist with royal duties. At his first editorial conference on February 6, 1962, he joined his new colleagues and then quickly left for lunch at Buckingham Palace to celebrate the tenth anniversary of the queen's accession. His appointment provoked immediate criticism from rival newspapers and later politicians who feared that the queen could be involved in controversy. This was a concern that brewed for a couple of months. In a letter to the new prime minister Sir Alec Douglas-Home in 1964, royalist lawmaker Sir Martin Lindsay complained that "royalty should not be used as a stunt." He argued that as the *Sunday Times* had been recently bought by provocative Canadian press baron Roy Thomson. Tony's association with the newspaper could drag the queen into political debate. Though the polar explorer turned politician had gotten his facts wrong—Thomson bought the newspaper group in the late 1950s—that did not stop him from warning the prime minister. "The Royal Family is far from popular with a large number of middle-class and working-class British people...the image of the Monarchy has been allowed to become tarnished."

⁓

His was not the only voice of dissent. It hadn't escaped notice that two months after the birth of their son, David, the royal couple left the infant in the care of royal nanny Verona Sumner and went on a three-week jaunt to Antigua in the Caribbean.

As Britain faced another punishing winter, the princess was panned for being "callous, selfish, and perverse," especially when it was later revealed that the entire first-class section of a Britannia aircraft was monopolized by her, Tony, a maid, and a detective, which meant that Margaret paid over £3,000 for a sixteen-seat space. This publicity seemed to confirm the charge that Margaret was profligate and spoiled. She stood her ground, complaining that the press were like "vultures waiting for an accident." The negative coverage, she admitted, left her "an absolute wreck" because "I had no way of hitting back."[32] Though the couple were seen as modern, fashionable, and fresh, these incidents reminded the public that they lived a life of privilege and indulgence. As royal writer Dennis Bardens complained, "This type of thing does great harm to the monarchy, which is traditionally chary of claiming privilege except as an inherent part of performing a duty."[33] In these more democratic times, when even the queen mother went by scheduled airline, Margaret's lifestyle, be it the restoration of her home or her sunshine holidays, suggested self-indulgence and conspicuous consumption at a time of economic belt-tightening.

It was all the more shocking for Margaret and Tony as this was the first time members of the royal family had been consistently criticized by the media and MPs for the cost of their upkeep. Since then it has become an integral part of the media narrative in assessing certain royals, notably Sarah, the duchess of York and more recently Harry and Meghan, the duke and duchess of Sussex. In the words of the new satirical magazine *Private Eye*, the newly minted earl and countess of Snowdon became "the two highest-paid performing dwarfs in Europe,"[34] symbols of a monarchy attempting to prove its continuing relevance. Indeed it was this abiding concern about remaining relevant that convinced the queen toward the end of the decade to give the go-ahead to a groundbreaking TV documentary, *Royal Family*, showing the royal family off duty and accessible.

For the most part, the queen had not been criticized for the cost of her travel or upkeep, not only because when she traveled abroad it was invariably on official diplomatic business, but because her holidays, like those of previous monarchs, followed the same domestic routine: Sandringham in the winter, Balmoral in the summer. She sympathized with her sister—and her brother-in-law—as she had asked them to undertake some overseas visits on her behalf. In the early days of their marriage, they attended royal marriages in Brussels and Norway, flew to Jamaica in August 1962 to grant the island country independence, and even came under the purview of Russia's secret service, the KGB, during a visit to Copenhagen, the Danish capital, in 1964. According to *Pravda* security correspondent Gennady Sokolov, agents planted bugs in their phone, cigarette lighter, and cigarette case in the hope of uncovering a scandal to embarrass the royal couple or the wider royal family. Ex-KGB chief Colonel Vadim Goncharov is later said to have listened in on "drunken parties" in which "most interesting, even scandalous" conversations were recorded.

It would not be long before he would really have something to excite his masters in the Kremlin.[35]

9

Cool Britannia

Decades before Prince Harry and his actress wife Meghan Markle were flagbearers of the exotic, progressive, and global, Princess Margaret and Lord Snowdon were established as Britain's hippest couple, peerless representatives of the "Swinging Sixties" and living proof that the monarchy could be both traditional and modern.

According to Lord Ardwick, editor of the *Daily Herald*, the Snowdons signified "a new kind of royalty," arguing, "they had far more contacts among writers and artists and so forth, not among stuffy courtiers. They became the new family model of fast traveling, hard-working, affluent young people—but at a price, a cost that was not always welcome."[1] Together, this bohemian couple raced through the streets of London on Snowdon's motorcycle or in his new Mini, visiting street markets, jazz clubs, and theaters.

Such was their appeal that even First Lady Jacqueline Kennedy was deeply disappointed when neither the princess nor her husband was present at a dinner in honor of President

Kennedy, which was held at Buckingham Palace in June 1961. Internationally, they were the royal version of Elizabeth Taylor and Richard Burton—sophisticated, artistic, and raffish. Once Margaret tried on the 29.4-carat diamond ring that was given to Taylor by her third husband, Mike Todd. She joked that it was "vulgar." Liz replied, "Yeah ain't it great." Vibrant, dynamic, and glamorous, Margaret and Tony captivated the nation in the early years, injecting new life and energy into what Prince Philip called "the Firm."

Everything from their fashions to their crowd—naturally "in"—was a playful counterpoint to the queen and her court. If the Snowdons were deemed "hip plush," the queen was "starchy matron"—her fashions were still chosen by her dresser since childhood, Bobo MacDonald. Just as her father had done, it was Tony who guided Margaret's style, urging her to adopt simpler, skimpier trends to mirror the taste and temper of the time. Though she never wore miniskirts, her skirts and dresses were still much shorter than those of other royal women. She also experimented with caftans, lace stockings, and modern costume jewelry, and at one point the princess was voted just behind Grace Kelly in the annual "World's Best Dressed Woman" contest.

Unlike the queen's unalterable look, Margaret's hairstyle was constantly changing, from glossy bobs to elaborate, high-reaching coiffures adorned with hairpieces. Nor was she afraid to showcase daring trends: pale lipstick, heavy eyeshadow, long earrings, and a provocatively low neckline. Tony's clothes were just as modish: velvet jackets, voile shirts, and barrow boy caps. He even wore a white polo neck instead of black tie to formal events.

While the queen and Prince Philip remained on British soil for their holidays, Margaret and Tony quickly became members of the international jet set and were much sought-after guests of the rich and powerful. At a time when travel abroad was exclusive and expensive, their holidays on a millionaire's yacht or villa excited awe and jealousy in equal measure. In September 1963, when the queen and the rest of the royal family were at Balmoral, the Snowdons holidayed on a private Aegean island owned by Greek shipping tycoon Stavros Niarchos, which came fully stocked with game birds for shooting parties. The following year it was the turn of the British-born Aga Khan IV to fly them on his private plane to the exclusive resort of Costa Smeralda on the Italian island of Sardinia, where they were able to water ski, sail, snorkel, and sunbathe in relative privacy. They returned to the island often. On one occasion, Aga Khan IV's yacht, the *Amaloun*, hit a rock and started to sink. Tony dove into the water, and the others took to a life raft, from which they were rescued by a passing boat. Significantly, the first person Margaret contacted to say all was well was the queen.

That escapade did not dim their enthusiasm for all things Italian, and it became a favored holiday destination. In the summer of 1965, for example, the couple drove to Rome in Tony's Aston Martin to see the sights and to be received by the pope in a private audience. The paparazzi, which began in Rome, stalked them constantly, one photographer observing, "You have to remember that Princess Margaret and Elizabeth Taylor are the two most wanted women in the world."[2]

Most years thereafter, Margaret would visit the pope's private garden. It was a pilgrimage of sorts, the beginning of what would become a long flirtation with the Church of Rome. Margaret was a high church Anglican, which was also known as Anglo-Catholic, a branch of the Church of England that adhered closest to Catholicism in its formality and resistance to modernization.

∾

Once the Snowdons moved into their newly renovated, twenty-room home at Kensington Palace in March 1963, an invitation to supper or for a sing-along around the grand piano became the hottest ticket in town. Their social circle reflected their bohemian bent, singers, musicians, artists, and writers all beating a path to 1a Clock Court. Their servants did not mind working eighteen-hour days when they had the chance to glimpse luminaries such as designer Mary Quant; writer Edna O'Brien (Margaret did a good impression of the writer's breathless, confiding speech patterns); actor Peter Sellers and his wife, Britt Ekland; ballet dancers Rudolf Nureyev and Margot Fonteyn; and trendsetting hairdresser Vidal Sassoon. They even befriended the Beatles, with John Lennon famously nicknaming the couple "Priceless Margarine" and "Bony Armstrove." On one occasion George Harrison asked Margaret to get his drug possession charges dropped. She declined. "I adored them because they were poets as well as musicians," the princess later recalled.[3]

Their parties were replete with the rich and famous. The comedian and musician Dudley Moore would play the piano; Cleo Laine and her jazz musician husband, John Dankworth, would sing; John Betjeman, a future poet laureate, would tell stories. Often, Princess Margaret would join in playing the piano and singing tunes from her favorite musicals. When the lights were out at Buckingham Palace, they were still blazing until the early hours at the Snowdons' salon—invariably at Margaret's bidding. Established in her own home for the first time in her life and with baby number two on the way, Margaret's life was scintillating, busy, and happy. She could even share the mutual joys and difficulties of pregnancy with her sister as the queen gave birth to her fourth child, Prince Edward, in March 1964. She and Prince Philip made a modest concession to modernity: For the first time, Prince Philip was present at the birth, which took place in the Belgian Suite at Buckingham Palace.

During this time, the differing personalities of the two sisters became more sharply delineated and formalized as Margaret established her own home and social circle. At last she had her own salon, where the princess, a performer and extrovert at heart, could literally hold court. By contrast, her sister focused her attention on her horses and dogs; her people were the country set who followed the jumps and the flats. Animals never broke her trust, let her down, or came to her with difficult problems. The rhythms of mating, birth, weaning, training, and racing were and are her abiding pleasure.

As an insider described, the queen is "not a people person, she's a horse person, a dog person, likes being on her own. She finds it easier to relate to horses and dogs than people and has an extraordinary empathy with them."[4]

Just as Margaret was comfortable with the singers and actors who thronged her new home, so the queen was at her most relaxed with fellow racing folk. On one occasion she was at lunch with her trainer Captain Cecil Boyd-Rochfort at his stables, Freemason Lodge, in Newcastle. For dessert crème brûlée was served. The caramelized topping was so hard that no one at the table could break into it. To everyone's astonishment, the queen slipped off her high-heeled shoe and smashed it down onto the dessert, cracking it into pieces. "She felt comfortable with her own people," explained Sean Smith, author of *Royal Racing*. "There is no need for airs and graces. She has known them for decades."

❧

While Margaret inhabited a social halfway house, befriending
the era's popular icons as well as those with a handle before
their first name, Elizabeth's friends and acquaintances came
almost exclusively from the landowning aristocracy—she first
knew her fourth prime minister Sir Alec Douglas-Home as
the owner of land in Scotland—or those from the Guards
regiments, such as Lord Plunket and Lord Porchester, her racing manager, who got to know her during the war. When her
mother won the Whitbread Gold Cup with Special Cargo,
Colonel Bill Whitbread and his wife, Betty, held a dinner party
for the queen mother. After dinner they adjourned to another
room to watch the race on TV one more time. They were a
chair short, so the queen sat on the floor, clearly comfortable
with the racing crowd she was with. It was hard to imagine her
being so relaxed with Margaret's friends.

Like her father, the queen was uncomfortable around artists and the avant-garde. Uninterested in discussing literary
or cultural issues, the queen preferred the familiar terrain of
politics, world affairs, and horses. In those days, she remained,
as a friend observed, nervous whenever meeting "people of a
higher academic field."[5] It was a world her younger sister relished, which became ever more apparent when she began to
mix with academics from Oxford and Cambridge.

❧

Trust was always an issue, hence the reliance on familiar faces,
on the tried and tested. The portrait artist Pietro Annigoni captured the essential distance and loneliness that was attendant
on the queen's position. Her cousin Margaret Rhodes observed:

"I don't think she has [a best friend]. There is no way one can get that close to somebody in that position. She is surprisingly outgoing to someone she feels she can trust. But then there can't be that many."[6] During her reign it has been her loyal dressers, notably Bobo MacDonald and later Angela Kelly, who had kept her company during the long stretches of tedium the position entails.

Arguably, for all their differences, her sister was the queen's closest friend and, along with her husband, most stalwart and loyal supporter. Though Margaret was the undoubted queen of the smart set, she was always the supporting act to her sister, never the star of the show. She gave a telling clue as to the origin of this family drama when she said, "I've never suffered from second daughter-itis. I've never minded being referred to as the younger daughter but I do mind being referred to as the younger sister." This was a question of place and position in the royal hierarchy. As the royal historian Michael Nash observed, "While her father was King, her own position was more elevated. She was in the mainstream. Immediately after he died, she became a collateral branch of the family. The same thing will happen with Princess Anne, Prince Andrew and Prince Edward when they cease to be the Sovereign's children."[7]

Since she was a little girl she was the one drawn to the spotlight, the one who loved being the center of attention, whether the audience was just her father or, during the war, a table full of eager Guards officers. Now it was her sitting room at Kensington Palace where she reigned supreme, singing show tunes as she sipped her Famous Grouse whisky.

She was, however, undoubtedly loyal to her sister—just as she was to her friends, a characteristic that pleased the queen.

Her role, as she told writer Andrew Duncan, was to support her sister in her difficult and isolated position. "In my own humble way I've always tried to take some of the burden off my sister. She can't do it all you know. And I leap at the opportunity to help."[8]

⌒

Unlike her sister, who, by disposition and position, stayed with the tried and traditional, Margaret was a trailblazer. She mixed in company where few had ever encountered royalty, so they didn't know the form, unlike those who surrounded the queen. She was at one dinner party when a latecomer arrived, stripped off his motorbike leathers, took one look at Princess Margaret, and cried, "I didn't know this was a Princess Margaret looka-like contest." Cue general laughter.

It worked both ways. At another dinner party, the actor Vivien Merchant, an anti-monarchist, refused to shake her hand when they were introduced. It was a tart realization of the price she sometimes had to pay for traveling outside the traditional royal comfort zone.

She was a pioneer in trying to remove the barriers of snob-bery and protocol—but not all. Woe betide the conversational partner who said "your sister" or "your father." They received the "Windsor glare." Though she struggled to turn on the elec-tric kettle, when she was a guest at a weekend party she liked to chip in, whether it be laying the fire—a particular pleasure—stripping wallpaper, or washing up. She hankered after a life more ordinary—but not too ordinary. Royalty mattered most. It was a social tightrope she walked all her life. As Tony's business manager Peter Lyster-Todd observed: "I often stayed with them for weekends and you never quite knew what you were going to get; friendly Margaret or talking to 'Ma'am.'"[9] It became a common refrain. While drag artist Danny La Rue found Margaret "witty and highly intelligent," he maintained, "you always knew you were in the presence of a princess."

There was always a barrier, a self-conscious line few crossed, Windsor glare or not.

As one observer noted, "No one seemed to behave naturally when she was there. She tried her best but it always came across as condescension. She had that royal way of moving on, of not wanting to be left too long with anyone. She never really seemed to belong to that arty world."[10]

The classic example was at the home of irreverent critic Kenneth Tynan, who asked Tony if after dinner he could screen a graphic homosexual film about two prisoners in love, directed by the French novelist and playwright Jean Genet. Would the princess mind? Tony thought it would do her good. However, once the room went dark and the guests, including playwright Harold Pinter, watched the screen, the atmosphere began to freeze as the graphic gay love affair was played out in front of the queen's sister. Fortunately, comedian Peter Cook lightened the mood, delivering an improvised commentary. Within minutes everyone, including the princess, was rocking with laughter. In spite of this unusual and intimate after-dinner entertainment, Tynan, the great iconoclast, bowed to her, kissed her hand, and said, "Thank you ma'am." Royalty had to be treated with due courtesy—even after watching blue movies.

༄

It was a film of quite a different kind that the royal couple helped make for the queen's thirty-ninth birthday in April 1965. The Snowdons joined Peter Sellers and several other friends in making a fifteen-minute home movie as a gift for

Her Majesty. At one point in the amateur film Sellers, who played the Great Berko, proclaimed that in a world record time of eleven seconds flat he would perform his celebrated impression of the Princess Margaret. He then disappeared behind a screen, flung various articles of clothing into the air, and a few seconds later, the actual princess emerged, curtsying and grinning before retreating behind the screen.[11] The queen loved the movie and showed it frequently.

Within months, in November 1965, the princess and her husband were on a professional movie set, rubbing shoulders with the likes of Mary Pickford, Charlton Heston, Maurice Chevalier, and James Stewart at Universal Studios in Studio City, Hollywood. The three-week, five-city tour of the United States was the chance to fly the flag for Britain and take time to enjoy the sights, courtesy of their host, Margaret's longtime American friend Sass Douglas, who organized the tour. Besides Los Angeles, the couple charmed San Francisco's old-money families, dazzled New York's Upper East Side aristocracy, and greeted locals in small-town Arizona—Sass's home state— before schmoozing President Lyndon Johnson at a black-tie dinner held at the White House. Even so, the royal couple, who had performed numerous successful overseas visits on behalf of the queen, found themselves the subject of constant criticism—even though many thought the trip a triumph.

While the tour was followed with intense interest by the media, palace officials watched in horror as the trip devolved into utter mayhem. The getting-to-know-you visit was supposed to show Americans just how sexy and unstuffy the British royals could be. Who more qualified to do that than the House of Windsor's grooviest couple, Margaret and Tony? Instead, as one columnist put it, the visit caused "plenty of trouble."

The jamboree cost the equivalent of $500,000 and many lost tempers. An aircraft of the Queen's Flight was sent out to back up a Lockheed JetStar, which an obliging President Johnson had provided. In addition, British Airways lent them a VC10 jet. Their entourage, which was substantial, included a Mayfair hairdresser, Rene Moulard; two menservants; two maids; a detective; a secretary; a lady-in-waiting; a private secretary; and the deputy captain of the Queen's Flight.

What followed after touchdown was a litany of missed appointments, canceled public engagements, and highly publicized social snubs. The princess, with her dangerous mix of highfalutin' formality and fun-loving affability, was difficult to read. One instant she could be all friends together; the next she would be the daughter of the king-emperor astride her high horse.

At a party at the Beverly Hills Hotel, the princess sent a message across the room to say that she would like to hear Judy Garland sing. The singer was incensed by the lordly tone and the trivializing of her talent. She said, "Go and tell that nasty, rude little princess that we've known each other long enough and gabbed enough in ladies' rooms that she should skip the ho-hum royal routine and just pop over here and ask me herself. Tell her I'll sing if she christens a ship first."[12]

Then, when Margaret met with President Johnson and his wife Lady Bird, she made full use of her "actressy" nature. According to one observer, who saw her at a ball at New York's Waldorf Astoria Hotel, "It's a put-on; campy; tongue-in-cheek camp. She's doing an impersonation of herself." Princess Margaret—always the performer—loved opportunities where she could showcase her "star" nature, becoming an exaggeration of her own public persona.

The couple was subject to a flurry of critical headlines from both sides of the political divide, the left-wing *New Statesman* magazine describing her tour as a "private rubber-necking trip to the American fun centers," while the right wing *Sunday Express* called it a "holiday frolic among the tinsel princes and princesses of Hollywood."

After her return to London in late November, questions were asked in the House of Commons about her behavior. In a private report, the British ambassador Sir Patrick Dean, reported, diplomatically, "They worked hard and played hard. It was a mistake that so much of their time was spent with and organized by Miss Douglas. It was not always possible to persuade the American public that HRH and Lord Snowdon were serious as well as gay people." When the princess spoke of returning to the States in 1973, the then British ambassador, Lord Cromer, torpedoed the suggestion. Margaret's private secretary Lieutenant Colonel Burnaby-Atkins was told, "Lord Cromer is not at all keen on having the Princess in the United States, possibly for some time to come. This is mainly due to the behavior of some of HRH's friends, who tend to take such visits lightly."[13]

With headlines like LUXURY TOUR, WHO PAYS, and OWN HAIRDRESSER, the impression was left in the public mind once again that the princess was neither pulling her weight nor proving to be cost-effective. Once established, this narrative would dog her for the rest of her life, no matter how many public engagements she undertook on behalf of the queen.

The wheels were beginning to come off—not just in terms of her public image but the couple's private behavior. Similar in so many ways, the personality traits that had at first united now gradually divided them. It was Margaret's tragedy that consciously and subconsciously she fell for a man who exhibited similar personality traits to herself rather than her sister.

Tragically, it soon became apparent that, in the worst sense, Margaret and Tony were "two peas in a pod," both strong-willed, competitive, centerstage people used to getting their way. The princess had long been indulged and coddled, while Tony was magnetic and ambitious, bolder and more conniving than Margaret herself. With their personalities "too alike, too selfish,"[14] as friends recalled, they were bound to clash. In the battle of wills that followed, Snowdon, as the queen's biographer Sarah Bradford noted, was much better at being nasty than Margaret.

Though the earliest years of their marriage were happy and stimulating, Snowdon soon chaffed at the bars of the royal cage—as his friends had predicted.

Before they married, Margaret's lady-in-waiting Lady Elizabeth Cavendish, who first introduced them, asked the princess if she could genuinely cope with Tony's "bohemian world." When Lady Elizabeth explained that he would be here, there, and everywhere with his professional commitments and would not always be home for dinner, Margaret dismissed her concerns, believing that their passion and deep connection would overcome all obstacles.

For all her surface royal sheen, Margaret was a surprisingly shy, insecure woman, more so than her sister, and once marital hostilities began, it was very easy for Snowdon to knock her off her perch. In the beginning he could pass off his casual controlling cruelties as practical jokes.

In the summer of 1963, when the couple stayed with wealthy Greek shipowner Stavros Niarchos on his private island, Spetsopoula, friends on a nearby island threw a party to celebrate Margaret's thirty-third birthday. When Tony arrived, he brought presents for everyone—except his wife. Then, as the two were getting ready for the barbecue that night, Margaret shouted from upstairs, "Oh, darling, what shall I wear?" Tony replied, "Oh, I think that ball gown you wore last week." Margaret, suspecting nothing, arrived at the dinner dressed to the hilt while all the other guests wore casual jeans and sandals.[15] These kinds of jokes in disguise progressively undermined her self-confidence as well as her trust in her husband. As the years ticked by, the photographer's controlling behavior could be described as mental cruelty.

For all her differences with her sister, she saw the queen's successful marriage as a template she should imitate. Like Tony, Philip was an alpha male, creative, bombastic, and strong-willed but accepting of his secondary role in the marriage. As he had once told a friend, "This is my destiny—to support my wife in what lies ahead for her."[16] In the early years, Snowdon performed this role exactly as Margaret had imagined, a smiling, gracious, and deferential addition to her retinue. Once he began working for the *Sunday Times*, he reverted to type, a workaholic with a wandering eye. An early riser, he was working when Margaret, after a long night carousing, was still in bed, often until shortly before noon. After a row he might send her a note, loving but firm, suggesting that she drink less and retire to bed earlier. Given her later health problems, this note could be interpreted as a husband's fond concern for his wife. He had the ability, which she found ultimately frustrating, of skillfully laying every problem with the marriage at her door. She knew instinctively that if she started complaining to her sister or mother, they wouldn't want to know. They had experienced a lifetime of Margaret's rudeness and self-absorption, so they likely would side with the angelic and courteous Tony. The queen knew it had been a long struggle for her own husband to adapt, so she sympathized with Tony's juggling act, working as a photographer and on design projects such as the aviary at the London Zoo as well as undertaking national and international royal duties.

The couple began to move in different worlds. Though she had longed to create a life outside royal circles, at moments of personal tension she fell back on the familiar, namely the formalities and superficialities of the royal world. In this world, her natural habitat, it was others who had to compromise to her standards and requirements. But as Tony began to exhibit a growing need for independence, she became increasingly possessive, calling him on assignments, at restaurants, or at the homes of friends. Lacking Elizabeth's economy of emotion, Margaret could not accept that someone had "out-royaled her." Since she was a little girl she had used her personality and position to get away with murder. As the gloves came off in their marriage, she began to realize that she had finally met her match.

Though the queen was aware of the backstage drama in her sister's marriage, she simply watched and waited, hoping that matters would resolve themselves.

The cracks remained, as Tony found his duties as consort increasingly tedious and burdensome. He snapped, "I am not a member of the royal family. I am married to a member of the royal family."[17] He focused fiercely on his job at the *Sunday Times*, traveling around the world on assignment, both for still photography and filming documentaries. It was creatively fulfilling, but it was a world that was alien to the princess. Though she pleaded with him to let her join him on projects, he flatly refused, saying that he wanted to be as anonymous as possible. Meanwhile, Margaret remained at home, pregnant and bored. As the sisters faced the challenges of pregnancy together,

Elizabeth fretted over the effects of the deteriorating marriage on her sister. She knew that Margaret's doctor—worried that marital strain was endangering her second pregnancy—had even warned Tony directly about his behavior.

While the pregnant princess marked time, Tony was busier than ever, shooting portraits of the likes of Charlie Chaplin, Sophia Loren, and David Hockney. He also designed the impressive Snowdon Aviary at the London Zoo, which opened in October 1964. Most important, he began to evolve into a progressive voice for change, championing the disadvantaged, dispossessed, and disabled.[18] Not only did he photograph blind and deaf children, as well as victims of rubella, but he also started making award-winning TV documentaries about old age, mental health, disability, poverty, and children. He was delighted that the queen watched his work, the sovereign complimenting him fulsomely on his efforts. As Snowdon's star rose, Margaret's only claim to fame continued to be an accident of birth—a truth she shrank from her entire life.

The seeds of discontent were now sown. Rows she could bear—at least they signified some emotional engagement. It was the silent treatment she dreaded. He would arrive home late and then head straight to his basement workroom, often ignoring his wife's requests to meet with guests. Instead, he would simply shut his door and leave Margaret at a total loss over what to do next.

With the birth of their second child, Sarah Frances Elizabeth, on May 1, 1964, by cesarean section, there was a temporary truce. Tony had his assistant fetch a huge bouquet for Margaret from the florist. Ever conscious of the royal protocol that the queen must know of the baby's birth and its sex before the press, Tony instructed the assistant, "If they do it up in pink ribbon, hide it—otherwise the press'll know that it's a girl."[19] An hour after the birth, Tony visited his wife and new daughter, then dutifully telephoned the queen and queen mother who came to see the infant in the severe black of court mourning following the death of the king of Greece. It was not an auspicious omen.

10

"I Hate You"

In the months following Sarah's birth, close friends could see that there was undeniable strain in the Snowdons' four-year marriage. Though there was a frost between the couple, they were attentive, loving parents who clearly adored their two children.

As Tony's business manager Peter Lyster-Todd observed, "I would stay at their home for the weekend and they could not be more charming involved parents. She was an affectionate mother and there was no sense there was strain between the couple. When the children were away it was a very different story. Things were very brittle then."[1]

Behind the mask of civilized companionship, the truth was that they were clashing more frequently and more bitterly. While abroad on photographic assignment, Snowdon began having casual flings, some of which he would pursue when he returned to London. On one occasion Margaret's close friend Lieutenant Colonel "Johnny" Johnston visited the couple at Kensington Palace for dinner. Before leaving, he and the princess went to look for Tony so that Johnston could say goodbye. "We went into his room and he was on the phone," Johnston recalled. "It was obvious he was talking to someone he shouldn't have been. He had been caught in the telephonic equivalent of *in flagrante delicto*."[2] After he left, the couple had a huge row, with insults traded and objects thrown.

As her marriage deteriorated more rapidly, Margaret found herself in a desperate emotional spiral. He found her insistent needs stifling. A highly sexual young woman, she could not handle Tony's neglect and increasingly hungered for male attention. With Tony away on business and the children cared for primarily by their nanny, Margaret sought reassurance with the tall, darkly handsome Anthony Barton, Tony's friend from Cambridge, who was a Bordeaux wine producer and godfather to their daughter, Sarah. Given that Barton was such a close friend of the family, friends have speculated that Tony deliberately set him up with Margaret. Even Snowdon's former boss Jocelyn Stevens agreed, "I've no doubt that Barton was originally encouraged by Tony. If you yourself are playing around, then your conscience is eased if your partner does the same."[3]

In early 1966, with Tony abroad in India for the *Sunday Times*, Barton visited Margaret at Kensington Palace—allegedly at Tony's suggestion. That evening, Margaret made her move. "Let's go to bed," she boldly told a startled Barton, who replied, "No, I think our relationship's not that." The princess then inched closer and cooed, "Well, I think you could be a bit more cuddly."[4] A short-lived but passionate dalliance followed, until Margaret tearfully confessed to Barton's wife, Eva, over the telephone. According to a friend of the Barton family, Margaret divulged the secret because she "obviously enjoyed the role of *femme fatale*, a typical Leo—devious, destructive, and jealous." Whatever her motivation, if the princess hoped that the affair would stoke Snowdon's jealousy and bring him back, she was sorely mistaken. He did not just continue with the same behavior; it was now magnified.

Later that year, Margaret experienced another betrayal over the issue of their family's country home. When his uncle, Oliver Messel, offered to renovate the family's Old House in Sussex, Tony jumped at the opportunity. Margaret, meanwhile, wanted their country retreat to be a place that they planned jointly. She much preferred Sunninghill, which her sister had offered her so that they could be closer together. Unable to agree, they brought in an arbiter, who sided with Margaret, recommending they build something new at Sunninghill.

Although Tony outwardly complied with this decision, he secretly proceeded with expensive and immediate renovations of Old House. When Margaret discovered that he had backed out of their deal, she claimed she felt "crushed." She later told gossip writer Nigel Dempster: "Tony broke up the whole marriage by going there. We were going to build a house at Sunninghill by the lake where we water-skied and then, without telling me, he went off and started Old House."[5] Valiantly trying to hide her disappointment over her husband's devious fait accompli, Margaret attended the opening ceremony of their new country home. The queen mother snipped the ribbon and the queen led the cheering. Margaret only went there a few more times before refusing to visit altogether.

Around this time, a tragedy put all their marital troubles into perspective and, for a time, drew the family together. On October 21, 1966, the students and teachers at Pantglas Junior School in Aberfan, a village in Wales, were about to start their lessons when the entire schoolhouse was buried in an avalanche of mining waste. According to one survivor, "There was a roar like the end of the world."[6]

As the hours went by, it became apparent that scores of children and adults at the school were buried beneath the lava-like slurry. One of the most haunting memories was the long period of silence in the midst of the frantic digging as the rescue teams listened for voices underneath the mountain of rubble. None were heard. The final toll was staggering: 144 people dead, 116 of them children—half of Aberfan's child population.

The queen learned of the tragedy shortly after it occurred but waited eight days to visit. It was argued that her decision was made for practical reasons. "People will be looking after me. Perhaps they'll miss some poor child that might have been found under the wreckage," she reportedly said. Her courtiers made the argument to go, but she was resolute in remaining at Buckingham Palace. Instead her brother-in-law became the first member of the royal family to reach the scene of devastation, traveling by overnight train in a second-class compartment, a shovel tucked into his overnight bag.

At first, he tried to help with the digging, but soon realized he was only getting in the way of the rescue teams. So he then visited homes and hospitals, brewed cups of tea, and tried to comfort the bereaved relatives. After seeing the bodies of dead children in the morgue, he wrote a heartfelt note to Princess Margaret: "Darling, it was the most terrible thing I have ever seen... I tried to ring you again this morning but you weren't awake yet... It was all so awful seeing grown men, really tough miners, crying and crying. One turned to me and said: 'I've lost both mine—Tony, you'll understand, because you have two as well.'"[7] In a telephone message he asked Margaret to "Kiss the children for me."[8] When he later told the queen mother about his experiences, it was hard to hold back the tears as he talked about "the worst day of his life."[9]

Both Snowdon and Prince Philip, who arrived the following day, were praised for their compassion and approachability. The queen's delay in visiting, her former private secretary Lord Charteris later admitted, was the "biggest regret" of her reign.[10] Once she arrived, the sheer heartbreaking desolation touched her in a way that few events ever have. "Aberfan affected the Queen very deeply, I think when she went there. It was one of the few occasions in which she shed tears in public," her former private secretary Sir William Heseltine revealed. "I think she felt in hindsight that she might have gone there a little earlier. It was a sort of lesson for us that you need to show sympathy and to be there on the spot, which I think people craved from her." Her private acknowledgment of her own misjudgment deepened her growing and deepening respect for the correct instincts displayed by her brother-in-law.

While the Aberfan disaster brought Tony and Margaret together, it was short lived. By Christmas that year, the princess was imbibing too much of the festive spirit, smoking and drinking excessively. The princess, melancholic and despairing, took to calling friends in the dead of night to vent her grievances. One friend recalled, "She would ring at one or two in the morning and one would dress and go round and there she'd be in floods and the whisky bottle would be empty and he'd be in the basement."[11]

In the New Year she was admitted to King Edward VII's Hospital while her husband was working in Japan. While supposedly there for a "checkup," rumors abounded that the princess had made a cry for help, overdosing on pills and alcohol. The previous weekend, Margaret had telephoned a friend while he was hosting a party. She threatened that if he did not come check on her immediately, she would throw herself from her bedroom window. The friend frantically phoned the queen at Sandringham, who replied calmly, "Carry on with your house party. Her bedroom is on the ground floor."[12] The queen's response matched that of the queen mother and other members of the royal family. They lived in a world where illness was dealt with by going for a long walk, and mental illness was ignored altogether. Like the queen's approach to central heating—"if you are cold put on a sweater"—her response to sickness, especially her sister's, was brisk and no-nonsense.

A generation later, Princess Diana would experience similar uncomprehending indifference when she suffered from the eating disorder bulimia nervosa.

Yet even though the princess tended toward melodrama—as the queen knew all too well—it was impossible to deny the reality of her current depression. Soon after her hospital visit, she began another brief liaison, this time with Robin Douglas-Home, an aristocratic nightclub pianist and well-known womanizer who numbered Princess Margaretha of Sweden and possibly First Lady Jackie Kennedy among his many conquests. Coincidentally, Robin's uncle was Sir Alec Douglas-Home, who had been appointed amid great criticism—much of it directed at the queen—to succeed Harold Macmillan as Conservative prime minister in 1963. With Snowdon off in Japan, Margaret and Robin began meeting at Kensington Palace or at Robin's small home on Cromwell Road. According to one report, they were discovered by a servant in flagrante delicto on the sofa at Kensington Palace. She stared at the servant until he left the room and then carried on as though nothing had happened.

An experienced and attentive seducer, Robin made the princess feel desirable again. On Valentine's Day 1967, she wrote him a gushing letter: "Darling, thank you for a perfect weekend... Thank you for making me live again. Thank you for being gentle when it was unexpected, which gave me back my self-confidence. Thank you for everything nice, which everything was. With best love." She signed the letter simply "M."—something that she only did with Tony and that only Tony called her.[13]

Again she wrote: "I think all the time of you. This is a bleak time for love. Not many people are lucky enough to have known a love like this. I feel so happy it has happened to me."

How the letters surfaced in an American magazine was a subject Margaret agonized over soon enough, and the feverish press speculation about the affair forced Snowdon, then in New York, to make a public statement denying a marital crisis. Tony told jostling reporters, "Nothing has happened to our marriage. When I am away I write home and telephone like other husbands in love with their wives."[14] This lie especially wounded Margaret, as one of their main disagreements was over Tony's failure to call while he was away. Still, Tony continued to maintain the façade, issuing another statement on February 26, 1967: "Talk of a rift is totally unfounded. It's news to me and I would be the first to know. I am amazed." His imperturbable discretion was duly noted inside Buckingham Palace, where the mantra was "deny, deny, deny." Meanwhile, Margaret and Tony agreed to make a public gesture of reconciliation. In early March Margaret flew to New York to meet her husband at Kennedy Airport, and they then departed for the Bahamas, the couple staying at Jocelyn Stevens's holiday home at Lyford Cay. At this point separation, not to mention divorce, remained unthinkable—for the sake both of their children and the image of the monarchy.

Upon her return from the Bahamas, Margaret broke off her month-long affair with Robin, telling him, "It has to be done this way for appearance's sake." Even though he was an accomplished Lothario, he was shattered by his dismissal. From then on he went downhill, and he committed suicide eighteen months later. Margaret did not attend his funeral. Their priority was to protect themselves—and the reputation of the queen.[15]

At this time Margaret had other suitors, notably Peter Sellers, who was madly in love with her. He told clairvoyant Maurice Woodruff that he wanted to marry her and asked him to predict the best date. It was however, like his confession that he had an affair with Sophia Loren—a fantasy.

In spite of the façade of togetherness, the construction of Margaret's house on the island of Mustique was a clear sign that the couple was going their separate ways. Tony had made no secret of his loathing of the island or the people who owned it. Once it was completed, Margaret visited twice a year in February and late autumn. She would usually arrive alone, never with the children, who were left in the charge of nanny Verona Sumner. Always organized—like her sister—she even had special "holiday" jewelry reserved only for Mustique, namely a faux ruby-and-paste necklace and earrings, along with various coral items.[16] One of her abiding pleasures was collecting shells on the beach, her new consuming passion evident to visitors, who were asked to admire her displays.

Soon enough, though, Mustique became synonymous with Margaret's extravagant and excessive lifestyle, a fact that overshadowed her continued commitment to her royal duties. Without the clearly defined duty and noble commitment that Elizabeth displayed toward the crown, Margaret merely appeared to be a royal hanger-on, sponging off the public.

Her routine bread-and-butter engagements and in particular her fundraising work for the Royal Ballet and the children's charity NSPCC were conveniently ignored. As her popularity ratings plummeted, the princess was crestfallen at being so willfully underappreciated. It was as if flying to the Caribbean on holiday was a crime against the country—and the monarchy. Invariably, the controversy over her holidays dovetailed with questions about her allowance from the Civil List, the monies set aside to pay for the monarchy. Tabloid headlines demanded IS SHE WORTH IT? and DOES SHE EARN IT? In turn these attacks were accompanied by deliberately low figures for her public engagements.[17] She put on a brave face, saying, "I've been misreported and misrepresented since the age of seventeen and I gave up long ago reading about myself."[18] While much of routine royal work is tedium personified—as Snowdon soon discovered—the knack was to show interest in the uninteresting, and it was not a technique Margaret ever fully mastered. As a result, she earned more bad marks for seeming bored and ungracious and simply going through the motions. While the queen would always strive to appear engaged and responsive, Margaret's visits would often end early, the princess eager to return home.

She needed no encouragement to attend the investiture of her nephew Prince Charles at Caemarfon castle in July 1969. The princess was eager to see how her husband, who had been asked by the queen to organize the event, had articulated his vision of meshing ancient and modern elements for a ceremony, last performed in 1911, where the Prince of Wales dedicated his loyalty to the queen.

In the preamble to the big day, the queen and the rest of the family had taken part in the making of a documentary, *Royal Family*, which followed the Windsors for a year. While reluctant film star Princess Anne thought the project was a "rotten idea," more than 350 million people from around the world begged to disagree, tuning in to watch the royals at home and off duty. Among other delights, Prince Philip was filmed barbecuing, and the queen was shown taking young Prince Edward shopping for ice cream in Ballater. Significantly, the queen was seen cradling young Lady Sarah Armstrong-Jones in her arms on the royal yacht *Britannia* as the royal party sailed around the Scottish coast.

As was their routine, Sarah's parents were in the Mediterranean on board a friend's yacht. "I think sometimes the Snowdon children used to think of the Queen as mum," observed a friend.[19] Certainly she took a special interest in Sarah, who was born just a couple of months after Prince Edward, perhaps wanting to shield her niece from the difficulties facing her parents. During their childhood, Sarah and her brother David spent most of their summer holidays with the queen or queen mother at Balmoral and Birkhall. Sarah learned to ride under the tuition of the queen, eventually entering horse riding competitions, carefully watched by her aunt. In many ways, Elizabeth assumed the role of surrogate mother, doting on them as children and later encouraging them in their respective careers.

The projection of the queen as a normal mother rather than a remote symbol was the abiding success of the documentary, revolutionizing public attitudes toward the monarchy. It augured well for the investiture, though threats of violence from Welsh nationalists ensured that everyone was on tenterhooks, particularly Prince Charles. Thankfully the ceremony, movingly traditional but also cleverly modern, went without a hitch, and Snowdon received universal praise for his creation, especially as it had been achieved on a minuscule budget.

The queen, who had had her doubts about Tony's vision, was perhaps the most enthusiastic. In a long letter of thanks and congratulations, she admitted that at first she was skeptical that his dramatic interpretation would work. She was delighted to be proved wrong, describing the ceremony as "spectacular and breathtaking."[20] Her respect for his undoubted brilliance grew accordingly. In the investiture honors list, where she gave those involved in the historic ceremonial her personal awards, she made Snowdon a knight of the Grand Cross of the Royal Victorian Order, one of the most coveted awards she could grant.

A few weeks later, after spending time on Peter Sellers's yacht in the Mediterranean, the Snowdons flew to the Far East in September for a three-week tour of Japan, Hong Kong, Cambodia, Thailand, and Iran. The trip was grueling, filled with official engagements from early morning until late in the evening. Their hard work brought scant recognition, particularly for the princess, and the endless pressure caused a further rupture in their strained relations. By the end of the tour, they were no longer on speaking terms. At a reception held at the British embassy in Tehran, a fellow guest recalled the princess entering the room with a face like thunder and immediately asking for a drink. Then she put a cigarette in a long holder and began puffing away, all the while making no effort whatsoever to engage in small talk with other guests. It was clear that her marital problems were preventing her from behaving in the manner expected of her, a cardinal sin in the eyes of the queen and queen mother, who thought performing one's *devoir* or duty was a primary strength of the monarchy.

Matters came to a head with Margaret's discovery of her husband's affair with Lady Jacqueline Rufus Isaacs, the model daughter of the marquess and marchioness of Reading, who were neighbors of Tony's near Old House. Tony had often stopped by to share meals with the Reading family and met Lady Jackie when she was only fourteen. The unsuspecting Margaret actually liked Lady Jackie, who was fourteen years her junior, even adding her to the Kensington Palace invitation list.

During their affair, Snowdon would pick her up on his motorbike from the central London boutique where she worked and, after checking the coast was clear, spirit her away. On one occasion they drove to the Isle of Wight, where they boarded a speedboat and raced around the island, smoking joints during their high-speed escapade. Another time there was a near miss when Margaret dropped by Old House without warning. Jackie had quickly made herself scarce by hiding in the trunk of Tony's Aston Martin. Nonchalantly, Snowdon told John Larkin, their chauffeur, to take his Aston Martin to the village of Staplefield Green to get more petrol. Once he drove away, Larkin, knowing what was going on, stopped the car. Lady Jackie climbed out and coolly walked home across the fields.

During the festive season that year, the Snowdons visited one of Margaret's favorite nightclubs, Les Ambassadeurs. Photographers noticed that Margaret sat at one table, while Snowdon sat at another with Lady Jackie. Nothing could be proved, though Britt Ekland admitted observing "a closeness between the couple."[21] They continued their affair regardless, and even when Snowdon had an operation, it was noted that Lady Jackie visited the London Clinic more frequently than his wife. Margaret was deeply humiliated, lamely telling a friend, "I could nurse him, you know. When I was a Girl Guide I got a badge for nursing."

Eventually, in early 1971, a New York newspaper summoned up the courage to announce their affair—only to be met with flat denials from Lord Reading, Lady Jackie, as well as Buckingham and Kensington Palaces. Under pressure from her father, Lady Jackie admitted the truth, and the Readings threatened to have Snowdon horsewhipped for abusing their trust. The public revelation of his affair with Lady Jackie led to "open warfare" at Kensington Palace. A sign of Margaret's devastation was that she would sob on the consoling shoulder of Larkin, her chauffeur. Given the fact that she could spend an entire road journey without uttering a civil word to her driver indicated the depths of her despair.

Even though she had engaged in her own flirtations and occasional flings, she believed that she had done so only to feel desired again, while Tony's betrayal bordered on revenge. Even in the early years of her marriage, she had a covetous eye for the opposite sex. The princess had a decided technique for meeting potential paramours. As a member of the royal family, she realized that she had to initiate contact. Her friend Anne Glenconner was a reliable conduit, the princess sending her to a table at a restaurant or a ball to ask the chosen beau to come and join her. Lady Glenconner recalled: "She liked the gentlemen very much. If she saw somebody she would say: 'Who's that, I'd like to meet him.' Then I would ask who he was and bring him up."

At one ball in the 1960s, Mick Jagger and his then girlfriend Chrissie Shrimpton, the younger sister of model Jean, were at one table, Princess Margaret and Peter Sellers at the head table. The singer was invited to join them, leaving Chrissie on her own. She recalled: "So I went up to him while he was chatting to PM [Princess Margaret] and said: 'I'm leaving.'" As she started to walk out, Jagger stood up suddenly, making the table rattle and came after her. The Rolling Stones front man later got to know Margaret much better when he bought a place on Mustique. One Christmas he played the elf to Margaret's Santa Claus, the duo handing out presents to workers' children on the island.

Actor Brian Cox almost got a very unexpected twenty-third birthday present in June 1969 when Margaret came backstage after watching his performance in *In Celebration*, a mining drama set in the Midlands. He played a hooded figure, and it was clear that the princess was intrigued by the man behind the mask. The young actor was wearing a red shirt given to him for his birthday and was, in his words, still "glistening" after a shower. He recalled: "She put her fingers on my shirt, and said: 'This is a lovely shirt.' And she started to run her fingers down the inside of my shirt. And I went: Uh oh! What do you do when you're being touched up by a royal?" His costar James Bolam could see what was going on and went "Ooooh" out of the side of his mouth. The princess only had eyes for the future Oscar winner and kept saying that he looked so wonderfully hooded onstage that she wanted to know more about him. Cox recalled: "She was an extraordinary creature. I excused myself and said: 'Thank you, ma'am,' and it came to a natural end."[22] A former naval equerry recalls a similar encounter, the princess lasciviously looking him up and down when they were first introduced on board a BAe 146 jet of the Queen's Flight.[23]

The princess's sporadic flirtatious encounters were one thing, Snowdon's longtime affair with the daughter of his nearest neighbor another. For the moment, though, Margaret and Tony continued with their usual policy of keeping up appearances and ignoring the gossip. In the winter of 1972, they met in Barbados and made sure that photographers captured them embracing and staring lovingly into each other's eyes. However, behind the scenes, the Lady Jackie affair marked the beginning of the end of Margaret's marriage. By 1973, the Snowdons were barely on speaking terms, communicating largely through the princess's private secretary Lord Napier. They tried to avoid one another as much as possible, and if they had to spend time together, they would inevitably get involved in a row. Peter Sellers's secretary, Hattie Stevenson, recalled, "They used to say the most awful things to each other. I can remember dinner parties and they'd argue right across the table."[24]

It was soon evident to the inner circle that Tony was cleverer at being nasty, prepared to go to all manner of lengths to upset and wrong-foot his wife. Tony even resorted to writing cruel one-liners, such as "You're fat and I hate you," which he tucked away in her glove drawer, among her hankies, or inside her books. There was such a paper blizzard of unpleasantness that she couldn't bring herself to open her chest of drawers. Instead, she asked the maid to do it for her. One note said, "Twenty Four Reasons Why I Hate You." A crushed Margaret confided to a friend, "I can't think of twenty-four reasons to hate ANYBODY." And not every note was elaborate: One hidden in her bedside book simply declared, "I hate you."[25]

Battle was now joined in public, too. If she was singing at the piano, he would mimic her sarcastically or perform a mock curtsy behind her back. When they attended an official engagement together in the same car, he would roll down the window so that the sudden breeze would muss up Margaret's carefully styled hair. She frequently complained that Tony would purposely reduce her to tears before a grand event so that she would look puffy-faced and red-eyed. On occasion they even quarreled in the queen mother's presence, screaming at each other across the drawing room at Clarence House. One argument devolved into such animosity that the queen mother whispered to her page, Billy Tallon, "Come on, William, we're going—into the pantry. We're not privy to this."[26]

At some point Prince Philip's private secretary Lord Rupert Nevill became so concerned about their increasingly volatile marriage that when they came to stay with him, he arranged to have the subsequent row secretly recorded and had the tapes sent to a Harley Street psychiatrist for analysis. His verdict on the anonymous voices: "This lady needs help—and she needs it soon."[27]

But even as their relationship grew more vindictive, they remained sexually involved, their bitter arguments serving as a kind of foreplay.[28] According to one close friend, "It was the last thing to die in their relationship. Had it not been for the sex, their marriage would have collapsed far sooner. They had an incredible lust for each other. They would touch and squeeze each other in front of friends and strangers alike. There were times when they couldn't keep their hands off each other and one could sense them straining at the bit in their eagerness to get to the bedroom."[29]

❧

Princess Margaret described his sexual domination herself, saying that he would fling open the bedroom door and stand before her naked. "Well, what could I do?"[30]

This constant seesawing between passion and hostility took a toll on Margaret's health as she chain-smoked and drank whisky to numb her misery. While Tony remained slender and fashionable, she gained weight and started looking uncharacteristically frumpy. For once, the quality that had set her apart from her sister—her looks—now became a source of ridicule. The satirical magazine *Private Eye* went so far as to publish a cartoon depicting Snowdon telling Margaret, "Shut up you fat bitch and keep smiling."[31]

Though la Clock Court had become Dysfunction Junction, Margaret still "neither wanted nor approved of divorce,"[32] partly for the sake of the children, her religious faith, and her pride, and partly because she didn't want to disappoint the queen. Both sisters still associated divorce with their uncle's abdication to marry Wallis Simpson, the shameful event that had brought them to this moment in the first place. Both the queen mother and the queen were completely opposed to the idea, not just because of the harm to the children but because of the negative impact on the monarchy as well.

Furthermore, the queen remained very fond of Lord Snowdon, who managed to act in the most affable, solicitous manner toward her even as he harassed his wife in private. Both the queen and queen mother tended to believe that much of the blame lay at Margaret's door. From their vantage point, Snowdon was beyond reproach, with his wit, natural finesse and talent as well as his impeccable manners. Since they did not see him often, the darker aspects of his temperament remained strategically hidden. By contrast, the queen knew only too well that Margaret could be arrogant, spoiled, and inconsiderate. She appreciated that only Tony could persuade Margaret to fulfill royal engagements that she didn't want to attend. Whenever the princess tried to invent excuses for backing out, Tony would act as mediator and persuader. After he spoke to her privately, Margaret would invariably announce, "I think I will go after all."[33] Thus the sympathy cards were stacked against her because Tony had endeared himself to the two women in her life who were closest to her. It more than rankled.[34]

Then along came Roddy.

11

"My Darling Angel"

In the summer of 1973, Roddy Llewellyn was working as a lowly researcher at the College of Arms in central London when out of the blue he received a phone call from a complete stranger that would change his life forever. In the process it would rupture relations between the queen and her sister and place the monarchy on trial.

On the other end of the phone was Princess Margaret's lady-in-waiting, Anne Glenconner, who explained that she was organizing a weekend party at Glen, their home in Peeblesshire in the Scottish Borders, and that a guest had dropped out at the last minute. Would he like to take his place to make up numbers?

She explained that she had been given his name by her husband's aunt, Violet Wyndham, who knew his father, the Olympic gold medalist show jumper Sir Harry Llewellyn. As a sweetener she offered to pay his train fare to Edinburgh and promised that her husband, Colin, would pick him up from the station. Oh, and by the way, she added, Princess Margaret would be present. Roddy accepted the intriguing invitation and started to pack. So began an adventure that would rock the House of Windsor.

When the stranger on the train arrived at Edinburgh station, Colin took him for lunch at the Café Royale bistro, where he met Princess Margaret and Colin's son, Charlie. The princess, who knew his father, immediately clicked with the rather shy young man who was nearly eighteen years her junior. Though not the alpha male type she usually was attracted to, Roddy had other social gifts. When he was in top form he was a marvelous raconteur, able to hold his own around any dinner table. Even the loquacious comedian Kenneth Williams was impressed, recalling in his diaries: "He's one of the few people I've ever come upon who knows how to tell a story."[1]

From the beginning, though, there was a sexual undercurrent between the princess and the pauper. Margaret, hearing that he didn't have a pair of swimming trunks, insisted on taking him to a store, where he modeled a tight pair of Speedos, colloquially known as "budgie smugglers," emblazoned with a Union Jack design. By the time they arrived at Glen, the duo were on the verge of holding hands. The chemistry was so obvious that Anne Glenconner said to her husband, "Oh gosh, what have we done?"[2]

What they had done was introduce the princess to someone who would lift her spirits at a time when she was arguably at the lowest ebb in her life. Her marriage, now a sour, empty husk, was over in all but name, as Tony had embarked on a serious affair with the woman who would become his second wife, Lucy Lindsay-Hogg, the daughter of an Irish clothing manufacturer. In the beginning she worked as a film assistant for a documentary he and broadcaster Derek Hart were making. The professional very soon turned to personal, their

budding romance helped by the fact that they were work colleagues and could pass off meetings in public as related to
their current project. Margaret, lonely and neglected, found
the perfect pick-me-up with the inoffensive, somewhat inex-
perienced twenty-five-year-old. Until the princess came into
his world, he had led a nomadic, aimless existence. He was a
young man who was prone to depression and had kept himself
afloat with a series of odd jobs. In company he was amusing:
He could hold a tune and liked a sing-along—a perfect foil for
Margaret. During their time at Glen he joined her in a jaunty
rendition of her favorite, Glenn Miller's "Chattanooga Choo
Choo," while she sported a red dress in the style of a Southern
belle and he pranced around in a mini kilt.

Roddy was entertaining, he was thoughtful, but above all he
was kind, a quality that had been in distinctly short supply for
the last few years of Margaret's married life. His effect on her
was immediate. Before the young man whom she called "my
darling angel" came into her life, she was a wreck. Her drinking was seriously out of control, and she was getting heavier
through comfort eating. Now she had lost weight, cut down her
alcohol consumption, and regained her zest for life. Once they
returned to London, Roddy moved into his own apartment in
Fulham, which the princess helped decorate. Unbeknownst
to him, it was only two doors away from the home of Snowdon's photographer friend Bob Belton. Snowdon took perverse
delight in blocking in Margaret's Rolls-Royce with his own car
when she visited her youthful lover.

Though Roddy had put a spring in Margaret's step, the
queen and queen mother hoped against hope that the Snowdons could resolve their differences and put their marriage
back on track—at least for the sake of the children. The
arrival of Roddy on the scene merely complicated an already

difficult situation. In public Margaret and Tony continued to call each other "Darling" and were attentive to one another. They behaved as a couple on formal royal occasions, such as the twenty-fifth wedding anniversary of the queen and Prince Philip at Westminster Abbey, though the irony of the celebration was not lost on the warring couple.

In reality they were living such separate lives that when Tony went into a London hospital for a hernia operation in November 1973, his mistress was his most frequent visitor. When Margaret, who was in the country with friends when the operation took place, finally visited him, she was upset to find Lucy by his bedside. But of course, it worked both ways. When Roddy returned to London, the princess was delighted to entertain him at her palace home or at the Chelsea home of the Tennants. Not so her husband, who demanded, "Tell your friend to keep out of my house!"[3] before heading off to spend the night with his mistress.

While Tony was able to conduct his affair with discretion, Margaret was more exposed, given the media interest in her life. Yet the circle of secrecy held, and Margaret invited Roddy to join her in Mustique in February 1974, with the Glenconners in attendance.

The aspiring landscape designer, who replanted the garden at Les Jolies Eaux during his stay, soon got into the island rhythm: late breakfasts overlooking the breathtaking blue waters of Gelliceaux Bay, lazy but competitive games of Scrabble on the terrace, picnic lunch at Macaroni Beach, dinner, charades, and singing in the evening. One of the favorite games was for a guest to recite a limerick, and once they completed the verse, the watching throng would join with a raucous chorus. Singer Dana Gillespie, who played Mary Magdalene in the first London musical production of *Jesus Christ Superstar*, recalls the evening when the woman she called "Ma'am" delivered her ditty. It went:

There once was a man from St Pauls
Who did a turn on the halls
His favorite trick was to stand on his dick
And freewheel off the stage on his balls.

Dana recalled: "When that comes out of Ma'am's voice it is exquisitely hilarious."[4]

Not so funny was the stressfully schizophrenic nature of Margaret's life once she returned to London. After the relaxed Caribbean idyll with Roddy, she was with her husband in May for an official visit to the United States to watch the famous Kentucky Derby and attend a performance of the Royal Ballet in New York. Because of their bright smiles and friendly body language, few, if any, of the attendant members of the media had a clue about the seething cauldron of despair and indifference brewing beneath the surface.

When someone pointed out that the duchess of Windsor was staying in the Waldorf Towers—the same hotel as Margaret and Tony—he suggested they go to see her. Though Margaret bridled—doubtless thinking of the reaction of her mother—she was soon convinced, and the couple spent fifteen minutes with the now reclusive duchess whose intersection in the life of Margaret's uncle had shaped her own life forever. Snowdon's media instincts proved true—the photograph of the duchess and the princess went around the world, demonstrating that the public was still fascinated by the woman who caused a king to abdicate his throne all those years ago.

Whatever sense of conciliation the trip might have suggested to the outside world was shattered when the princess asked her husband to move out that June. He refused. Caught in the middle of this marital grinding machine, Roddy, inoffensive but somewhat fragile, was faced with an angry husband on one side and an older, more worldly lover who became increasingly possessive and demanding, both emotionally and sexually. Confused, bewildered, and well out of his depth, he got out of Dodge and went on the run, heading to Heathrow airport and taking a flight to Turkey, where he traveled the country for several weeks on a bus as he tried to recover his shaky equilibrium. When he returned, his friends were concerned that he had suffered a mental breakdown, and indeed, for the next three weeks he was an inpatient at the Charing Cross hospital before going back to the family home in Wales.

⁓

His collapse had direct consequences for the queen and the crown.

Roddy's sudden disappearance left Margaret in tatters. Unable to sleep, she ended up taking too many tranquilizers and had to cancel all her royal engagements. On November 15, 1974, it was announced that she had caught a severe chill, which, given her heavy smoking and drinking, was believable. However, rumors persisted that she had tried to commit suicide. After leaving the hospital, she retreated to her bedroom and refused to leave. Her friends had to rotate caring for her day and night until exhaustion finally pushed one of them to call the queen and explain the reality of her sister's situation.

Though not naturally empathetic to sick people, the queen set aside her engagements and drove to Kensington Palace to see the ailing princess. "I feel exactly like the night nurse taking over from the day nurse,"[5] she said. Helped by her maid, Margaret was led out to the car, which then whisked her and her sister away for a recuperative weekend together at Windsor—and a chance to find out what was really going on in Margaret's life. She was able to take a more robust stance with her sister than any of her ladies-in-waiting. As nonroyals, they may have tactfully suggested a course of action but found their advice ignored. They could suggest but not command. The queen was able to go where a diplomatic lady-in-waiting feared to tread. While the queen was always reluctant to become directly involved in her sister's dramas, always hoping that they may resolve themselves, on this occasion "big sister" came to the rescue. Indeed Margaret's lady-in-waiting Lady Glenconner always argued that the four-year age gap between the sisters ensured that Margaret was, ultimately, more compliant. "There would have been more rivalry if there had been less of an age gap," she now says.[6]

The next twist in the marital drama shocked even Margaret's imperturbable sister. In June 1975, after recuperating in the Welsh countryside, Roddy joined a commune at Surrendell, a forty-seven-acre farm in Wiltshire, where some of his aristocratic friends, along with various actors and artists, were attempting to create a self-sufficient community. For extra income, they opened a restaurant, with Roddy, now elevated to the position of head gardener, providing fresh produce from the farm's market garden. Now much calmer, he and Margaret resumed their relationship but without the intensity and neediness that had characterized the first frenetic few months. The Surrendell commune had a peaceful ambiance that gave Roddy the space, both physical and mental, to heal himself and his royal relationship, which they now described as a "loving friendship." As communication with the commune was difficult, the

Tennants, once again, acted as go-betweens. Every Thursday Roddy drove from Surrendell to their house in Chelsea to see Margaret, who arrived from Kensington Palace with a picnic hamper.

After listening to Roddy's tales of life in a commune, Margaret decided that she wanted to visit to see what all the fuss was about. On one occasion she even spent the night there. Her decision created front-page headlines around the world and caused panic at the palace.

Margaret arrived by Rolls-Royce and sent her driver to find accommodation in the village. Then she joined fellow residents in a game of mah-jongg, noting that she was rather rusty, as it was the first time she had played since she was a child. Later, drink and ubiquitous cigarette in hand, she joined with the rest of the throng singing show tunes in front of the blazing log fire after the party had returned from a local restaurant. That night Princess Margaret stayed in the most comfortable bedroom while Roddy slept in his blue Ford Transit van. In the morning Roddy brought her a cup of tea in bed. It is as well he did, as she struggled to work the on-off switch of an electric kettle. (Her sister was little better—she was unable to run her morning bath without assistance.) After her morning cup of tea, Margaret donned rubber boots and helped him in the garden.

A later arrival was actor Helen Mirren, sex symbol, Shakespearian stage star, and member of the radical Socialist Workers Party. Though there was an initial frisson, the two women bonded—both were strong, independent, and rather rebellious and had a healthy interest in sex. Margaret would have found it amusing to know that the young radical firebrand she first met in a Wiltshire farmhouse would one day play her sister in an Oscar-winning movie, *The Queen*. Margaret may have noticed, too, that Roddy seemed somewhat smitten by Helen. As he later told writer Ivan Waterman: "She was very striking, irresistibly delicious. There are very few women I have met who exude sex from every pore but she was and is one."

⁓

Another visitor who also caught his attention and would ultimately change Roddy's life was Tania Soskin, the daughter of film producer Paul Soskin. When he reflected on that first meeting with the woman who later became his wife he said, "I knew she was the one."[7]

In a summer when punk bands like the Sex Pistols put two fingers up at the establishment, Surrendell was seen as a provocative outpost of skinny-dipping, free love, and pot smoking. When news of Margaret's presence leaked out, the lane outside the farm was packed with reporters and cameramen. Roddy made himself scarce, and the commune's days were numbered when the police subsequently discovered almost three hundred cannabis plants under cultivation.

The discovery of an illegal marijuana farm and headlines such as MARGARET'S DARLING ANGEL ON THE DOLE![8]— suggesting that jobless Roddy was claiming benefits from the state—were incendiary. Margaret's visit to a hippie den of iniquity—as the tabloids saw it—was a colossal mistake. While the queen sympathized with Margaret's marital difficulties, she was not so forgiving of her sister's retreat to a colony of aristocratic hippies or her relationship with a rootless dropout. As for Prince Philip's view, it was not difficult to imagine.

This association could only bring calumny. The exasperated queen, her patience exhausted, lamented to her private secretary, Lord Martin Charteris, "What are we going to do about my sister's guttersnipe life?"[9] She had always felt responsible for her sister and worried about what to do with her. No more so than now. In her heart she had hoped that Margaret and Tony could at least have lived under the same roof while leading independent lives; monarchy was all about appearances. Snowdon, as a talented photographer, knew that better than most—including, it seemed, his wife. While the queen was more flexible and forgiving about the issue of divorce than her mother, they were both deeply concerned that Princess Margaret could become the first member of the royal family to divorce since Henry VIII and Anne of Cleves in 1540.

Events, however, were now moving apace. In October Margaret and Tony were due to undertake a ten-day tour of Australia. Margaret could no longer continue the charade, telling her private secretary Lord Napier that if Tony went, she wouldn't go. So it was decided to pretend that Tony had to stay home for work commitments and that Margaret would go with her lady-in-waiting Anne Glenconner instead. Naturally, the Australian media sensed marital discord, but by giving briefings to reporters during a twelve-hour train ride from Canberra to Melbourne, Margaret was able to tame the local press for the time being. However, she was only putting off the inevitable.

Snowdon, his own affair a secret, took the moral high ground and wrote a letter to the queen at the end of 1975 clarifying his view on their failed marriage. He stated that he could no longer tolerate their turbulent life at Kensington Palace: "The atmosphere is appalling for all concerned—the children, the staff, the few remaining loyal friends and she and I both."[10]

The queen responded three weeks later, admitting that the delay had been caused by her despair over his letter. She suggested that she was already aware of how unsustainable the situation had become, but she pleaded with Snowdon not to take any hasty steps before Christmas. Snowdon, deeply respectful of the queen's wishes, took a vow of silence, as requested.

Behind the scenes, though, the palace began frantically preparing for the worst. The queen certainly did not want the situation to come to a head in 1977, the year scheduled for her Silver Jubilee, an event several years in the preparation. This historic event was one of the waypoints in the queen's reign, a grand pageant that was seen as a reaffirmation of the compact between the monarchy and the crown. The queen—and other members of the royal family—accepted as a matter of course that private and personal issues were sacrificed in the name of duty and obligation to the monarchy. The crown came first. This was graphically demonstrated by Queen Mary, who, shortly before she died in March 1953, made it clear that court mourning must be limited so as not to interfere with the upcoming coronation. She placed duty before self to her very last breath.

During the queen's reign, however, Margaret and her personal problems kept getting in the way of major royal events. Her love affair with Group Captain Peter Townsend had, at one point, threatened to overshadow the coronation, an action that would have been unforgivable. Now, as preparations were under way for the Silver Jubilee, it was feared that Margaret's marital issues may now rain on her sister's parade.

The queen's response was essentially practical—how and when the separation announcement could be made so that it was in the best interests of the Snowdons' children and without affecting the tentpole royal events that took months to plan and prepare for. She and her ministers thus decided that the best time to announce a separation would be Easter 1976, as the children, David and Sarah, could receive the news quietly when they were at home for the holidays.

There were other considerations. Just a few days after Snowdon's letter was handed to the queen, her prime minister, Harold Wilson, told her that he intended to resign in March 1976. He would only stay on if Margaret created further calamity for the queen or if there was an outbreak of terrorist violence in Northern Ireland, which was convulsed by paramilitary conflict in the long struggle for Irish independence. "I'm not going to leave her on her own," the outgoing prime minister told a royal aide.[11]

Through a twist of fate, the palace got the timeline they desired—though at great cost to Princess Margaret. On February 1, 1976, fuzzy photos taken by New Zealand photographer Ross Waby appeared in the Sunday tabloid *News of the World* showing Margaret and Roddy sitting side by side at Basil's Bar on Mustique. He was wearing his Union Jack swimming trunks, and she was in a modest one-piece bathing suit, though the tabloids preferred to call it a "skimpy bikini." These pictures looked just intimate enough to be compromising, although just to make sure that readers focused only on the princess and her boyfriend, they cropped out the princess's friends Viscount Thomas Coke and his wife, Valeria, who were sitting at the same table as Margaret and her "tanned toy boy."

As the row exploded, the same tabloid seemed to have a man positioned in the room with the queen when she called Margaret on the long-distance telephone. "How could you do this to me, to the family, to the monarchy," she was quoted as saying. "How could you have been so silly?"[12] Even if the quotes were tabloid make-believe, for many they had the ring of truth.

For the princess it was a disaster, not just in terms of public relations but with respect to the two women who mattered most in her life, the queen and queen mother. As much as they loved Margaret, they were very fond of Snowdon and felt that the princess must shoulder much of the blame for the end of the marriage. They weren't privy to the detailed ins and outs of the breakdown, but they knew Margaret's character. As her friend and biographer Christopher Warwick observed, "They didn't realise the depths of Margaret's despair. They remembered her as the trickster, the prankster, the little girl getting things her way. There was a feeling it was mainly her fault."[13] This conclusion was emphasized in the official biography of the queen mother by William Shawcross, where Roddy Llewellyn's name alone is linked to the marriage breakdown. There is no mention of Snowdon's long-term relationship with Lucy Lindsay-Hogg, whom he eventually married.

Nor was her name mentioned in the tabloid stories that greeted the publication of pictures of Margaret and Roddy in Mustique. In the public's mind, Lord Snowdon was a hard-working documentary maker and photographer whose work with the impoverished, the elderly, and other disadvantaged groups had earned much acclaim. He was seen as the wronged party in this marital breakdown, his relationship with his girlfriend unknown to the wider public. The story became more than just about an extramarital relationship but also about whether the taxpayer was inadvertently paying for Margaret's holiday in the sun.

∽

Meanwhile, at Kensington Palace, Lord Snowdon summoned Lord Napier to his office and demanded an explanation for the photos. The exasperated Napier pointed out Tony's hypocrisy, saying that Tony knew perfectly well that Margaret and

Roddy were in a relationship, just as he himself was having an affair with TV producer Lucy Lindsay-Hogg. The major difference was that Tony had been able to conduct his affair with discretion.

Not hearing the answer he wanted, Tony buzzed his secretary, Dorothy Everard, and proclaimed, "Dotty. We're moving out."[14] Then, turning to Napier, he stated, "We'll be out by the end of the week." An overjoyed Napier now had to find a way to relay the news to the princess in Mustique, where long-distance calls were not very private, so he used a simple code. Once she was on the line he cryptically told her: "Ma'am I have been talking to Robert and he has given in his notice."

After a pause, the princess said, "I'm sorry, Nigel, have you taken leave of your senses? What exactly did you say?" Napier repeated, "Robert has given notice." After another long pause, Margaret finally realized that Tony's third Christian name was Robert. Without batting an eyelash, she replied, "Oh, I see. Thank you, Nigel. I think that's the best news you've ever given me."[15]

True to his word, Tony promptly moved out of Kensington Palace and then wasted no time in writing to the queen again to say that he had been publicly humiliated and was the injured party. Initially the queen had asked the couple to try to resolve their differences. When that strategy failed, she asked them at the very least to remain civil in public and conduct their private lives with discretion. Snowdon had done this; Margaret and her boyfriend had made the front pages. Whatever she thought—or knew—of Snowdon's extramarital relations, at least he had passed the test of privacy. Finally and very reluctantly the queen admitted that the pretense had to end. As with Margaret's romance with Peter Townsend, she had kicked the can down the road, hoping that the Snowdons could reach a civilized accommodation. They obviously couldn't. They decided that an immediate separation was the best way forward. The two children were to stay with their mother at Kensington Palace, while their father could visit them freely and would also receive a six-figure sum from Margaret in order to purchase his own property. On March 19, 1976, the separation was officially announced from Kensington Palace: "HRH The Princess Margaret, the Countess of Snowdon, and the Earl of Snowdon have agreed mutually to live apart. The Princess will carry out her public duties and functions unaccompanied by Lord Snowdon. There are no plans for divorce proceedings."[16]

The D-word. Divorce, or the prospect of divorce, had cursed the House of Windsor again. The queen made it clear through her press secretary Ronald Allison that no pressure had been placed on either party by her. The only pressure had been to encourage the warring parties to find a way forward together. That policy had clearly failed.

The queen was dismayed by this turn of events, saddened by the prospect that her sister might never find happiness. She was aware also that for a deeply religious woman, Margaret must have gone through agonies to come to this lonely decision. Yet she was a woman who gave in to the temptation of the flesh, again and again. She craved love and companionship inside and outside of marriage. Her faith was both a blessing and a curse. It gave her comfort but also brought her guilt. Did Margaret look to the Almighty to forgive her sins so that she could continue to live by whatever moral code she chose? Over the years it seems that her search for happiness and contentment ultimately compromised her deep religious commitment. Her behavior was all the more complex, as the princess herself opposed divorce. The queen also knew how proud Margaret was and how loyal, not just toward herself but toward the institution of the monarchy. Yet she didn't always behave in a way that burnished the name of the House of Windsor. She had two implacable taskmasters: the values of the monarchy and the morality of the Church of England. She had set herself an almost impossible bar to measure herself against, and all too often her actions compromised her standards.

What troubled the queen as well was her keen appreciation of the human cost behind the blaring headlines, namely the effect on the children, David and Sarah. She adored the Snowdon children and appreciated Lord Snowdon as a fine father. In the months after the separation, she made it her business to spend time with the children, ensuring that they took holidays with her at Balmoral and jolly weekends at Windsor. "They loved the Queen and she loves them," a friend observed.[17]

The very same day as the separation announcement, Snowdon flew off to Australia to prepare for an exhibition of his photographs. Once in Sydney, he appeared on television, looking utterly disconsolate as he delivered his prepared statement. "I am naturally desperately sad in every way that this had to come. I would just like to say three things: firstly to pray for the understanding of our children; secondly to wish Princess Margaret every happiness for her future; thirdly to express with the utmost humility my love, admiration and respect I will always have for her sister, her mother, and her entire family."[18] It was a public relations coup, and Princess Margaret commented acidly, "I have never seen such good acting."

As for Roddy, he sensibly kept his head down, hiding out at the farm of his friend Diane Cilento, the ex-wife of actor Sean Connery. In a brief statement, he told the Press Association,

"I much regret any embarrassment caused to Her Majesty the Queen and the royal family, for whom I wish to express the greatest respect, admiration and loyalty." He thanked his family and friends for their support and then asked for privacy. That wasn't likely to happen.

∽

Meanwhile Margaret licked her wounds and spent time with her mother, at Royal Lodge, or with friends who kept her company during the long lonely days at Kensington Palace. Duty, or as the queen mother liked to say, *devoir*, was the elixir that brought her back to life. She made state visits to Monaco, Morocco—where she said it was like being kidnapped—Cyprus, Italy, and the United States. Brightening the occasional evenings was a new friend, Elton John, who enchanted both the princess and her mother when he gave private royal command performances at Royal Lodge. Perhaps the highlight of a difficult year was her attendance as guest of honor at Colin Tennant's fiftieth birthday extravaganza on Mustique, now the island of choice for the international jet set. In the buildup to the elaborate "Gold Night" fancy dress ball, Colin had the sand and palm trees painted gold. Of course the guests wore gold costumes, and the princess, her skin specially darkened, looked suitably alluring in a bejeweled caftan and turban. She danced the night away, not with Roddy, who remained in England to study for a horticultural diploma, but with an even younger man, the island's artist in residence, Andrew Hewkin.

The following year saw the first visit to Mustique by the queen and Prince Philip, the couple arriving on board the royal yacht *Britannia* during the Silver Jubilee celebrations in November 1977. If it was a gesture of reconciliation and a chance for Margaret to show her sister that the island was not a Caribbean outpost of Sodom and Gomorrah, then it was a resounding success. After viewing Les Jolies Eaux and enjoying a picnic on the beach, the queen went swimming—a very rare occurrence—in Macaroni Bay, while Prince Philip went snorkeling in Black Sand Bay, where he could see sharks giving birth. When the royal couple first arrived, the islanders' costumes caught the queen's eye: They were dressed in clothing dating back to Victorian times. "I had no idea that Mustique was in a Victorian time warp," the queen, somewhat perplexed, said to her sister.[19] Margaret explained that Colin Tennant's mother had bought a job lot of ancient fancy dress for the locals, thinking it would be fun. After explaining the joke, Margaret then proceeded to show the queen around her island "kingdom."

In spite of media speculation that Roddy would be in residence on the island, during the queen's brief visit he was flying from London to join the princess later. He intended to arrive after the queen and Prince Philip had left. As he waited in Barbados for his connecting flight to Mustique, the royal party boarded the Concorde to return to London. At that moment eagle-eyed photographers captured Roddy boarding an island hopper, which caused the trainee gardener to be accused of trying to draw attention to himself. He passed off his proximity to the royal party as "awful bad timing."

Even though the queen disapproved of Roddy, he remained a central part of Margaret's life, soothing, consoling, and reviving her depleted spirits. They became more public, attending the theater together, on one occasion with Margaret's friend, Lord St John Stevas; swimming in the Buckingham Palace pool; and jointly hosting dinner parties at Kensington Palace. Once guests got used to the absence of Tony, they found her new lover agreeable, amusing, and thoughtful toward the princess. That mattered a lot, especially after the years of embarrassing antagonism from Tony.

The gardener was keen to branch out. With the encouragement of the princess, he endeavored to exploit his singing ability and signed an album deal to record a collection of easy listening standards. His album, titled *Roddy*, attracted much comment and publicity but, after briefly charting on the BBC, it sank without trace. However, he did sing a duet with Petula Clark, which was broadcast on French television. This venture was followed by a lucrative offer to promote a controversial new nightclub in Battersea, south London, called Bennett.

Inevitably, he was accused of cashing in on his association with the princess, who remained his biggest cheerleader. After fulfilling his commercial obligations, in March he flew out to Mustique to join Margaret on her regular spring holiday. Within hours of arriving he was taken ill, suffering a gastrointestinal hemorrhage. As it could be a life-threatening condition, he was flown to a hospital in Barbados for observation. Two days later he was visited by the princess, who spent her time sunning herself as Roddy slowly recovered. Once again her timing could not have been worse.

The sour narrative of the pleasure-loving, self-indulgent princess and her boy-toy lover was now fixed in the popular imagination. His illness coincided with a Parliamentary review of payments to members of the royal family on the Civil List, the funds allocated to members of the royal family by the taxpayer. The princess was dubbed a "royal parasite" by one lawmaker while another complained that she had only fulfilled eight engagements in the previous three months, at a cost of around £14,000. Roddy didn't help their cause when he returned to Britain and told reporters, "I shall go on seeing Princess Margaret when and where I want. Let them all criticize—I don't mind. I certainly don't believe that Princess Margaret has done anything to give the royal family a bad name, as suggested."[20]

Lawmakers, bishops, and the public begged to differ. Unlike the Townsend affair and her romance with Snowdon, Margaret was now a separated mother of two youngsters. In the public's mind the blame for the collapse of her marriage was largely laid at her door, and Roddy Llewellyn was seen as instrumental in encouraging her self-indulgent behavior. The wave of disapproval and vitriol was now lapping round the gates of the monarchy, and it was deeply concerning for the queen and her advisers. As much as she loved her sister, she was baffled by her fixation with a much younger man who did not seem worthy of her attention or affection. In April the tabloid *Sun* newspaper claimed that the queen had told her sister to choose between her royal duties or her lover. "GIVE UP RODDY OR QUIT," it shouted.[21] Though the story, known in the trade as a "flier," as it was based on shaky or nonexistent information, was false, insofar as Margaret had never discussed with her sister renouncing Roddy or her allowance, it struck a popular nerve. Undoubtedly, though, the queen was concerned about her sister and felt that she was going through a bad patch in her life. As one of her friends told historian Ben Pimlott: "The queen sometimes found it hard to cope with Princess Margaret. She wondered: 'What am I going to do with her?'"[22]

As her former private secretary Lord Charteris admitted, "She thought the Princess was behaving badly."[23] Her previous prime minister Harold Wilson had offered to delay his retirement to deal with this difficult family matter; now the hot potato landed in the lap of his successor, the avuncular James Callaghan. Among the options discussed was whether Princess Margaret should be removed from the Civil List and allowed to lead a private life. According to the *Daily Telegraph*, the queen strenuously objected to this proposal, pointing out how much her sister did to support her and the monarchy. She had been given a bad rap. There the matter remained—for the time being.[24]

Still, the Roddy factor remained toxic. An opinion poll published in April 1978 showed that nearly three-quarters of the public felt that the relationship harmed Margaret's standing as a member of the royal family.[25] Their love affair pushed buttons deep in the national psyche—if he had been older and wealthy, would they have cared as much? Margaret was the original cougar, so dangerous that many wanted her caged. There was a double standard operating here. While Snowdon and his partner were barely mentioned by the media, the narrative centered on Margaret and her boy-toy lover. She was scrutinized in much harsher light than a man would be in her position, as their affair took place at a time when older women dating younger men had not yet been accepted by the mainstream.

At the same time there was also the simple matter of climate. As increasingly strike-bound Britain shivered and moaned, with mounds of uncollected trash filling the streets, the sight of Margaret enjoying the sunshine was too much for some to take—as too were pictures of Roddy in the royal Rolls-Royce being chauffeured to Heathrow.

ᕙᔕ

After an angry near riot outside Bennett nightclub in Battersea, where irate residents clashed with partygoers, it was suggested that Roddy, who was viewed, unfairly, as the public face of this disastrous enterprise, make himself scarce and fly to Morocco.

The divorce and the vicious publicity surrounding her relationship with Roddy had taken a severe toll on Margaret's health. She was unable to attend her daughter's confirmation on April 5, 1978, because of a severe case of flu and then, after a brief rally, found herself in an isolation ward at King Edward VII Hospital suffering from hepatitis. Her doctors asked her to refrain from drinking alcohol and stick to barley water instead. On May 10, just before she was released from the hospital, the official divorce statement was announced from Kensington Palace. It said that after a separation of two years the royal couple had "agreed that their marriage should formally be ended." The following day, when she was released, the appearance of the newly divorced princess shocked many. Gone was the gamine, glamorous woman of yesteryear. Margaret looked gray, exhausted, and very middle-aged. Under her doctor's advice, she suspended official engagements for a month.

In her incapacitated state the princess appeared an unlikely ally of the queen. In her divorce statement, however, she made it clear that she had no plans to remarry and intended instead to commit the rest of her life to serving the queen.

To emphasize the point, while he was in Morocco Roddy told journalists that he would never marry Princess Margaret, as personal reasons would prevent it. That was a relief all around. He added for good measure, "I don't consider myself in any way responsible for the divorce."[26]

In the summer of 1978 she was well enough to drive to Glen to join Roddy and the Glenconners to celebrate their fifth anniversary and then on to Balmoral for her forty-eighth birthday. In September she flew to the South Pacific to represent the queen at the granting of independence to the island of Tuvalu, but once more illness struck her down. The princess, who was staying on board the New Zealand frigate *Otago*, suffered a debilitating attack of viral pneumonia, waking in the middle of the night unable to breathe and with such a high temperature that she lapsed into delirium. "I very nearly died," she later revealed.[27] She was flown to the nearest hospital in Sydney, where she recuperated for nine days before continuing with the rest of her program. The princess, contrary to her public image, was determined not to let anyone down, even though she had every reason to cancel the tour.

Margaret's hedonistic lifestyle, her younger lover, and her passion for the tropics made her seem exotic, unpredictable, and decadent—perhaps rightly so. After her divorce, her image inspired a subgenre of newspaper stories, television documentaries, and even a big-screen movie centered around her apparently lascivious behavior. The woman who loved ballet, the theater, and theological discussion no longer existed in the popular imagination.

Her brief encounter on Mustique in the early 1970s with British gangster and part-time actor John Bindon sparked this explosion of interest. A few years later, in 1978, he was acquitted of the murder of another East End rogue, John Darke. After his release, his girlfriend, baronet's daughter Vicki Hodge, negotiated a £40,000 fee with the *Daily Mirror* for Bindon to serialize his life story with the emphasis on his alleged relationship with Princess Margaret.

He had openly boasted about having sex on the beach with the princess, with Hodge backing up his claims, noting that when they first met over lunch on the island, Margaret was intrigued by "his cockney accent, his rhyming slang, and dirty jokes."[28] Hodge recalled, "When I saw them together, they were magnetized to each other, they were obviously involved.

You could tell it in their body language. The fact that I was his girlfriend didn't really matter. It was, 'Step aside, baby.'" Bindon also claimed that when he returned to London, the princess continued to see him, sending her car to pick him up for trysts at the palace.

Though tantalizingly salacious, for the most part Bindon's memoirs were untrue or exaggerated. He arrived on the island as a guest of his friend Dana Gillespie, who was sharing a house with composer Lionel Bart. Tennant asked Dana to join the princess for lunch and bring along her houseguests. During lunch the princess was indeed amused by Bindon, who was, according to Dana, "hilariously funny. Ma'am was giggling away." However, she never went for a private walk with the gangster. "There were so few of us that we never moved from the table."[29]

Over the years the story gained a life of its own and became the inspiration for TV documentaries. It was even used as a plot element in a 2008 movie called *The Bank Job*, which suggested that Britain's security forces used criminals to break into a bank to recover compromising pictures of Margaret and Bindon having sex.

Not that life on Mustique was a sunshine version of a vicar's tea party. Another photograph that made its way onto the front page of the *News of the World* showed Roddy, Colin Tennant, and island manager Nicholas Courtney photographed by the princess in various poses on the beach, all of them stark naked.

While the photograph caused another media firestorm, what really hurt was the news in December 1978—just after she returned from an official tour of Japan—that Tony and his lover Lucy Lindsay-Hogg had married at the Kensington register office. Margaret was completely taken aback by the news, stunned that he had moved on so quickly. Tony's remarriage, just five months after their divorce, merely tied the bow on what Margaret called the "worst year" of her life.

So when the queen mother suggested asking Tony over to Royal Lodge for a festive lunch, that was the last straw. If she needed any further evidence that her family would never accept Roddy and continued to, in her eyes, idolize her ex-husband, this was proof positive. In any case, Roddy's continued presence in her life was rapidly becoming a mixed blessing. While he gave her much-needed solace and support, he was frequently making headlines for all the wrong reasons. In the New Year he was arrested for drunk driving and fined and banned from driving for eighteen months, a verdict that damaged his gardening business. Later in the year the husband of actress Naima Kelly, whom Roddy was taking home when he was arrested, was said to be naming him as a co-respondent in their marriage breakup. The story proved to be false but still prompted further embarrassing headlines.

Not to be outdone, shortly after the assassination of Earl Mountbatten in Ireland in the fall of 1979, Margaret flew to the United States for a two-week tour to raise funds for the Royal Opera House. At a dinner in Chicago, she was seated next to Mayor Jane Byrne, who told her that she had attended Mountbatten's funeral in London as part of an American delegation. "The Irish—they're pigs," the princess was reported as saying, a sentiment that caused Mayor Byrne, who was Irish herself, to leave the function early. Though her private secretary issued a statement saying no such comment was made, the damage was done, and Irish American demonstrators took to the streets in San Francisco and Los Angeles. There was even the discovery of an IRA plot to assassinate Margaret in Los Angeles, information that gave rise to presidential-level security thereafter. A proposed visit to Washington the following year was canceled because of the prospect of pro-IRA demonstrations.

⌒

Inside the royal family it was accepted that Roddy brought comfort to the princess, but the monarchy continued to pay a high price. While the queen mother occasionally entertained Roddy at Royal Lodge—anything for the quiet life—the queen still refused to invite him to any of her private homes. Roddy had only met her once, and under deeply embarrassing circumstances. At Royal Lodge, wearing only a shirt and underpants, he went looking for the Snowdon children's nanny, Verona Sumner, to sew on a button. When he finally found Sumner, she was talking to the queen. "Please forgive me, Ma'am, I look so awful," Roddy stuttered. "Don't worry, I don't look very good myself," the queen answered politely before exiting the room.[30]

Matters came to a head in the summer of 1980 as the family planned the celebrations for Margaret's milestone fiftieth birthday. While Roddy was still a fixture, accompanying her and her children to shows, parties, and other social events, there was a family rift over his presence at her party.

The family planned to celebrate the actual date, August 21, at Balmoral, sans Roddy, but to have an additional party at the Ritz hotel on November 4 for all her many friends. Naturally Margaret wanted Roddy to be included among the favored group of forty guests who would arrive first for a celebration dinner. Her sister did not want Roddy to attend at all, not even with the one hundred other guests who would arrive later to dance. She felt his presence would overshadow the party itself.

As indulgent of her sister as the queen had been throughout her life, this was an indulgence too far. The Roddy affair had attracted public derision and hilarity in equal measure.

Margaret's name and reputation had been sullied by that relationship, which had flourished during her separation and subsequent divorce from Lord Snowdon. When she was on a visit to Canada in her fiftieth year, on July 23 the *Toronto Sun* unleashed a trenchant editorial. "She is out West being given the top hat and curtsy treatment as if she were something special rather than a Royal Baggage who has, by her lifestyle, forfeited all right to respect and homage."

This was the kind of criticism from the normally ultraloyal Canadian media that sent shivers down the spines of courtiers at Buckingham Palace. Roddy was now toxic, his presence staining the name and reputation of Princess Margaret and, by association, the monarchy. With Margaret's divorce, the long-held notion of members of the House of Windsor representing a model family was becoming increasingly unrealistic. Roddy's presence further undermined public faith in the monarchy. If the queen was present at an event involving Roddy, it would be akin to giving it official approval.

❦

As the queen made clear to Margaret, she had to protect the monarchy before her sister. She was acting as sovereign first, sister second. Over the years the queen had done everything possible to accommodate and welcome the men in Margaret's life. Not this one. While his erratic, increasingly publicity-seeking behavior was one thing, the queen drew the line at his perceived involvement in the first-ever royal divorce in well over four hundred years. The queen's first priority was the monarchy, not her family, although for the most part they were one and the same. It was a course she maintained in the decades to come. For many years after the prince and princess of Wales divorced in 1996, the queen and her senior staff would not receive Camilla Parker Bowles, as she was seen as partly responsible for the breakdown of the fairy-tale marriage.

Possibly for the first time in their lives, the sisters were in direct conflict, though no one would have guessed it that August. They joined the queen mother to publicly celebrate her eightieth birthday, both collecting flowers from well-wishers at Clarence House.

The deadlock was only broken when the sisters brokered a compromise. It was agreed that the ever-loyal Tennants, who would have expected to be at the top table, would take Roddy out to eat first, then he would arrive with the less important guests for the dancing. That evening Roddy steered well clear of the queen and Prince Philip, dancing with Princess Margaret only after the monarch had left.[31] Many guests at the party wondered how long this increasingly awkward relationship would last. They did not have long to wait.

During Margaret's birthday evening Roddy was nursing a secret. A few weeks before, on October 9, at a party at Stringfellows nightclub to celebrate his thirty-third birthday, he was reunited with attractive, dark-haired fashion designer Tatiana "Tania" Soskin. Margaret wasn't present, as it was felt it would be further exploitation of Roddy's friendship with Princess Margaret. Soon Roddy and Tania began seeing each other, and within a matter of months they decided to marry. Roddy broke the news to Margaret in February 1981 while they were on holiday in Mustique. Margaret was shocked but understanding and utterly gracious, urging him to propose as soon as possible. After returning from Mustique, she cheerfully admitted: "I'm really very happy for him. Anyway, I couldn't have afforded him much longer!"[32]

Margaret even threw a small luncheon party at Kensington Palace for Roddy and Tania shortly before they announced their engagement on April 4, 1981.

With the end of their eight-year relationship, Princess Margaret observed, "I'm back to where I started with Peter, but this time *I'm* divorced."[33]

She may have lost a friend, companion, and sometime lover, but she had regained a sister. From now on she rededicated herself to supporting the queen, recognizing that she would always be in her shadow. It was her destiny. As she commented, "Still playing second best after all these years, I guess I'll be second best to my grave."[34]

Though she didn't appreciate it yet, in 1981 there was a new kid in town, one who would overshadow everyone—including her sister.

12

Bud and Her Rose

The comparisons may have prompted a wry smile to play across her face. When Prince Charles was born she was pushed down the royal pecking order, forever known as "Charlie's aunt." Now that he had chosen Lady Diana Spencer as his bride, Princess Margaret was quietly put out to pasture and Diana became the media's latest chew toy. In the old days, when she was lauded for her beauty and glamour, she was matched with Hollywood star Elizabeth Taylor. No longer. Ironically, when Taylor came to London in 1982 to star in a stage play, it was the Princess of Wales who was chosen to meet her.

For Margaret it was something of a relief that she was no longer in the media crosshairs, though she and the queen watched with mounting concern as her next-door neighbor at Kensington Palace was now the main target. The queen invited newspaper editors to Buckingham Palace and politely asked them to give a modicum of privacy to the newest member of "the Firm." Margaret did her bit, too, to make Diana feel at home, taking her to the theater, joining her for social events, taking her shopping, and essentially showing her the ropes. Diana was full of appreciation for her royal guardian angel. "I've always adored Margo. I love her to bits and she has been wonderful to me from day one," she told me.[1] When Diana returned home from the hospital with baby William, Margaret gathered up the staff and rushed outside with them to wave handkerchiefs and tea towels as mother and baby drove by.

So much that Diana was going through reflected Margaret's own experience. When Diana said clothes weren't her prime concern, that too was Margaret's thinking. As she recalled, "The fashion writers insisted on treating her, as they did me, as if we were unreal figures straight from *Dynasty*."[2] There were even Dynasty Diana headlines about Diana's fashion choices.

When Diana returned from her honeymoon in August 1981, Margaret helped her navigate the social nuances of the Balmoral summer holiday with the rest of the clan. But from the outset, she felt herself an outsider, with her husband always deferring to the queen or queen mother rather than taking her needs into account. The early signs that all was not well with the fairy tale came when Diana stayed in her room rather than joining in with the rest of the family for picnics or barbecues. Her seeming refusal to fit in irritated the queen.

Princess Margaret came to her rescue, suggesting to the queen that Diana was having difficulties adjusting to her role and that she should cut her some slack. "Let her do what she likes," said Margaret, feeling that her sister was being too black and white. "Leave her alone and she will be all right."[3] The queen, who avoids family confrontation if at all possible, took her sister's advice.

As much as Margaret was an early Diana fan, her primary concern was assisting the queen. With Roddy fading into the background, Margaret became a one-woman Praetorian guard for the queen, doing and saying things that she instinctively knew that her sister agreed with but, for various reasons of polity and diplomacy, could not express herself.

Margaret could be intimidating, infuriating, and exasperating, but the queen loved the woman with the eager mind, crisp response, and waspish wit.

She was also secretly thrilled that Margaret regularly bettered the queen's bombastic husband in argument. The queen, Margaret, and the queen mother made for an impenetrable trio who spoke on the phone most days—sometimes in French or mimicking an accent. They had their own lives and circles, but in the end they relied on one another. As Mountbatten's private secretary John Barratt noted, "The royal family is very inward-looking and finds it hard to welcome strangers, and the Queen, particularly, finds it very difficult to relax unless she is surrounded by those with whom she feels at home."[4] With Margaret, Elizabeth felt the most at home, despite being temperamentally worlds apart. The queen tolerated in Margo many things she wouldn't accept from anyone else for a moment.

❧

Just as Princess Elizabeth had vowed to dedicate her whole life, whether it be long or short, to the monarchy, so in the new decade Margaret pledged herself to the crown. "Everything I do is to support the Queen and to help her."[5] Early in the New Year she created a fresh start for herself by undergoing an operation to remove her double chin; she also lost weight, which allowed her to wear more stylish clothes and brighter colors.

With her svelte frame and newly chiseled face, she seemed to gain greater confidence. While the queen stayed with the tried and tested, Margaret now looked, according to one fashion commentator, "startlingly slender, glamorous even, with softly waved hair, pink lipstick, and a relaxed smile."[6]

Throughout 1980, Margaret busied herself on behalf of her sister with official engagements, visiting West Germany, the Far East, and Canada. When she traveled overseas she always carried a small silver framed photograph of the queen, either hanging it on the wall or placing it on her dresser. In Britain, she filled her diary with visits—most of them unpublicized—to charities, regiments, and other bodies that she had long been associated with. Many of these functions remained second-string royal occasions—"All town clerks are the same," she once observed—but she had long recognized that this now was her role in life.

She became the first member of the royal family to visit people with AIDS—but no one noticed. Years before Diana hit the headlines around the world when she shook the hand of an AIDS patient at the Middlesex hospital in April 1987, Margaret was meeting and hugging patients at the Lighthouse AIDS center in west London.

The following year, as a sign of the new, relaxed Margaret, she appeared on the long-running radio show *Desert Island Discs*. Rather than soul standards—she was known for donning a wig and belting out Sophie Tucker's "Red Hot Mama"—she picked flag-waving tunes like "Rule Britannia!" and "Scotland the Brave." She joked that if she were alone on an island, she would dance like a ballerina and "would probably have been beautiful" because the world wouldn't be watching her for once.[7]

For once there were no dramas around her men friends. Age appropriate, discreet, and acceptable, there were no lurid headlines now about her choice of companions. Her name was linked to wealthy Italian banker Mario d'Urso, several years her junior, after she stayed at his family villa in Amalfi. Then there was Irish property owner and antique dealer Ned Ryan, who used his gift of the gab to seduce Margaret out of bed before her usual eleven o'clock hour and join him at six thirty in the morning at Bermondsey antique market to look for prime pieces of silver. He was her court jester, with Margaret enjoying his banter and the fact that she was rarely recognized during her early-morning jaunts. But perhaps her most serious suitor was Eton-educated businessman Norman Lonsdale, a widower descended directly from the duke of Wellington, who accompanied her on holidays to Italy and wined and dined her around London.

Love came full circle when, in 1992, Group Captain Peter Townsend arrived at Kensington Palace for a reunion after thirty-four years. He was much older, grayer, and slower than in their romantic heyday, but when asked how he was, she stated simply, "He hasn't changed at all."[8] After lunch and a long chat on the sofa, they said goodbye to what might have been. They never saw each other again.

It was a senior civil servant called Derek Jennings whose influence came closest to causing a royal rift. A top official at the Department of the Environment, he converted to Catholicism and later became a priest. Their discussions led Margaret, a High Church Anglican, to consider converting herself. A dinner party he organized at his home in Chelsea in 1988 was, Margaret later described, "one of the most rewarding, fascinating and satisfying nights of [my] life." She returned to Kensington Palace on a spiritual high. The princess told Cardinal Hume that she had met Pope Pius XII many years before and admitted that she was so nervous that she couldn't stop shaking. Since then her interest in Catholicism had grown, and the princess visited the pope's private garden most years. Tempted as she was by the prospect of joining the "bells and smells" of the Catholic church, it was, according to Father Jennings,[9] her loyalty to the queen, who is the supreme governor of the Church of England, that stayed her hand. Once again, Margaret's wants were secondary to the needs of the state. Six years later, in 1994, her cousin-in-law the duchess of Kent became the most senior royal to convert to the Catholic faith.

No doubt the queen was pleased by Margaret's decision to figuratively remain by her sister's side. In recognition of her service, on Margaret's sixtieth birthday on August 21, 1990, the queen conferred upon her sister the Royal Victorian Chain, the highest-ranking award in the Royal Victorian Order. It is presented by the monarch as a "personal token of high esteem and distinction." Of the ten current living recipients, six are former and current heads of state. In a royal world dominated by place, precedent, titles, ribbons, medals, and garters, this was indeed a signal honor, a gesture of affection and respect from Margaret's big sister. In Britain, honors are awarded for achievement, merit, or long service and are normally presented by the queen or another senior member of the royal family at Buckingham Palace. The honors list comprises knights, dames, and various appointments under the Order of the British Empire. The use of the word *Empire* regularly attracts criticism as outdated and anachronistic, though there are no immediate plans to change the name. From time to time senior American figures such as philanthropist Bill Gates are included. He was made an honorary knight in 2005.

The next few years would bring the sisters together in a way neither had experienced since the days of the Blitz. In adversity they were united in common purpose, Margaret proving herself time and again a loyal and devoted sister who was prepared to do the heavy lifting on behalf of the sovereign. "The Queen always came first in her thoughts," said her lady-in-waiting Janie Stevens. "She was always saying, 'my poor sister' whenever anything went wrong."[10]

Fortunately for Elizabeth, Margaret was there for her in 1992, the queen's *annus horribilus*. The worst year of the queen's reign began with the separation in March of the duke and duchess of York and continued with the divorce in April of her daughter Princess Anne from Captain Mark Phillips. This was followed by a devastating fire at Windsor Castle in November. When the queen, dressed in a green rain mac and matching hat, came to visit the smoldering ruin, she looked utterly devastated. The castle, an icon of Britain's history, had also been her home for most of her life. She retreated to Royal Lodge and spent the weekend with Margaret and her mother, almost inconsolable. "The symbolism of the Windsor Castle fire was not lost on anyone inside the family," Diana recalled.[11]

The queen's miserable year was rounded off with the separation of the prince and princess of Wales in December. In between there was the publication in June of *Diana: Her True Story*, which revealed her difficulties inside the royal family as well as her husband's long-standing affair with another man's wife. A few weeks later came the embarrassment of the so-called Squidgygate tapes, in which Diana was secretly recorded on the telephone talking to an amorous admirer, James Gilbey (who called her "Squidgy") and criticizing the royal family. While this made for blushing royal encounters, nothing matched the hide-behind-the-sofa embarrassment that followed the publication of pictures of the duchess of York having her toes sucked by her "financial adviser" John Bryan by the side of a villa pool in the south of France while her two young daughters, princesses Beatrice and Eugenie, looked on.

Unfortunately for Fergie, the publication in a Sunday tabloid coincided with her visit to Balmoral Castle to discuss future arrangements now that she was separated from Prince Andrew. She came down to breakfast with everyone silently reading the pictorial exposé on the newspaper front pages.

Years later, Fergie described the awkwardness of the breakfast tableau: "It would be accurate to report that the porridge was getting cold. Eyes wide and mouths ajar, the adults were flipping through the *Daily Mirror*."[12]

Margaret pointed out that Fergie had no real way out. "What do you all do?" she observed. "We all had to come down to breakfast anyway."[13] After reading the newspapers privately in her sitting room, the queen summoned Fergie. As her friend the writer Ingrid Seward recalled, "The Queen was furious, absolutely furious. I think partly because she loved Fergie so much. She just couldn't believe Fergie could have been so stupid to allow this to happen."[14]

Philip told her bluntly, "You should get to a nunnery or a madhouse."[15]

That was but the opening salvo. Margaret, no stranger herself to compromising pictures, sent Fergie a withering letter in which she wrote, "You have done more to bring shame on the family than could have been imagined. Not once have you hung your head in embarrassment even for a minute after those disgraceful photographs. Clearly, you have never considered the damage you are causing us all."[16]

There were real double standards here, as Fergie immediately recognized. After all, she had no idea the compromising pictures were being taken by a French paparazzo who spent days hiding in nearby bushes. By contrast, Margaret was the photographer when three naked men pranced before her on Mustique. There were other embarrassments, too, notably the publication of love letters she sent to her piano-playing lover, Robin Douglas-Home. The hypocrisy was not lost on the errant duchess. As she looked at the assembled company, she thought to herself, "There but for the grace of God go the lot of you."[17]

Nonetheless, Margaret's letter of rebuke reduced Fergie to tears, and she sent the princess a huge bouquet, hoping for her forgiveness, but they were returned. Margaret had never warmed to the boisterous, bouncy redhead and considered her coarse and greedy. As she grew older she became grander and looked down her nose at the daughter of Prince Charles's polo manager. She was noticeably absent from the christenings of Fergie's daughters, Beatrice and Eugenie, and the princess would have doubtless agreed with the withering comment by the queen's former private secretary, Lord Charteris: "Sarah Ferguson was not cut out to be a royal princess in this or any other age."[18] He called her "a vulgarian, vulgar, vulgar, vulgar," sentiments that would have found an echo with Margaret.[19]

෴

Prince Philip was also no fan of Fergie's, but he did want to help salvage the marriage of the prince and princess of Wales, if possible. During the summer of 1992 and beyond, he wrote Diana a series of letters, ranging from the accusatory to the sympathetic and affectionate. Margaret, having gone through a bitter separation herself, felt the sensible solution to the War of the Waleses was an early divorce. She complained that when she raised the subject with Prince Charles, he didn't listen to her advice. "As I talked to him, I noticed his eyes roaming around the room," she told Kenneth Rose.[20] She lamented his decision to admit his adultery on prime time television and to serialize his authorized biography, written by broadcaster Jonathan Dimbleby, in October 1994, precisely the same week as the queen was making a historic tour to Russia. Although Margaret was upset on her sister's behalf that the publicity surrounding Charles's book might overshadow the long-awaited Russia visit, she was guilty of doing the same thing herself, as when the queen and Prince Philip toured the Netherlands in 1958 and a surprise visit to London by Group Captain Peter Townsend to see Margaret at Clarence House had eclipsed the queen's tour.

While the queen was prepared to allow the Waleses' marriage to plod on in the forlorn hope that there could be a reconciliation, Margaret was under no such illusions. Delay only tarnished the monarchy. Margaret complained to a friend, "Poor Lilibet and Charles have done everything they can to get rid of the wretched girl, but she just won't go."[21] In view of Diana's tragic death, this sounds harsher than it was intended at the time. The queen's sister wanted the warring parties to face up to their responsibilities and grasp the nettle of divorce. She was further confirmed in her conviction that there should be a divorce when Diana gave her famous television interview in November 1995, during which she questioned Prince Charles's fitness to be king; observed that there were three people in her marriage, "so it was a bit crowded"; and spoke of her ambition to be the queen of people's hearts. It was this last statement that stung the queen and her sister into action. It was a seemingly innocent remark, but given Diana's hostility toward the royal family, it was no doubt calculated as a veiled insult to the sovereign.

In the early days of the Waleses' separation, Margaret had

given Diana the benefit of the doubt, writing to Prince Charles and informing him that she was going to continue her association with his estranged wife. That association stopped dead the moment she questioned the queen—and her husband—in public. Once her staunchest supporter in the family, Margaret sent Diana a "wounding and excoriating" letter following her controversial performance on the BBC *Panorama* program. She accused her of letting everyone down—including herself. She had obviously been "incapable of making even the smallest sacrifice," she wrote. Noticeably, she had refrained from writing to Prince Charles, who was the first member of the royal family to admit his adultery on prime time television. She was doing exactly what she complained about during her own separation and divorce from Lord Snowdon—she was solely criticizing the errant wife for her behavior. In Diana's mind, her controversial television interview was a riposte, however ill judged, to the original documentary about her husband.

Diana was devastated by Margaret's hostility. From that day forward Margaret became her fiercest critic and most implacable opponent. She welcomed the queen's decision to ask the couple to divorce as soon as legally possible and supported the move to remove her appellation, Her Royal Highness.

Margaret experienced a deep sense of hurt and betrayal as she watched Diana's historic interview. She had considered herself an ally, a guide, and a friend who had invested time and effort in integrating the princess into the rarefied royal world. She had encouraged the queen, sometimes against her better judgment, to indulge her whims and caprices. This, she thought, is how she repaid the royal family. She was angry and upset, so much so that after the interview she threw out every magazine with Diana's picture on the cover. Not only did she cut off all contact with the princess, but she made it clear to her children that she did not want them fraternizing with the enemy. So complete was the split that in July 1996, when Diana bought a present for Sarah's first baby, she timidly passed it on to Margaret's chauffeur Dave Griffin and asked him to deliver it.[22]

It was the backlash to her TV confessional and her subsequent divorce that informed the royal family's initial reaction to the news of her death in a Paris underpass in August 1997. Apart from being the mother to the two princes, Harry and William, she had no standing inside or contact with members of the royal family. The last time she had seen the queen was the previous March. Margaret and other royals had had nothing to do with her for several years. She was a figure from the past, essentially an independent private individual who was no longer a member of the royal family.

The way Margaret and the queen navigated their way through the funeral week said much about their different priorities and positions. How the two sisters responded to Diana's death in the coming days highlighted their differing temperaments as well as their constitutional status.

Margaret was her sister's alter ego, saying the things that as queen she might think but could not possibly comment on. She was the head of the House of Windsor but also the head of state. It made for conflict.

Like her sister, Princess Margaret ached for Princes William and Harry. "Terrible to lose your mother at that age, and with little Harry's birthday only a few days away," she said.[23] As far as Margaret was concerned, that sympathy extended only so far.

At Balmoral, in the early conversations about the next steps into what was the unknown, Margaret's view was that the family should have as little to do with the funeral as absolutely necessary. She complained bitterly about the "fuss the unfortunate girl who married my nephew has caused."[24]

A private funeral for a private citizen was her verdict. She was not the only one. The queen mother had never been an admirer of the late princess and instinctively sided with her grandson, Prince Charles. Her primary concern was for her great-grandchildren and not a former member of the family. However, with unprecedented crowds gathering outside the royal palaces, the queen was eventually convinced by the cadre of senior royal advisers, including prime minister Tony Blair, of the need for a special funeral for a special lady. Throughout what became known as the queen's worst week, Margaret continued her rearguard action, believing that she was articulating what her sister truly felt but was reluctant because of her position to put into words.

She did not think that Diana's coffin should rest in the Chapel Royal, nor did she feel that the Union Jack should fly at half-mast above Buckingham Palace—a subject of anger and rancorous debate among the increasingly resentful crowds mourning the death of the "people's princess."

Once she returned to Kensington Palace, Margaret grumbled over the smell of rotting cellophane-wrapped flowers—five feet deep in some places—piling up outside the gates near her home.[25] She expressed her bafflement that this "floral fascism" defined this unique moment in royal history. "It was like Passchendaele," she complained to Peter Stothard, editor of the *Times*, describing how the lawns were churned into mud by mourners. Even by her standards it was a remarkably insensitive comment, especially by speaking to a journalist; she had no way of knowing if her comments would be published. The mud of Passchendaele was a symbol for the thousands of soldiers who died in a "senseless" military battle during the First World War. By contrast, the mud on the grounds of Kensington Palace was caused by the affectionate respects paid by thousands of well-wishers to the late princess. "The Di thing was all too much," she continued. "The flowers on the paths everywhere were just awful." After consistently dissing the late princess, both before and after the funeral, Margaret then switched gear and intimated that she was speaking for her when discussing the mawkish public response. "Diana would have hated it. She would not have wanted all that fuss about her. She would have insisted that the flowers went straight to hospices."

As far as Margaret was concerned, it was the frenzy, or rather her perception of the frenzy, that she hated. Brought up never to show feelings in public, Margaret and her sister found the wailing and keening hard to understand. As Anne Tennant recalled, "Princess Margaret didn't like any of the emotionalism one bit." She believed the grief was hysterical, "rather like Diana herself. When she died she got everyone to be as hysterical as she was."[26] At the time those who believed in the British avoidance of grief, a stiff upper lip, were set against those who exhibited the trembling lower lip. Diana was seen as the latter, Margaret and other members of the family the former. They did not believe in showing private grief "on a public sleeve." At the same time, the dismissal of Diana as mentally unstable dovetails with the response of many, inside and outside, to her television interview.

The day of the funeral symbolized the differing formal reaction to Diana's death by the queen and Margaret. As they stood outside the gates of Buckingham Palace waiting for the gun carriage carrying her body, somewhat bizarrely, Margaret was talking to her sister about improving the lavatories at Kensington Palace. Then, as the funeral cortege passed by, the queen respectfully bowed her head while Margaret gave the most cursory of nods, looking for all the world like she wanted to be elsewhere. She never forgave Diana for what she saw as her betrayal of the royal family, not even in death. Later, inside Westminster Abbey, she and the rest of the royal family remained silent and stony faced when the congregation joined with the thousands outside in applauding Charles Spencer's eulogy, which in praising Diana also took a swipe at the chilly House of Windsor.

Before Margaret left for her delayed holiday in Tuscany, she wrote an appreciative note to her sister, thanking her for "how kindly you arranged everybody's lives after the accident and made life tolerable for the two poor boys. There, always in command, was you, listening to everyone and deciding on all the issues. I just felt you were wonderful."[27] Ironically, the funeral week had seen the queen responding and reacting to events, rather than controlling them. She had been agitated and alarmed by the hostility of the crowds, though when she returned to London from Balmoral she showed the composure and steely resolve that comes with a lifetime of training.

For months after Diana's death, Margaret did her best, within her personal sphere, to expunge her memory from the royal family's private record, destroying scores of personal letters written by Diana, Princess of Wales, to the queen mother.

The queen's sister ordered that several "large black bags of papers" be taken from her mother's London residence, Clarence House, and burned, because Margaret decided "they were so private." The queen mother's official biographer, William Shawcross, observed, "No doubt Princess Margaret felt that she was protecting her mother and other members of the family. It was understandable, although regrettable from a historical viewpoint."[28] Yet she knew that the royal family had their own well-protected archive in the Round Tower at Windsor Castle, where vetted historians were allowed to view some royal papers. Her own correspondence with Peter Townsend was kept there, with strict instructions that it was not allowed to be seen until 2030, a century after her birth and eighty years since their affair first hit the headlines.

Margaret seemed to feel Diana's decision to, as she saw it, betray the royal family by airing dirty laundry in public much more keenly than others. They were hurt by her actions but not consumed by it. The queen mother, for example, thought it was a mistake for both Charles and Diana to talk publicly about their marriage—and left it at that.

Writer Petronella Wyatt was rather less diplomatic about Margaret's feelings toward her onetime neighbor: "No one hated Diana except perhaps Margaret. She wasn't a bit upset when Diana died."[29] Hers was an uncharacteristically vehement reaction, a sense that she had been personally let down after investing so much emotional capital in the late princess.

∽

The royal family "doesn't do sick." If you feel unwell, take an aspirin and carry on. They learn, almost at the knee, that hundreds, often thousands, of people are relying on them to arrive, wave, smile, and bless them with the magic of monarchy. So when Margaret had her first stroke in February 1998, just six months after Princess Diana's death, she tried to take it in stride and carry on. It was fortunate that her stroke, which occurred over dinner at the end of her three-week holiday in Mustique, was moderate. She was first taken to a hospital in Barbados and then flown to London for further tests at a private hospital. Though the queen and her mother were among the first to hear of her condition, Margaret was keen to play down the aftereffects and resume her social life as soon as possible. She didn't want to be considered an invalid.

Though she strived to look alert and lively, she tired easily. Gradually, though, she resumed her public duties, attending an arts reception hosted by the queen at Windsor Castle, visiting the Chelsea Flower Show at the Royal Hospital, and celebrating Trooping the Colour, the ceremonial military display to mark the queen's official birthday, held every second Saturday in June. In any case, she knew that she wouldn't get much sympathy from her sister and mother—nor did she want any. The princess didn't need to be told that she was expected to soldier on, as her father had done when he was ill.

The following year, in March 1999, Princess Margaret had a serious mishap during her holiday in Mustique. While stepping into the bath to wash her hair, she badly scalded her feet due to a faulty thermostat. The soles of her feet were so badly burned that she was unable to walk and had to be confined to bed. Unfortunately she was unable to stay at Les Jolies Eaux, as her son, David Linley, who had been bequeathed the property, had rented it out. Instead she stayed at a friend's beach house, sitting in the dark with the curtains drawn, cantankerous and depressed. After a few days, her lady-in-waiting Anne Glenconner, who had flown from London to nurse her, was at her wits' end.

With Margaret's feet showing little sign of improvement, Lady Glenconner suggested that they return to London to receive specialized treatment. Margaret refused, saying she was not well enough. In the end Lady Glenconner contacted Buckingham Palace and spoke directly to the queen. Elizabeth then spoke to her sister and managed to convince her to fly home on the Concorde, which she did, with her legs propped up on a milk crate. "The Queen was wonderfully understanding, concerned and supportive," recalled Lady Glenconner.[30] Once home, she was treated with, among other things, leeches, though even this medieval remedy was unable to accelerate the healing process by much.

Colin Glenconner had his own theory about Margaret's accident, believing that it was a cry for help. He felt that the princess was craving sympathy from her sister and mother after receiving little comfort from family members following her first stroke—even though she didn't want to be treated as an invalid.

He said, "Let's face it, Princess Margaret was a depressed person and in the royal family you are not allowed to be depressed. In her circle you didn't mention the word."[31] Her sadness was compounded by the fact that her son, Lord Linley, had put Les Jolies Eaux, the only place she had ever owned, on the market.

The queen did ban wheelchairs from Balmoral and Sandringham in an attempt to encourage her ailing sister to walk. "Come on," she told her during their Balmoral holiday. "Put away your sticks and practise walking."[32] The queen felt that her sister was malingering and was, in the beginning, not unduly sympathetic to her plight. She was from the "pull yourself together" school of kindness—especially where her sister was concerned. A family friend cautioned: "No one is allowed to be ill in that family. But the family's lack of understanding is making the princess' moods even blacker."[33] This, though, was not the first time that she had suffered from depression. She had been treated off and on by psychiatrist Mark Collins, who worked at the Priory Clinic. He had initially been called in to help when Roddy Llewellyn had impetuously flown to Turkey, leaving Margaret bereft and alone.

∽

As she slowly recovered, Margaret had her Ford Galaxy SUV modified to take her wheelchair, which she now preferred to walking. Her mother, by contrast, was determined to walk to the end of her life. When they both went to Buckingham Palace for a function, the queen had a footman waiting outside the top floor elevator with a wheelchair for her mother. Instead, Margaret would sit down in the chair, leading her sister to exclaim, "For God's sake Margaret, get out. That's meant for Mummy."[34] Margaret performed a similar trick at a party held at Windsor Castle on June 21, 2000, to celebrate the queen mother's centenary and Margaret's seventieth birthday. The queen, according to one onlooker, was left "fuming" when the birthday girl absconded with her mother's wheelchair yet again.

Several months later, on January 4, 2001, Margaret suffered a second stroke while she was with the queen and the rest of the family at Sandringham. Although it was initially described as "mild," she was still admitted to King Edward VII's Hospital for ten days. Before she left the hospital, she had her hair done so that she would look her best for the TV cameras waiting outside. By early March, she seemed to finally be on the road to recovery, more positive, eating again, and able to walk without a cane—or use of a wheelchair. She even threw out her gray and khaki outfits and went back to wearing vibrant colors, especially red and gold. Her noticeable improvement came as a relief to the queen, who had been "worried sick" about her sister. On March 15, they shared dinner together with their mother. But the relief was again short lived. About two weeks later, Margaret suffered a third debilitating stroke, which left her incapacitated and once again using a wheelchair. Her eyesight was also affected; the princess very quickly almost entirely lost her vision. She struggled in the next weeks to restore some movement in her legs and did manage to regain partial sight. In June, she surprised everyone when she insisted on attending Philip's eightieth birthday service at St. George's Chapel, Windsor. After the queen had delivered a few words in tribute to her husband, she announced, "And now, my sister has something for you." Minutes later, a dancer from the Royal Ballet School entered the hall, followed by twenty of his peers. Margaret had organized a special birthday version of the hornpipe for her brother-in-law.[35]

Her celebratory mood did not last long. Margaret spent most of her time in her dimly lit bedroom, listening to the radio, and stopped virtually all socializing. Now dependent on others to help her with the simplest tasks, she felt embarrassed and undignified. As her cousin Margaret Rhodes put it, "All her life she has been the sparkling one, but since her [first] stroke three years ago, she has lost that particular facility to sparkle."[36] Once a lover of male company, she now wanted only a few close female friends to visit and read to her. On one occasion, the princess asked Anne Glenconner to read aloud a book from Roddy Llewellyn about plant seeds. Though Glenconner found it boring, Margaret was genuinely thrilled by the topic and urged her friend to continue.

When the queen visited her sister for afternoon tea, she found Margaret in a curmudgeonly mood, even though Lady Glenconner was keeping her company. Soon after she arrived, Margaret insisted on listening to *The Archers*, a soap opera, and said "Shhhh" every time the queen tried to initiate a conversation. It was just like the old days in the nursery, though this time, rather than Crawfie, Lady Glenconner took control, firmly telling Margaret, "Ma'am, the Queen is here, and she can't stay all that long. Would you like me to help pour the tea?" She then turned off the radio, poured each of them a cup of tea, and left the room. With Lady Glenconner smoothing the way, Princess Margaret and the queen could then proceed with a proper conversation.[37]

On August 4, 2001, two months after Philip's birthday party at Windsor, Margaret made a rare appearance to attend her mother's 101st birthday celebrations outside Clarence House. Since Philip's party, Margaret had deteriorated, and both the queen and queen mother tried to dissuade her from attending, as they felt that she would be upset by the reaction of people to her appearance. She insisted on attending, although she looked a sad, pathetic shell of the glamorous, vibrant woman she once was. Even though she wore dark glasses to protect her eyes and sat in a wheelchair with her arm in a sling, she uncharacteristically took great pleasure from the occasion, happy to support her mother on her big day for what turned out to be the last time.

She spent Christmas and New Year with the family at Sandringham, but the onetime star of charades and sing-alongs around the piano kept to her room and refused to eat. Once again Anne Glenconner came to the rescue, wheedling her out of bed, settling her down to watch *Antiques Roadshow* on TV, and even convincing her to eat a jam tart. When her sister was told of that small triumph, she responded with surprise and gratitude: "A jam tart." It was a rare moment of levity.

For the most part she preferred to be on her own and refused to even speak on the phone to her family. One afternoon the queen mother, frustrated at not being able to speak to her daughter on the phone, arrived without warning and went straight into her bedroom.

For a time she did speak to Lord Snowdon on the phone,

and Roddy Llewellyn came to visit, but toward the end she refused to allow any male visitors, saying, "I look so awful now." At one point Margaret complained to her maid: "If only I were a dog, I could be put down."[38]

On February 8, 2002, Princess Margaret suffered yet another stroke. She died early the next morning in King Edward VII's Hospital with her children at her bedside.

Within hours of her death Buckingham Palace released "with great sadness" a statement on behalf of the queen, announcing that "Her beloved sister HRH Princess Margaret died peacefully in her sleep at 6.30am." Later, the queen informed the queen mother.

∽

Princess Margaret's dying wish was honored—to join her beloved papa at St. George's Chapel at Windsor, where the funeral service was to be held. First the queen went to Kensington Palace, where Margaret's coffin was in her bedroom, surrounded by her favorite photographs, seashells, and other cherished artifacts. Her children, David Linley and Lady Sarah Chatto, were waiting by the front door together with long-serving members of her staff. The queen went into the room and for a few solitary minutes said her final goodbye to her younger sister. Then her coffin, draped in her standard and adorned with a spray of white lilies and roses, made the twelve-minute journey to the queen's chapel at St. James's Palace, her hearse preceded by Scottish pipers.

On February 15, the day of the funeral, the queen mother was brought by helicopter from Sandringham and then taken to the service at St. George's Chapel, Windsor, in a wheelchair. Margaret's rose-colored coffin was already at the altar when she arrived, the organist playing melodies from *Swan Lake* before the service began—a touching reminder of Margaret's love of ballet. Always a meticulous planner—a quality she had inherited from her feared grandmother, Queen Mary—the princess had chosen the music, prayers, and hymns for her own final farewell.

After the service, as the coffin was borne out of the chapel, the queen mother managed with great difficulty to struggle to her feet in a final sad acknowledgment of her daughter. The queen, too, seemed overwhelmed by the loss of the sister she spoke to on the telephone every day. As the coffin was placed into the hearse, one hand gripped that of her niece, Sarah Chatto, the other brushed away a tear.

Out of the stillness came the sound of a Scottish lament, "The Desperate Battle of the Birds," chosen by her daughter. It served as a metaphor for her tumultuous life, so full of promise and glamour yet dwindling into loneliness and despondency. She was at once imperious and haughty as well as loyal and thoughtful. As all would attest, she was never dull.

In the popular imagination, Princess Margaret was a fast-living socialite who spent most of her time partying or lounging about in the Caribbean. But less well known to outsiders was that she dedicated her life to serve her sister and to uphold the values of monarchy that her sister represented. It was a quality the queen appreciated in full measure; time after time the queen defended her from what she considered to be unfair attacks by lawmakers and others. As Reverend Canon Barry Thompson eulogized, Margaret should be remembered not only for her mischievous and vivacious nature, but also for her "loyalty and sense of duty; her faithfulness toward her family and her friends; her energy and enthusiasm; her quick wit and sound advice, and for her depth of knowledge and her love of life."

After the service the coffin was taken to Slough crematorium, Margaret becoming the first member of the royal family in over sixty years to be cremated. At her express wish she made the final journey on her own, without any family or friends accompanying the hearse to the crematorium. As there was no space in the royal crypt for a coffin, she chose to be cremated to ensure that her ashes could be next to her beloved father—as she always wanted.

Among the four hundred guests who came to say goodbye were friends from the world of show business, including singer Cleo Laine and her musician husband, John Dankworth; actresses Dame Judi Dench and Felicity Kendal; as well as director Bryan Forbes and his wife, Nanette Newman.

There were no politicians or dignitaries, just people who had known the princess during her lifetime. After the service the queen took Anne Glenconner to one side and thanked her for bringing Roddy Llewellyn into Margaret's life. She told her, "I'd just like to say Anne it was rather difficult at moments but I thank you so much for introducing Princess Margaret to Roddy, he made her really happy." This was quite a remarkable turnaround by the queen, who had previously banned him from her houses and had fought tooth and nail to stop him from attending Margaret's fiftieth birthday party. It seemed as if the queen had learned, through her own travails with her children and their marriages, to be more accepting and understanding of others. She had been judgmental of her sister's relationship with Roddy, even though, as she now came to appreciate, he stood by her through the good times and, toward the end, the bad.

Less than two months after Princess Margaret's death, the queen mother passed away on the afternoon of Easter Saturday at Royal Lodge at Windsor, with her eldest daughter by her side. Her final resting place had been reserved next to her husband in St. George's Chapel. It was a moment the queen had been dreading. She had told friends that her biggest nightmare was losing her mother and sister at the same time. It was a considerable blow to the queen, though she took much consolation from the outpouring of affection from the public for her much-loved mother. Some 200,000 members of the public filed past her coffin to pay their respects. In a broadcast to the nation, the queen expressed her thanks for the public's expressions of support and sympathy. Later she admitted that if she had also had to speak about the death of her sister, as calm and phlegmatic as she was, she would not have been able to get through the broadcast without breaking down, as her heart was so full.

While death is humanity's greatest leveler, for the Windsor sisters it only confirmed the dynastic gulf between them. In striking contrast to Princess Margaret's modest funeral arrangements, far more elaborate plans will mark the passing of Queen Elizabeth II. In 1952, when her father died, broadcaster Richard Dimbleby announced, "The sunset of his death tinged the whole world's sky." The same could be said about the queen, as the preparations for both her death and its ceremonial aftermath—code named Operation London Bridge—have been extensively considered since the 1960s. Even by comparison to Diana's funeral and that of the queen mother, the queen's passing will have unparalleled repercussions for the nation and world. While a few onlookers watched Margaret's funeral, it is expected that the line for the lying in state for Queen Elizabeth, which will be held at Westminster Hall, will be at least thirteen miles long.

On a more intimate level, Margaret's death concluded a complex saga of two sisters united yet divided by love and duty. One preferred the routines and rhythms of a rooted traditional aristocratic lifestyle; the other invented herself as a daring, flirtatious partygoer mingling with celebrities, artists, and bohemians. She embraced the exotic and the subversive, creating a life for herself outside of the confines of Britain.

Yet, as historian Ben Pimlott observed, it is too simplistic to accept that "while the Queen must be portrayed as an icon of seriousness, opposite qualities must be found in her sister."[39] In less noticed private moments the lines between the two women were blurred, the sisters often remarkably similar in behavior and thought.

For all their differences, both sisters shared one enduring, deeply rooted trait: loneliness. Both sisters were universally known and almost constantly surrounded by people. Yet in so many ways, they remained indecipherable to everyone but each other. Always at the center of public attention, neither ever fully enjoyed "normal" relationships. It was from this position of magnificent isolation that the sisters forged their inseparable, intuitive bond. One was a "bud," the other a "rose," but both were grafted from the same branch.

Acknowledgments

Members of the royal family are often best explained and understood by comparison with another. Though princes William and Harry come to mind, perhaps the most intriguing— certainly the longest lasting—royal double act is between HM the Queen and her younger sister, Princess Margaret.

I have my agent, Steve Troha, and Gretchen Young, my editor at Grand Central, to thank for suggesting that this relationship, intriguing but neglected, was ripe for further exploration.

During this journey I have been guided by those who have known both sisters at various stages and places in their lives. I would like to extend my sincere thanks to the following for their insights and witness: Charles Azzopardi, Michael Bonello, Basil Charles, Phil Dampier, Dana Gillespie, Carmen Glenville, Tony Grech, David Griffin, Eric Milligan, former Lord Provost of Edinburgh, Michael Nash, Professor Jonathan Petropoulos, Dr. Frank Prochaska, Paul Reynolds, Ingrid Seward, Ian Shapiro, Sean Smith, Dr. Micallef Stafrace, Professor Andrew Stewart, Robert and Dee Hornyold Strickland, Professor John Taylor, Marjorie Wallace CBE, and Christopher Wilson.

I would also like to thank my researchers Dawn Kuisma, Claudia Taylor, Camille J. Thomas, Andrina Tran, and Marisa Xuereb in Valetta, Malta, for their hard work in difficult circumstances. At Grand Central I would like to again thank my editor, Gretchen Young, for her forensic focus, as well as assistant editor Haley Weaver and copy editor Lori Paximadis.

In a world of lockdowns and a deadly pandemic, a big shout-out to my wife, Carolyn, for her love and support.

Andrew Morton

Pasadena, November 2020

Notes

1. Rising of the Sun and the Moon

1. Bradford, *Elizabeth*, 7.
2. Edwards, *Royal Sisters*, 45.
3. Edwards, *Royal Sisters*, 11.
4. Ziegler, *King Edward VIII*, 199; Rose, *King George V*, 392.
5. "The Tragic Heroine of *The Crown*: Princess Margaret's Life in Pictures," *The Telegraph*, December 9, 2017.
6. Aronson, *Princess Margaret*, 174.
7. Warwick, *Princess Margaret* (2000), 124.
8. Princess Margaret profile, *Sunday Telegraph*, August 20, 2000.
9. Seward, *Royal Children*, 61.
10. Edwards, *Royal Sisters*, 16.
11. Shawcross, *The Queen Mother*, 257.
12. Shawcross, *The Queen Mother*, 307.
13. Jennifer Ellis, ed., *Thatched with Gold: The Memoirs of Mabel, Countess of Airlie* (London: Ulverscroft, 1992), 180.
14. Aronson, *Princess Margaret*, 45.
15. Edwards, *Royal Sisters*, 25.
16. Seward, *The Queen and Di*, 80.
17. Morrow, *The Queen*, 11.

18. Dismore, *Princess*, 73.

19. Morrow, *The Queen*, 14.

20. Dismore, *Princess*, 93.

21. Bradford, *Elizabeth*, 33.

22. Edwards, *Royal Sisters*, 41.

23. Shawcross, *Counting One's Blessings*, 76.

24. Crawford, *The Little Princesses*, 17.

25. Warwick, *Princess Margaret* (2000), 47.

26. Shawcross, *Counting One's Blessings*, 208.

27. Warwick, *Princess Margaret* (2000), 48.

28. Jane Dismore, "The Royal Family at 145 Piccadilly," Intercontinental London Park Lane website, https://parklane.intercontinental.com/en/news/145-piccadilly.

29. Edwards, *Royal Sisters*, 45.

30. Morrow, *The Queen*, 13.

31. Dismore, "The Royal Family at 145 Piccadilly."

32. Edwards, *Royal Sisters*, 42.

33. Bradford, *Elizabeth*, 41.

34. Bradford, *Elizabeth*, 193.

35. Seward, *Royal Children*, 16.

36. Philip Lindsay, *Crowned King of England: The Coronation of King George VI in History and Tradition* (London: Ivor Nicholson and Watson, 1937), 258.

37. Bradford, *Elizabeth*, 99.

38. Matthew Dennison, "Inside the Diary of the Teenager Who Spent the War in Lockdown with the Future Queen," *The Telegraph*, April 28, 2020.

39. Dennison, "Inside the Diary," 49.

40. Edwards, *Royal Sisters*, 44.

41. Dismore, *Princess*, 78.

42. Ian Lloyd, "Revealed: The Little Girl the Queen Chose to Be Her Best Friend," *The Daily Mail*, July 25, 2014.

43. Lloyd, "Revealed."

44. Dismore, "The Royal Family at 145 Piccadilly."

45. Morrow, *The Queen*, 17.

46. Warwick, *Princess Margaret* (2000), 90.

47. Bradford, *Elizabeth*, 37.

48. Warwick, *Princess Margaret* (2000), 53.

49. Dismore, *Princess*, 104.

50. Warwick, *Princess Margaret* (2000), 55–56.

51. Edwards, *Royal Sisters*, 53.

52. Edwards, *Royal Sisters*, 53.

53. Morrow, *The Queen*, 14.

54. Bradford, *Elizabeth*, 34.

55. Craig Brown, *Ninety-Nine Glimpses of Princess Margaret*, 47.

56. Bradford, *Elizabeth*, 33–34.

57. Warwick, *Princess Margaret* (2000), 48.

58. Edwards, *Royal Sisters*, 11.

59. Edwards, *Royal Sisters*, 12.

60. Edwards, *Royal Sisters*, 13.

61. Edwards, *Royal Sisters*, 307.

62. Edwards, *Royal Sisters*, 63.

63. Bradford, *Elizabeth*, 2.

64. Edwards, *Royal Sisters*, 64.

65. Morrow, *The Queen*, 15.

66. Smith, *Elizabeth the Queen*, 4.

67. Warwick, *Princess Margaret* (2000), 81.

68. Morrow, *The Queen*, 21.

69. Edwards, *Royal Sisters*, 75.

70. Edwards, *Royal Sisters*, 78; Bradford, *Elizabeth*, 266.

71. Morrow, *The Queen*, 21.

72. Edwards, *Royal Sisters*, 78.

73. Edwards, *Royal Sisters*, 66.

74. Smith, *Elizabeth the Queen*, 11.

75. Mary Watson, "How Margaret Got Her Own Palace Brownie Pack," *Daily Mail*, February 1, 2014.

76. Edwards, *Royal Sisters*, 156.

77. Dismore, *Princess*, 120.

78. Anne Edwards, *Matriarch: Queen Mary and the House of Windsor* (New York: Rowman & Littlefield, 1984), 433.

79. Edwards, *Royal Sisters*, 17.

80. Crawford, *The Little Princesses*, 99.

81. Warwick, *Princess Margaret* (2000), 94.

82. Crawford, *The Little Princesses*, 102.

2. Sisters at War

1. Aronson, *Princess Margaret*, 70; Warwick, *Princess Margaret* (2000), 94.
2. Comer Clarke, "Kidnap the Royal Family…," *The Sunday Pictorial*, March 22, 1959.
3. Clarke, *England under Hitler.*
4. Clarke, *England under Hitler.*
5. Stewart, *The King's Private Army*, 124.
6. Hannah Furness, "Queen Mother Learned to Shoot Buckingham Palace Rats in Case Nazis Tried to Kidnap Royal Family," *Daily Telegraph*, April 30, 2015.
7. Stanley Olson, ed., *Harold Nicolson: Diaries and Letters, 1930–1964* (New York: Atheneum, 1980), 188.
8. Shawcross, *Counting One's Blessings*, 277.
9. Warwick, *Princess Margaret* (2000), 102.
10. Caroline Davies, "How the Luftwaffe Bombed the Palace, in the Queen Mother's Own Words," *The Guardian*, September 12, 2009.
11. Edwards, *Royal Sisters*, 89.
12. Bradford, *Elizabeth*, 87.
13. Warwick, *Princess Margaret* (2000), 101.
14. Morrow, *The Queen*, 22.
15. Warwick, *Princess Margaret* (2000), 106.
16. Shawcross, *The Queen Mother*, 586.
17. Glenconner, *Lady in Waiting*, 18.
18. Bradford, *Elizabeth*, 88.
19. Smith, *Elizabeth the Queen*, 8.
20. *Elizabeth and Margaret: Love and Loyalty* [TV program], Channel 5, September 26, 2020.
21. Rhodes, *The Final Curtsey*, 74.
22. Warwick, *Princess Margaret* (2000), 112–113.
23. *Elizabeth and Margaret: Love and Loyalty.*
24. Bradford, *Elizabeth*, 96.
25. Edwards, *Royal Sisters*, 87, 90.
26. Edwards, *Royal Sisters*, 87.
27. Richard Kay, "The Queen on the Couch," *Daily Mail*, September 23, 2020.

28. Edwards, *Royal Sisters*, 90.

29. Dismore, *Princess*, 66.

30. Bradford, *Elizabeth*, 100.

31. Bradford, *Elizabeth*, 100.

32. Edwards, *Royal Sisters*, 86.

33. Shawcross, *Counting One's Blessings*, 354.

34. *Elizabeth and Margaret: Love and Loyalty.*

35. Seward, *Royal Children*, 62.

36. Seward, *Royal Children*, 62.

37. Edwards, *Royal Sisters*, 92.

38. Duff Hart-Davis, ed., *King's Counsellor: Abdication and War: The Diaries of Sir Alan Lascelles* (London: Orion Publishing, 2006), 85, 211.

39. Henry Wallop, "Her REAL Highness…," *Daily Mail*, February 4, 2018.

40. Seward, *The Queen and Di*, 83.

41. Bradford, *Elizabeth*, 100.

42. Bradford, *Elizabeth*, 105.

43. Edwards, *Royal Sisters*, 122–123.

44. Bradford, *Elizabeth*, 105.

45. Bradford, *Elizabeth*, 107.

46. Edwards, *Royal Sisters*, 102.

47. Rhodes, *The Final Curtsey*, 87.

48. Howard, *The Windsor Diaries*, 71.

49. Howard, *The Windsor Diaries*, 117.

50. "Elizabeth's Journey," *Daily Telegraph*, February 12, 2012.

51. Howard, *The Windsor Diaries*, June 1942.

52. Howard, *The Windsor Diaries*, October 23, 1941.

53. Philip Eade, "The Romances of Young Prince Philip," *The Telegraph*, May 5, 2017.

54. Dismore, *Princess*, 175.

55. Howard, *The Windsor Diaries*, November 1941.

56. Katherine J. Igoe, "Did Princess Margaret Really Want to Be Queen?" *Marie Claire*, November 17, 2019.

57. Edwards, *Royal Sisters*, 123.

58. Elizabeth Grice, "What Was the Queen Like as a Teenager?" *Daily Telegraph*, October 2, 2020.

59. Shawcross, *Counting One's Blessings*, 366.
60. Warwick, *Princess Margaret* (2000), 144.
61. "Growing Up Royal: How Elizabeth and Margaret's Close Bond Was Tested by a 'Forbidden' Love,'" *Hello*, November 4, 2016.
62. Aronson, *Princess Margaret*, 85.
63. Hart-Davis, *King's Counsellor*, 211.
64. Pimlott, *The Queen*, 200.
65. Warwick, *Princess Margaret* (2000), 148.
66. Botham, *Margaret* (2012), 50.
67. Edwards, *Royal Sisters*, 126.
68. Mark Duell and Martin Robinson, "Dame Vera Lynn Dies at 103...," *Daily Mail*, June 18, 2020.
69. *The Way We Were*, BBC Radio 4, December 24, 1985.
70. Warwick, *Princess Margaret* (2000), 125.
71. Morrow, *The Queen*, 25.

3. Love in a Warm Climate

1. Victoria Glendinning, *Rebecca West* (New York: Knopf, 1987), 170.
2. Pimlott, *The Queen*, 81.
3. Sam Greenhill, "Revealed: The 'Devastatingly Attractive' Dashing Young Army Captain Who Set the Queen's Heart A-flutter at the Age of 19," *Daily Mail*, August 9, 2013.
4. Howard, *The Windsor Diaries*, February 15, 1945.
5. Pimlott, *The Queen*, 85.
6. Kitty Kelley, *The Royals* (New York: Grand Central, 1997), 59.
7. Ingrid Seward, "'I Saw Prince Philip and His Friend Penny...,'" *Daily Mail*, September 12, 2020.
8. Deborah Hart Strober and Gerald S. Strober, *The Monarchy: An Oral Biography of Elizabeth II* (New York: Broadway Books, 2002), 73.
9. Strober and Strober, *The Monarchy*, 73.
10. Bradford, *Elizabeth*, 114.
11. Richard Kay and Geoffrey Levy, "Inside the Very Amorous Marriage of the Queen and Prince Philip," *Daily Mail*, March 8, 2016.
12. Pimlott, *The Queen*, 97.
13. Maclean, *Crowned Heads*, 34.
14. Crawford, *The Little Princesses*, 178.

15. Edwards, *Royal Sisters*, 151.

16. Bradford, *Elizabeth*, 115.

17. Pimlott, *The Queen*, 112.

18. Bradford, *Elizabeth*, 115.

19. Edwards, *Royal Sisters*, 155.

20. Pimlott, *The Queen*, 115.

21. Townsend, *Time and Chance*, 159.

22. Glenconner, *Lady in Waiting*, 275; de Courcy, *Snowdon*, 65.

23. Graham Viney, "The Royal Express of Excess," *Daily Mail*, April 12, 2019.

24. Edwards, *Royal Sisters*, 159.

25. Edwards, *Royal Sisters*, 156.

26. Viney, *The Last Hurrah*, 270.

27. Edwards, *Royal Sisters*, 165.

28. Edwards, *Royal Sisters*, 165.

29. Viney, *The Last Hurrah*, 272.

30. Townsend, *Time and Chance*, 147.

31. Aronson, *Princess Margaret*, 92.

32. Edwards, *Royal Sisters*, 166.

33. Pimlott, *The Queen*, 119.

34. Edwards, *Royal Sisters*, 169.

35. Edwards, *Royal Sisters*, 170.

36. Edwards, *Royal Sisters*, 170.

37. Steph Cockroft, "How Prince Philip Curtsied to King George VI," *Daily Mail*, July 31, 2015.

38. *Prince Philip: The Plot to Make a King* [TV program], Channel 4, 2015.

39. Crawford, *The Little Princesses*, 209.

40. Seward, *Royal Children*, 35.

41. Pimlott, *The Queen*, 135.

42. Elizabeth Grice, "Royal Wedding: A Marriage Made in History," *The Telegraph*, March 25, 2011.

43. Warwick, *Princess Margaret* (2000), 132.

44. Pimlott, *The Queen*, 135.

45. Shawcross, *The Queen Mother*, 629.

46. Shawcross, *The Queen Mother*, 629.

47. Edwards, *Royal Sisters*, 183–184.

48. Sarah Gristwood, "Prince Philip: A Life of Duty and Devotion," *History Extra*, November 6, 2019.

49. Shawcross, *The Queen Mother*, 631.

50. Warwick, *Princess Margaret* (2000), 133.

51. Aronson, *Princess Margaret*, 99.

4. The Long Goodbye

1. Rhodes, *The Final Curtsey*, 45.

2. Wheeler-Bennett, *Friends, Enemies, and Sovereigns*, 754–755.

3. Townsend, *Time and Chance*, 182.

4. "Princess Elizabeth Visits Paris (1948)," The Court Jeweller, March 16, 2017, http://www.thecourtjeweller.com/2017/03/princess -elizabeth-visits-paris-1948.html.

5. Richard Kay, "How Meghan Markle Is Transforming the Royal Family…," *Daily Mail*, December 27, 2017.

6. Edwards, *Royal Sisters*, 187.

7. Craig Brown, *Ninety-Nine Glimpses of Princess Margaret*, 86.

8. Warwick, *Princess Margaret* (2000), 149–150.

9. Edwards, *Royal Sisters*, 197.

10. Noel Botham and Bruce Montague, *The Book of Royal Useless Information: A Funny and Irreverent Look at the British Royal Family Past and Present* (London: John Blake, 2012), 56.

11. Chloe Foussianes, "New Letters by Princess Margaret Reveal Love for Her 'Heavenly Nephew,' Prince Charles," *Town and Country*, March 13, 2019.

12. Edwards, *Royal Sisters*, 206.

13. Warwick, *Princess Margaret* (2000), 138.

14. Craig Brown, *Ninety-Nine Glimpses of Princess Margaret*, 122.

15. Edwards, *Royal Sisters*, 200.

16. de Courcy, *Snowdon*, 64.

17. Edwards, *Royal Sisters*, 210.

18. Edwards, *Royal Sisters*, 205.

19. Rhodes, *The Final Curtsey*, 98.

20. Aronson, *Princess Margaret*, 107.

21. Warwick, *Princess Margaret* (2000), 159.

22. Hadley Meares, "Why Princess Margaret Was the Worst Party Guest," *Biography*, June 21, 2019.

23. Townsend, *Time and Chance*, 185.
24. Warwick, *Princess Margaret* (2000), 155.
25. Edwards, *Royal Sisters*, 200.
26. Philip Ziegler, *Mountbatten: The Official Biography* (London: William Collins Sons & Co., 1985), 492.
27. Pimlott, *The Queen*, 162.
28. Ian Lloyd, "Our Samba Queen," *The Mail on Sunday*, November 22, 2015.
29. Morgan, *Edwina Mountbatten*, 444.
30. Morgan, *Edwina Mountbatten*, 444.
31. Townsend, *Time and Chance*, 196.
32. Edwards, *Royal Sisters*, 211.
33. Townsend, *Time and Chance*, 189.
34. Harry Wallop, "Her Real Highness," *Daily Mail*, February 2, 2018.
35. Aronson, *Princess Margaret*, 116.
36. Tam Dalyell, "The Duke of Buccleuch and Queensberry," *The Independent*, September 6, 2007.
37. Andrew Pierce and Richard Kay, "Margaret's Very Private Correspondence," *Daily Mail*, February 20, 2015.
38. Erin Blakemore, "The Governess Who Spilled the Queen's Secrets," *History*, December 14, 2017.
39. "Thank You for the Spiffing Stockings," *Scottish Daily Mail*, February 21, 2015.
40. "Mabel Strickland's 'nanny' dies aged 64," *Times of Malta*, March 17, 2005.
41. Pierce and Kay, "Margaret's Very Private Correspondence."
42. Pierce and Kay, "Margaret's Very Private Correspondence."
43. Seward, *My Husband and I*, 85.
44. Seward, *My Husband and I*, 84.

5. "Bad or Mad"

1. Pierce and Kay, "Margaret's Very Private Correspondence."
2. Shawcross, *Counting One's Blessings*, 444.
3. Pimlott, *The Queen*, 175.
4. John Hartley, *Accession: The Making of a Queen* (London: Quartet Books, 1992), 128.
5. Hartley, *Accession*, 130.

6. Hartley, *Accession*, 131.

7. Pimlott, *The Queen*, 179.

8. Wheeler-Bennett, *Friends, Enemies, and Sovereigns*, 133.

9. Edwards, *Royal Sisters*, 238.

10. Edwards, *Royal Sisters*, 242.

11. Williams, *Young Elizabeth*, 47.

12. Edwards, *Royal Sisters*, 244.

13. Shawcross, *The Queen Mother*, 656.

14. Aronson, *Princess Margaret*, 120.

15. Bradford, *Elizabeth*, 165.

16. Pimlott, *The Queen*, 199.

17. Warwick, *Princess Margaret* (2000), 178.

18. Aronson, *Princess Margaret*, 120.

19. Shawcross, *Counting One's Blessings*, 456.

20. Pimlott, *The Queen*, 185.

21. "Prince Philip: The Plot to Make a King," *Secret History*, Channel 4, July 30, 2015.

22. *The Royal Family*, PBS, March 2018.

23. Pierce and Kay, "Margaret's Very Private Correspondence."

24. Pierce and Kay, "Margaret's Very Private Correspondence."

25. Warwick, *Princess Margaret* (2000), 159.

26. Warwick, *Princess Margaret* (2000), 182.

27. Geoffrey Levy, "Doomed Affair That Blighted Her Life," *Daily Mail*, February 11, 2002.

28. Townsend, *Time and Chance*, 195.

29. Townsend, *Time and Chance*, 196.

30. Warwick, *Princess Margaret* (2000), 166.

31. Levy, "Doomed Affair That Blighted Her Life."

32. Levy, "Doomed Affair That Blighted Her Life."

33. Pimlott, *The Queen*, 220.

34. Townsend, *Time and Chance*, 197.

35. Townsend, *Time and Chance*, 198.

36. Elizabeth Longford, *Elizabeth R: A Biography* (London: George Weidenfeld & Nicolson, 1983), 205.

37. Townsend, *Time and Chance*, 198.

38. Longford, *Elizabeth R*, 152.

39. Bradford, *Elizabeth*, 187.

40. Kenneth Rose, *Who Loses, Who Wins: The Journals of Kenneth Rose: Volume 2, 1979–2014* (London: Weidenfeld & Nicolson, 2019), 65.
41. Warwick, *Princess Margaret* (2000), 186.
42. Edwards, *Royal Sisters*, 255.
43. Editorial, *Daily Express*, October 20, 1952.
44. Smith, *Elizabeth the Queen*, 81–82.
45. Williams, *Young Elizabeth*.
46. Smith, *Elizabeth the Queen*, 67.
47. Pimlott, *The Queen*, 209.
48. Edwards, *Royal Sisters*, 260.
49. Aronson, *Princess Margaret*, 126.
50. Edwards, *Royal Sisters*, 260.
51. Pimlott, *The Queen*, 193.
52. "Queen Elizabeth II: Mother and Queen (Part Two)," History of Royal Women, May 22, 2019, https://www.historyofroyalwomen .com/elizabeth-ii-2/queen-elizabeth-ii-mother-and-queen.
53. Edwards, *Royal Sisters*, 263.
54. Glenconner, *Lady in Waiting*, 74.
55. Edwards, *Royal Sisters*, 262.
56. Warwick, *Princess Margaret* (2000), 189.
57. Edwards, *Royal Sisters*, 263.
58. Pimlott, *The Queen*, 215–216.
59. Bradford, *Elizabeth*, 78.
60. Longford, *Elizabeth R*, 189.
61. Warwick, *Princess Margaret* (2000), 190.
62. Warwick, *Princess Margaret* (2000), 192.
63. Pimlott, *The Queen*, 219.
64. Pimlott, *The Queen*, 219.

6. "My Dear Prime Minister"

1. Pimlott, *The Queen*, 160–161.
2. Pimlott, *The Queen*, 160–161.
3. Pimlott, *The Queen*, 235.
4. Hannah Furness, "Queen Intervened to Make Prince Philip Regent," *Daily Telegraph*, December 1, 2014.
5. Furness, "Queen Intervened to Make Prince Philip Regent…"

6. Bradford, *Elizabeth*, 199.
7. Edwards, *Royal Sisters*, 278.
8. Townsend, *Time and Chance*, 197.
9. Edwards, *Royal Sisters*, 278.
10. Edwards, *Royal Sisters*, 281.
11. Robert Hardman, *Our Queen* (London, Hutchinson, 2011), 195.
12. Edwards, *Royal Sisters*, 282.
13. Townsend, *Time and Chance*, 212–213.
14. Bradford, *Elizabeth*, 200.
15. Townsend, *Time and Chance*, 217.
16. Hart-Davis, *King's Counsellor*, 400.
17. Edwards, *Royal Sisters*, 293.
18. Warwick, *Princess Margaret* (2000), 197.
19. Roya Nikkah, "Princess Margaret: Recently Unearthed Letter Sheds New Light on Decision Not to Marry," *Daily Telegraph*, November 7, 2009, https://www.telegraph.co.uk/news/uknews /theroyalfamily/6520837/Princess-Margaret-recently-unearthed -letter-sheds-new-light-on-decision-not-to-marry.html.
20. "Closed Extracts," August 16, 1955, Prime Minister Papers, 11/1565/1, National Archives, London.
21. Warwick, *Princess Margaret* (2000), 207–208.
22. Paul Reynolds, "Margaret Was Offered Marriage Deal," BBC News Online, January 2, 2004.
23. Edwards, *Royal Sisters*, 309.
24. Edwards, *Royal Sisters*, 310–311.
25. Warwick, *Princess Margaret* (2000), 205.
26. "Closed Extracts," August 16, 1955, Prime Minister Papers, 11/1565/1, National Archives, London.
27. Warwick, *Princess Margaret* (2000), 200.
28. Townsend, *Time and Chance*, 234.
29. Warwick, *Princess Margaret* (1983), 75.
30. Warwick, *Princess Margaret* (2000), 202.
31. Warwick, *Princess Margaret* (2000), 202; Townsend, *Time and Chance*, 236.
32. Townsend, *Time and Chance*, 231.
33. Warwick, *Princess Margaret* (2000), 209.
34. Longford, *Elizabeth R*, 220.

35. Townsend, *Time and Chance*, 238.
36. Bradford, *Elizabeth*, 207.
37. Morton, *Wallis in Love*, 218.
38. Townsend, *Time and Chance*, 227.
39. Townsend, *Time and Chance*, 221.
40. Willi Frischauer, *Margaret: Princess without a Cause* (London: Michael Joseph, 1977), 87.
41. Alice Vincent, "Carrie Fisher on the Kerfuffle Caused by Her Father's Affair with Princess Margaret," *Daily Telegraph*, December 8, 2016; Sam Creighton, "Princess Margaret 'Had an Affair' with 1950s Crooner Eddie Fisher," *Daily Mail*, March 24, 2016.

7. The Prince and the Showgirl

1. Chris Hastings, "When the Queen Told Churchill: Stop Making Me Sit through These Dreadful Films," *Mail on Sunday*, November 7, 2010.
2. Bosley Crowther, "The Screen in Review; 'Beau Brummell' Opens Run at Loew's State," *New York Times*, October 21, 1954.
3. Keith Dovkants, "Marriage and Indiscretion," *Evening Standard*, February 11, 2002.
4. Pierce and Kay, "Margaret's Very Private Correspondence."
5. Warwick, *Princess Margaret* (2000), 161.
6. Warwick, *Princess Margaret* (1983), 80.
7. Caroline Davies, "A Captivating Woman Who Was Courted by Many Suitors but Failed to Find Lasting Love," *The Telegraph*, February 11, 2002, https://www.telegraph.co.uk/news/uknews/1384451/A-captivating-woman-who-was-courted-by-many-suitors-but-failed-to-find-lasting-love.html.
8. Botham, *Margaret* (2012), 15.
9. Pimlott, *The Queen*, 226.
10. Bradford, *Elizabeth*, 264.
11. Seward, *My Husband and I*, 134.
12. Elizabeth Longford, *The Royal House of Windsor* (New York: Knopf Doubleday, 1974), 236.
13. Pimlott, *The Queen*, 271.
14. Gordon Rayner and Beth Hale, "Prince Philip's 'Passion' for Duchess," *London Evening Standard*, September 6, 2004.

15. Seward, *My Husband and I*, 137.

16. Seward, *My Husband and I*, 136.

17. Elizabeth Grice, "Sarah Bradford: Perhaps I Got It Wrong about the Duke of Edinburgh…," *Daily Telegraph*, December 3, 2011.

18. "Every Time I Talk to a Woman…," *Daily Mail*, September 27, 2006.

19. Pierce and Kay, "Margaret's Very Private Correspondence."

20. Jebb, *The Diaries of Cynthia Gladwyn*, 207.

21. Untitled, Box 6, Folder 32, Papers of Bruce Gould, University of Iowa Libraries, Iowa City, Iowa.

22. Aronson, *Princess Margaret*, 152.

23. Dennis Bardens, *Princess Margaret* (London: Robert Hale, 1964), 176.

24. Fiona MacCarthy, "Recalling the Lost Era of Debutantes," *Daily Telegraph*, March 16, 2008.

25. Warwick, *Princess Margaret* (2000), 221.

26. Warwick, *Princess Margaret* (2000), 222.

27. Bradford, *Elizabeth*, 287.

28. Andrew Morton, *Inside Kensington Palace* (London: Michael O'Mara, 1987), 133.

29. Bradford, *Elizabeth*, 313.

30. Unity Blott, "Who Is Prudence, Lady Penn?" *Daily Mail*, February 5, 2018.

31. Aronson, *Princess Margaret*, 156.

32. Barry, *Royal Secrets*, 167.

33. Bradford, *Elizabeth*, 243.

34. De Courcy, *Snowdon*, 151.

35. Warwick, *Princess Margaret* (2000), 220.

36. Aronson, *Princess Margaret*, 164.

37. Pimlott, *The Queen*, 241.

38. Barry, *Royal Secrets*, 58.

39. Warwick, *Princess Margaret* (2000), 209.

40. Warwick, *Princess Margaret* (2000), 210.

41. Townsend, *Time and Chance*, 279.

8. "Sex, Sex, Sex"

1. Warwick, *Princess Margaret* (2000), 213.

2. De Courcy, *Snowdon*, 51.

3. Botham, *Margaret* (1995), 101.

4. De Courcy, *Snowdon*, 73.

5. Aronson, *Princess Margaret*, 168.

6. Warwick, *Princess Margaret* (2000), 214.

7. Warwick, *Princess Margaret* (2000), 211.

8. Warwick, *Princess Margaret* (2000), 218.

9. Aronson, *Princess Margaret*, 172.

10. Warwick, *Princess Margaret* (2000), 223.

11. Warwick, *Princess Margaret* (1983), 95.

12. Dempster, *HRH the Princess Margaret*, 48–49.

13. Botham, *Margaret* (1995), 140.

14. Botham, *Margaret* (1995), 165.

15. Bardens, *Princess Margaret*, 189.

16. Warwick, *Princess Margaret* (2000), 224.

17. Warwick, *Princess Margaret* (1983), 97.

18. Aronson, *Princess Margaret*, 197.

19. Bradford, *Elizabeth*, 285.

20. Author interview with Victoria Charlton.

21. Andrew Alderson, "Lord Snowdon, His Women, and His Love Child," *Daily Telegraph*, May 31, 2008.

22. Elizabeth Angell, "The Strange Story of *A Very British Scandal*," *Town and Country*, January 1, 2019.

23. Smith, *Elizabeth the Queen*, 152.

24. Aronson, *Princess Margaret*, 199.

25. De Courcy, *Snowdon*, 93.

26. De Courcy, *Snowdon*, 95.

27. Chris Hastings, "Royals 'Cashing In on Titles...,'" *Daily Mail*, March 7, 2020.

28. Anne de Courcy, "The Unrepentant Lothario: Lord Snowdon and His Insatiable Appetite for Sex," *Mail on Sunday*, June 5, 2005.

29. Shawcross, *The Queen Mother*, 729.

30. Rose, *King George V*, 199.

31. Warwick, *Princess Margaret* (2000), 236.

32. Aronson, *Princess Margaret*, 215.

33. Bardens, *Princess Margaret*, 207.

34. Aronson, *Princess Margaret*, 209.

35. Will Stewart and Camilla Tominey, "KGB: We Bugged Royals," *Sunday Express*, December 23, 2012.

9. Cool Britannia

1. Warwick, *Princess Margaret* (2000), 240.
2. De Courcy, *Snowdon*, 123.
3. Aronson, *Princess Margaret*, 216–217.
4. Bradford, *Elizabeth*, 254.
5. Pimlott, *The Queen*, 240.
6. Bradford, *Elizabeth*, 253.
7. Author interview with Michael Nash.
8. Duncan, *The Reality of Monarchy*, 69.
9. Author interview with Peter Lyster-Todd.
10. Aronson, *Princess Margaret*, 219.
11. Peter Sellers, *I Say I Say I Say* [film], https://www.youtube.com/watch?v=Xos72Hfq6ME.
12. Aronson, *Princess Margaret*, 232.
13. Andrew Alderson and Peter Day, "Jet-Set Friends Got Margaret 'Barred' from US," *Sunday Telegraph*, September 14, 2003.
14. Warwick, *Princess Margaret* (2000), 240.
15. De Courcy, *Snowdon*, 118.
16. *The Royal Family*, PBS, March 2018.
17. Carroll, *Royal Pains*, 367.
18. Author interview with Marjorie Wallace.
19. De Courcy, *Snowdon*, 120.

10. "I Hate You"

1. Author interview with Peter Lyster-Todd.
2. Tim Heald, "Blue Movies and Casual Flings: The Amazing Truth about Princess Margaret's Marriage," *Evening Standard*, July 2, 2007, https://www.standard.co.uk/news/blue-movies-and-casual-flings-the-amazing-truth-about-princess-margarets-marriage-6594830.html.
3. Aronson, *Princess Margaret*, 234.
4. De Courcy, *Snowdon*, 142.
5. Botham, *Margaret* (1995), 204–206.
6. De Courcy, *Snowdon*, 148.
7. De Courcy, *Snowdon*, 150.
8. Interview with Victoria Charlton.

9. De Courcy, *Snowdon*, 150.
10. Rebecca Lees, "Aberfan: Queen's 'Biggest Regret,'" The Free Library, https://www.thefreelibrary.com/Aberfan%3A+Queen%27 s+%27biggest+regret%27.-a082244332.
11. De Courcy, *Snowdon*, 160.
12. Aronson, *Princess Margaret*, 276.
13. De Courcy, *Snowdon*, 154.
14. Botham, *Margaret* (1995), 245–246.
15. Warwick, *Princess Margaret* (2000), 245.
16. De Courcy, *Snowdon*, 174.
17. Aronson, *Princess Margaret*, 264.
18. Dempster, *HRH the Princess Margaret*, 176.
19. Bradford, *Elizabeth*, 357.
20. De Courcy, *Snowdon*, 192.
21. De Courcy, *Snowdon*, 197.
22. Erin Vanderhoof, "Brian Cox Remembers a Bizarre Interaction with Princess Margaret," *Vanity Fair*, January 14, 2020.
23. Aronson, *Princess Margaret*, 286.
24. Aronson, *Princess Margaret*, 256.
25. Craig Brown, *Ninety-Nine Glimpses of Princess Margaret*, 305.
26. De Courcy, *Snowdon*, 201.
27. "A Truly Modern Royal," *The Scotsman*, February 11, 2002.
28. De Courcy, *Snowdon*, 210.
29. Botham, *Margaret* (1995), 189.
30. De Courcy, *Snowdon*, 224.
31. Aronson, *Princess Margaret*, 257.
32. Warwick, *Princess Margaret* (1983), 138.
33. De Courcy, *Snowdon*, 225.
34. Aronson, *Princess Margaret*, 277.

11. "My Darling Angel"

1. Kenneth Williams, *The Kenneth Williams Diaries*, edited by Russell Davies (London: HarperCollins, 1993), 719.
2. Glenconner, *Lady in Waiting*, 171.
3. Warwick, *Princess Margaret* (2000), 256.
4. Author interview with Dana Gillespie.
5. De Courcy, *Snowdon*, 230.

6. Kayleigh Roberts, "Princess Margaret's Lady-in-Waiting Spilled the Tea about Her Relationship with Queen Elizabeth," *Harper's Bazaar*, March 7, 2020.

7. Ivan Waterman, "Princess and the Prime Suspect," *Mail on Sunday*, June 8, 2003.

8. Sandbrook, *Seasons in the Sun*.

9. Sandbrook, *Seasons in the Sun*.

10. De Courcy, *Snowdon*, 234.

11. Turner, *Elizabeth*, 183.

12. "Love, Lust, Scandal, and Honour," *News of the World*, February 10, 2002.

13. Christopher Warwick, *Elizabeth and Margaret: Love and Loyalty*, Channel 5.

14. De Courcy, *Snowdon*, 241.

15. Heald, "Blue Movies and Casual Flings: The Amazing Truth about Princess Margaret's Marriage."

16. Aronson, *Princess Margaret*, 279.

17. Bradford, *Elizabeth*, 398.

18. De Courcy, *Snowdon*, 242.

19. Glenconner, *Lady in Waiting*, 189.

20. Aronson, *Princess Margaret*, 264.

21. *The Sun*, April 5, 1998.

22. Pimlott, *The Queen*, 441.

23. De Courcy, *Snowdon*, 260.

24. Andrew Alderson, "The Passionate Princess Who Loved and Lost," *Daily Telegraph*, February 10, 2002.

25. Warwick, *Princess Margaret* (2000), 261.

26. Botham, *Margaret* (1995), 266.

27. Aronson, *Princess Margaret*, 273.

28. Elaine McCahill, "Princess Margaret's Scandalous 'Love Affair' with Gangster Who Had VERY X-rated Party Trick," *Mirror*, December 15, 2018, https://www.mirror.co.uk/news/uk-news/prin cess-margarets-scandalous-love-affair-13695172.

29. Author interview with Dana Gillespie.

30. Aronson, *Princess Margaret*, 308.

31. Aronson, *Princess Margaret*, 308.

32. Dempster, *HRH the Princess Margaret*, 188.

33. Dempster, *HRH the Princess Margaret*, 191.

34. Botham, *Margaret* (1995), 277.

12. Bud and Her Rose

1. Andrew Morton, *Diana: Her True Story in Her Own Words* (London: Michael O'Mara, 2017), 86.

2. Aronson, *Princess Margaret*, 297.

3. Seward, *The Queen and Di*, 65.

4. Aronson, *Princess Margaret*, 327.

5. Rocco, *Independent on Sunday*, October 3, 1993.

6. Aronson, *Princess Margaret*, 306.

7. Warwick, *Princess Margaret* (2000), 265–266.

8. Glenconner, *Lady in Waiting*, 275.

9. "Princess Wanted to Be a Catholic," *Sunday Times*, February 24, 2002.

10. Andrew Alderson, "Princess Margaret Dies," *Sunday Telegraph*, February 10, 2002.

11. Morton, *Diana: Her True Story in Her Own Words*, 337.

12. Daniela Elser, "The Toe-Sucking Photo That Ruined the Duchess of York," News.com, July 28, 2019, https://www.news.com.au/entertainment/celebrity-life/royals/the-toesucking-photo-that-ruined-the-duchess-of-york/news-story/abd664af0ab8944a6e9cd4bdc1b57446.

13. Pimlott, *The Queen*, 556.

14. Elser, "The Toe-Sucking Photo."

15. Seward, *My Husband and I*, 189.

16. Stephanie Nolasco, "Princess Diana and Princess Margaret's Secret Royal Feud," News.com, October 4, 2018, https://www.news.com.au/entertainment/celebrity-life/royals/princess-diana-and-princess-margarets-secret-royal-feud/news-story/5596c97f62b35cc47e87ddab969e51e0.

17. Seward, *The Queen and Di*, 200.

18. Bradford, *Elizabeth*, 451.

19. Rachel Borrill, "No Shock as 'Vulgarian' Fergie Leaves the Royal Fold," *Irish Times*, April 18, 1996.

20. Kenneth Rose, *Who Loses, Who Wins: The Journals of Kenneth Rose: Volume Two, 1979–2014* (London: Weidenfeld & Nicolson, 2019), 264.

21. Craig Brown, *Ninety-Nine Glimpses of Princess Margaret*, 329.
22. Andrew Morton, *Diana: In Pursuit of Love* (London: Michael O'Mara, 2004), 200.
23. Warwick, *Princess Margaret* (2000), 285.
24. Seward, *The Queen and Di*, 23.
25. Tina Brown, *The Diana Chronicles*, 415.
26. Craig Brown, *Ninety-Nine Glimpses of Princess Margaret*, 331.
27. Camille Heimbrod, "Princess Margaret Wrote 'Secret' Letter to Queen Elizabeth after Princess Diana's Death," *International Business Times*, October 24, 2018.
28. Andrew Morton, "Destroyed: The Letters That Fuelled a Royal Feud," *Sunday Telegraph*, September 20, 2009.
29. Petronella Wyatt, "Diana Rose from the Ashes of Her Marriage...," *Daily Mail*, June 29, 2019.
30. Glenconner, *Lady in Waiting*, 280.
31. "Colin Tennant Fears over Princess Margaret Illness," *Daily Express*, October 9, 2002.
32. Botham, *Margaret* (2012).
33. "The Private Hell of Princess Margaret," *Mail on Sunday*, August 22, 1999.
34. De Courcy, *Snowdon*, 349.
35. Warwick, *Princess Margaret* (2000), 302.
36. Warwick, *Princess Margaret* (2000), 303.
37. Glenconner, *Lady in Waiting*, 283.
38. Rose, *Who Loses, Who Wins*, 363.
39. Pimlott, *The Queen*, 198.

Select Bibliography

Airlie, Mabell, Countess of. *Thatched with Gold*. Edited by Jennifer Ellis. London: Hutchinson, 1962.

Aronson, Theo. *Princess Margaret: A Biography*. London: Michael O'Mara, 1997.

Barry, Stephen. *Royal Secrets: The View from Downstairs*. London: Random House, 1985.

Botham, Noel. *Margaret: The Last Real Princess*. London: John Blake, 2012.

———. *Margaret: The Untold Story*. London: John Blake, 1995.

Bradford, Sarah. *Elizabeth: A Biography of Her Majesty the Queen*. London: Penguin, 1996.

Brandreth, Gyles. *Philip and Elizabeth: Portrait of a Royal Marriage*. London: W. W. Norton, 2004.

Brown, Craig. *Hello Goodbye Hello: A Circle of 101 Remarkable Meetings*. New York: Simon & Schuster, 2012.

———. *Ninety-Nine Glimpses of Princess Margaret*. New York: Farrar, Straus & Giroux, 2017.

Brown, Tina. *The Diana Chronicles*. New York: Penguin Random House, 2007.

Carroll, Leslie. *Royal Pains: A Rogues' Gallery of Brats, Brutes, and Bad Seeds*. New York: New American Library, 2011.

Clarke, Comer. *England under Hitler*. London: Consul, 1963.

Crawford, Marion. *The Little Princesses*. London: Cassell & Co., 1950.

de Courcy, Anne. *Snowdon: The Biography*. London: Phoenix, 2008.

Dempster, Nigel. *HRH the Princess Margaret: A Life Unfulfilled*. London: Quartet, 1981.

Dismore, Jane. *Princess: The Early Life of Queen Elizabeth II*. Guilford, CT: Lyons Press, 2018.

Duncan, Andrew. *The Reality of Monarchy*. London: Pans, 1973.

Edwards, Anne. *Royal Sisters: Queen Elizabeth II and Princess Margaret*. Guilford, CT: Lyons Press, 1990.

Glenconner, Anne. *Lady in Waiting: My Extraordinary Life in the Shadow of the Crown*. London: Hodder & Stoughton, 2019.

Heald, Tim. *Princess Margaret, A Life Unravelled*. London: Weidenfeld & Nicolson, 2007.

Hoey, Brian. *At Home with the Queen*. London: HarperCollins, 2002.

Howard, Alathea Fitzalan. *The Windsor Diaries: 1940–45*. London: Hodder & Stoughton, 2020.

Jebb, Miles, ed. *The Diaries of Cynthia Gladwyn*. London: Constable, 1995.

Maclean, Veronica. *Crowned Heads: Kings, Emperors, and Sultans—A Royal Quest*. London: Hodder & Stoughton, 1993.

Morgan, Janet. *Edwina Mountbatten, A Life of Her Own*. London: HarperCollins, 1991.

Morrow, Ann. *The Queen*. New York: William Morrow, 1983.

Morton, Andrew. *Wallis in Love*. New York: Grand Central Publishing, 2018.

Pimlott, Ben. *The Queen: Elizabeth II and the Monarchy*. London: HarperCollins, 1996.

Rhodes, Margaret. *The Final Curtsey: A Royal Memoir by the Queen's Cousin*. London: Umbria, 2012.

Rose, Kenneth. *King George V*. London: Weidenfeld & Nicolson, 1983.

Sandbrook, Dominic. *Seasons in the Sun: The Battle for Britain, 1974–1979*. London: Penguin, 2013.

Seward, Ingrid. *My Husband and I*. New York: Simon & Schuster, 2017.

———. *The Queen and Di*. New York: Arcade, 2000.

———. *Royal Children*. New York: St. Martin's Press, 1993.

Shawcross, William, ed. *Counting One's Blessings: The Selected Letters of Queen Elizabeth the Queen Mother.* New York: Farrar, Straus & Giroux, 2012.

———. *The Queen Mother: The Official Biography.* New York: Knopf, 2009.

Smith, Sally Bedell. *Elizabeth the Queen: The Life of a Modern Monarch.* New York: Random House, 2012.

Stewart, Andrew. *The King's Private Army: Protecting the Royal Family during the Second World War.* Warwick: Helion & Co., 2015.

Thorpe, D. R., ed. *Who Loses, Who Wins: The Journals of Kenneth Rose, Volume 2: 1979–2014.* London: Weidenfeld & Nicolson, 2019.

Townsend, Peter. *Time and Chance: An Autobiography.* London: Collins, 1978.

Turner, Graham. *Elizabeth: The Woman and the Queen.* London: Telegraph Books, 2002.

Viney, Graham. *The Last Hurrah: South Africa and the Royal Tour of 1947.* Johannesburg: Jonathan Ball, 2018.

Warwick, Christopher. *Princess Margaret.* London: Weidenfeld & Nicolson, 1983.

———. *Princess Margaret: A Life of Contrasts.* London: Andrew Deutsch, 2000.

Wheeler-Bennett, Sir John. *Friends, Enemies, and Sovereigns: The Final Volume of His Autobiography.* London: Palgrave Macmillan, 1976.

Williams, Kate. *Young Elizabeth: The Making of the Queen.* Berkeley: Pegasus Books, 2015.

Ziegler, Philip. *King Edward VIII: The Official Biography.* London: Collins, 1990.

Photo Credits

Page 11: Evening Standard/Hulton Archive via Getty Images; Ray Bellisario/Popperfoto via Getty Images

Page 12: Anwar Hussein /EMPICS Entertainment via PA Images; Lichfield/Lichfield Archive via Getty Images

Page 13: Anwar Hussein/Getty Images News via Getty Images; PA/PA Archive/PA Images

Page 14: All photos Tim Graham/Tim Graham Photo Library via Getty Images

Page 15: Doug Peters/EMPICS Entertainment via PA Images; PA/PA Archive/PA Images

Page 16: Tim Graham/Tim Graham Photo Library via Getty Images

Index

About the Author

Andrew Morton is one of the world's best-known biographers and a leading authority on modern celebrity and royalty. Morton has written an extensive number of bestselling biographies, including books on Tom Cruise, Angelina Jolie, and Madonna, as well as the British royal family, such as the Duke and Duchess of Windsor, Prince Andrew, and Meghan Markle. His #1 *New York Times* bestselling biography *Diana: Her True Story*, which won international acclaim, was described by critics as a "modern classic" and "the closest we will ever come to [Princess Diana's] autobiography." He studied history at the University of Sussex, England, with a focus on aristocracy and the 1930s, and now divides his time between London and Los Angeles.